IMAGES
of America

VANISHING TACOMA

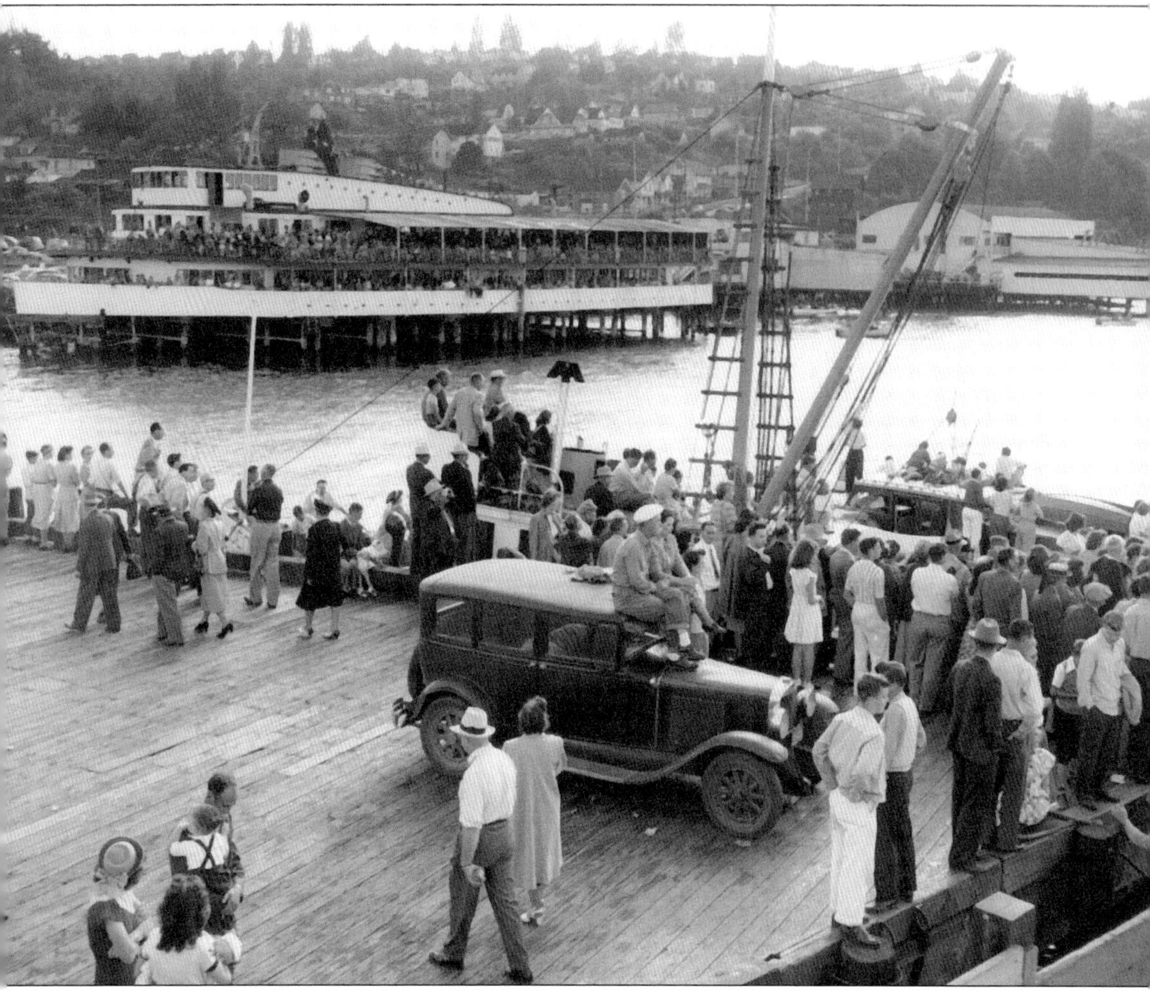

On August 29, 1848, Tacomans are gathered on the Old Town Dock to watch the Tacoma Athletic Commission Water Carnival originating from the Top of the Ocean Restaurant. The dock has been rebuilt many times over the years, with the last dock completed in May 2013. In this view, the little boy in the suspenders is Ron Karabaich, coauthor of this history. (Richards Studio, Tacoma Public Library.)

On the Cover: Some accidents do unexpected damage to buildings—in this case, the Bacon Block, located at 1151 Tacoma Avenue South. In 1935, a Pacific Oil truck, transporting gasoline, tipped over. The gasoline did not ignite as it flowed down Thirteenth Street past the Sampson Hotel, but the accident did cause a fire in the Manpie Imai grocery store in the Bacon Building. (Richards Studio, Tacoma Public Library.)

IMAGES
of America

Vanishing Tacoma

Caroline Gallacci and Ron Karabaich

ARCADIA
PUBLISHING

ISBN 978-1-4671-3028-8

Published by Arcadia Publishing
Charleston, South Carolina

Printed in the United States of America

Library of Congress Control Number: 2013931996

For all general information, please contact Arcadia Publishing:
Telephone 843-853-2070
Fax 843-853-0044
E-mail sales@arcadiapublishing.com
For customer service and orders:
Toll-Free 1-888-313-2665

Visit us on the Internet at www.arcadiapublishing.com

To all the health care professionals who have kept me from becoming part of Tacoma's vanishing landscape

Contents

ACKNOWLEDGMENTS

More of Tacoma might have vanished were it not for certain individuals who insisted that buildings be saved and created the governmental structure to make sure they were. As with all projects of importance, the names of men and women who dedicated their efforts are too many to list individually. Two, however, do deserve specific acknowledgement: former representative Norm Dicks, whose assistance led to the salvation of the Pantages Theater and Union Station; and Peter Callaghan, columnist for the *News Tribune*. Callaghan keeps his finger on the preservation pulse in the city, including new issues in the making. As of this writing, the future of Tacoma's totem pole is the topic of discussion, with a column printed on May 23, 2013.

As with every Arcadia Publishing history we have written, we have substantially relied on both the Tacoma Public Library Northwest Room Photograph Collection Index and the Housing and Building Index. Space requirements do not allow a complete numerical reference for the photographs provided by the library. These are, however, in both the author's and the Tacoma Public Library files. In addition to library sources, the collections of Ron Karabaich and Thomas R. Stenger were equally valuable. Unless noted otherwise, all photographs are from Ron Karabaich's collection.

Introduction

Cities change over time and go through generations of different landscapes. This phenomenon occurs both within the central business district and within the various neighborhoods and commercial districts radiating outward from the central core. Many people make decisions affecting these urban changes, including individual property owners and land developers, community and business organizations, and city officials carrying through a wide array of local ordinances. State and federal laws impact how cities develop over time. Then there are fires, earthquakes, other acts of nature, and the human factors of style and taste. All of these result in a rich mosaic of old and new.

One of the major challenges in telling the story of *Vanishing Tacoma* is the realization that "one person's junk is another's antique"—or "one person's historic landmark is another's eyesore." Perhaps the best photograph of the dilemma in Tacoma is an image published in the *Downtown Tacoma* history published by Arcadia in 2009. In it, a *Tacoma News Tribune* photographer caught a bus with a notice stating, "The best way to build a city is to never tear it down." The bus was passing in front of a building undergoing demolition.

While I have tried to retain a certain degree of neutrality in writing this book, there were times when that was not possible. My own personal biases are in play here. I was a member of the charter Tacoma Landmarks Preservation Commission appointed by Mayor Gordon Johnson and then worked as both historic preservation planner and officer. For those readers who are not familiar with Mayor Johnson, he was one of the first public officials to take a stand toward preserving Tacoma's heritage. Many still remember the night when he chastised an attorney for referring to his newly appointed commission as the "hysterical" landmarks board.

Another challenge while writing this book was that there were new preservation issues arising. Some were minor, such as the announcement that the Harbor Lights was to undergo interior renovation. The most controversial was a City of Tacoma announcement that the totem pole now lodged in Fireman's Park on South A Street might have to be removed because it was deteriorating. As I finish this introduction, I have encountered another—the unknown future of the neon sign for the Chiefton, a restaurant located on South Tacoma Way. Like these three instances, many other preservation issues have not yet come to be, and so they are not included in this book.

In chapter one of *Vanishing Tacoma*, the reader is introduced to a series of streetscapes that show the city's neighborhoods during the early years of Tacoma's development. This is to provide a starting point for the history that is to follow. In a general sense, this is the city before newer modes of transportation—primarily the streetcar and automobile—began to lead to new construction and, in some cases, the loss of older buildings.

Chapters two and three document how fires, earthquakes, flooding, and other acts of nature have affected Tacoma's urban environment. In both of these chapters, as with the ones that follow, questions of motivation, issues of health and safety, and public policy, come into play when deciding to replace or restore a lost resource.

Transportation is the focus of chapter four. As noted above, if there is one thing that transformed Tacoma, it was changes in how people moved about the city. And, as modes of transportation evolved over time, so did the impact that streetcars, automobiles, trains, and airplanes have had on the fate of buildings. Chapter five showcases the evolution of buildings in Tacoma, from wood-frame and brick buildings to steel-reinforced structures. Reasons why buildings changed over they years vary from building codes to the impact of the automobile. For example, many stores have been converted into parking garages. Whether or not these changes are a good or bad thing is primarily a matter of preference or nostalgia.

Chapter six deals with demolitions, which occur for so many reasons. While Tacomans do have their lists of unpardonable demolitions, with the loss of the Pierce County Courthouse heading the lot, many demolitions are more problematic in terms of public opinion. Demolition by neglect, such as city and county unwillingness to do anything to preserve the Luzon Building on Pacific Avenue and the municipal dock below the Murray Morgan Bridge, are difficult to explain. On the other hand, the federal constitution includes liberties that allow any property owner to do as he or she wills within reason. So, applauding or disproving those who choose to demolish is always going to be a difficult call.

Not all of Tacoma's significant past has vanished. As noted throughout this book, examples are provided as to the preservation of various buildings throughout the city. Once the Tacoma City Council established the Tacoma Landmarks Preservation Commission in the late 1970s, a conscious effort has been made to identify, designate, and protect known historic districts, buildings, structures, and sites. Since there are too many to list all of them in this publication, chapter seven highlights a few. As with everything related to this history, the list will constantly expand.

Chapter eight concludes the story of *Vanishing Tacoma* with the notion that for some Tacomans, whether or not a building—or other aspect of the urban landscape—is there does not matter. Memories and photographs are what matters. Some of these memories, such as mass transit, are transformed into today's urban amenities. Others remain as memories preserved in photographs, personal reminiscences, or in the mind's eye.

One

STREETSCAPES

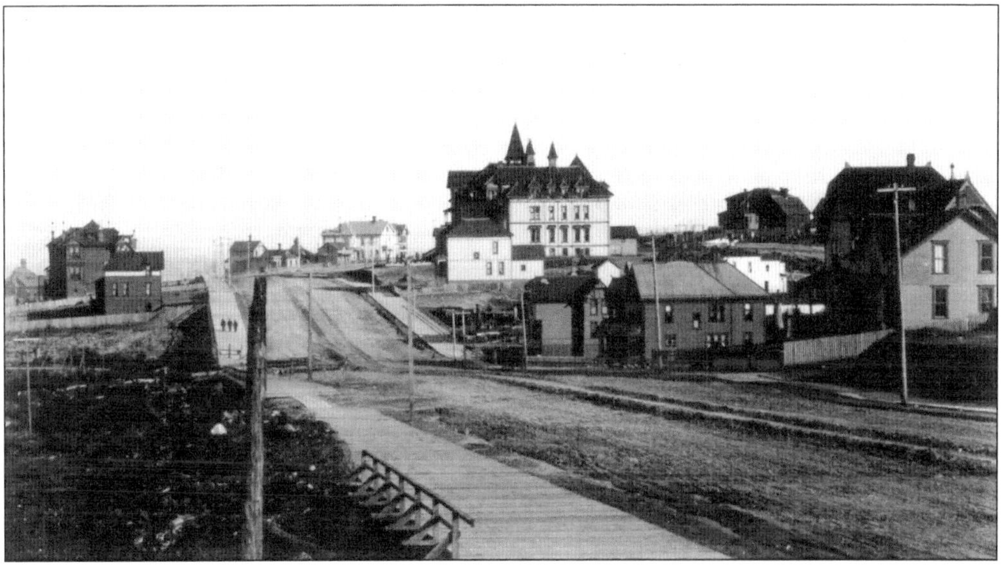

Vanishing Tacoma begins on North Tacoma Avenue looking east toward Division Avenue, the present-day Stadium Business District. I.S. Davidson photographed the street around 1888, and it appears that the road has been prepared for the streetcar tracks laid the following year. The large building on the right is Annie Wright Seminary, constructed in 1884. In the distant left is where Ranko's Stadium Pharmacy was eventually located in the late 1930s. In the distance and to the left of Annie Wright Seminary are two houses built in the mid-1880s for Walter J. Thompson and Henry Drum, which still remain on South St. Helens Avenue. In 1888, Drum became one of Tacoma's earliest mayors. Thompson was a banker. At the time Davidson took this photograph, this area was becoming a residential suburb, especially for those who could afford to move outside Tacoma's downtown. As streetcar lines moved continually outward, new residences arose, creating some of Tacoma's historic neighborhoods.

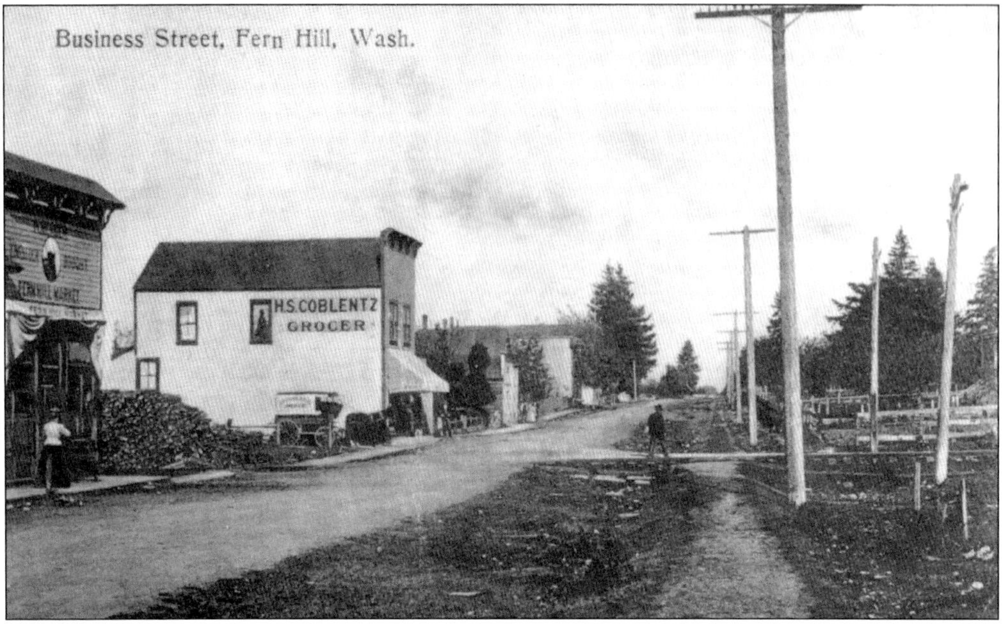

Fern Hill was developing as a crossroads settlement near the intersection of Indian Henry Trail (Park Avenue) and Byrd Mill Road (South Eighty-Fourth Street) before Tacoma was founded in 1873. This undated photograph shows the Byrd Mill Road, a link between the towns of Steilacoom and Puyallup. Indian Henry Trail ultimately connected the pioneer community northward to Tacoma. (Thomas R. Stenger collection.)

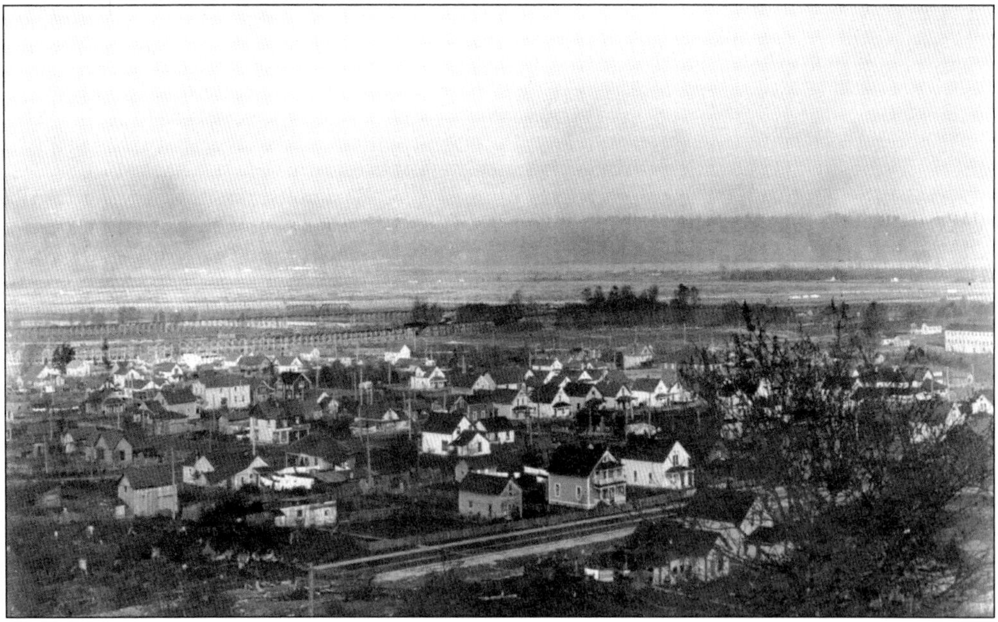

The homes seen here were for working-class families employed either by the railroad or nearby manufacturing and milling plants. The undeveloped land in the distance was a portion of the Puyallup Indian Reservation, with the school and hospital grounds on the right side of this undated photograph. The area would soon be called the Hawthorne neighborhood. (Thomas R. Stenger collection.)

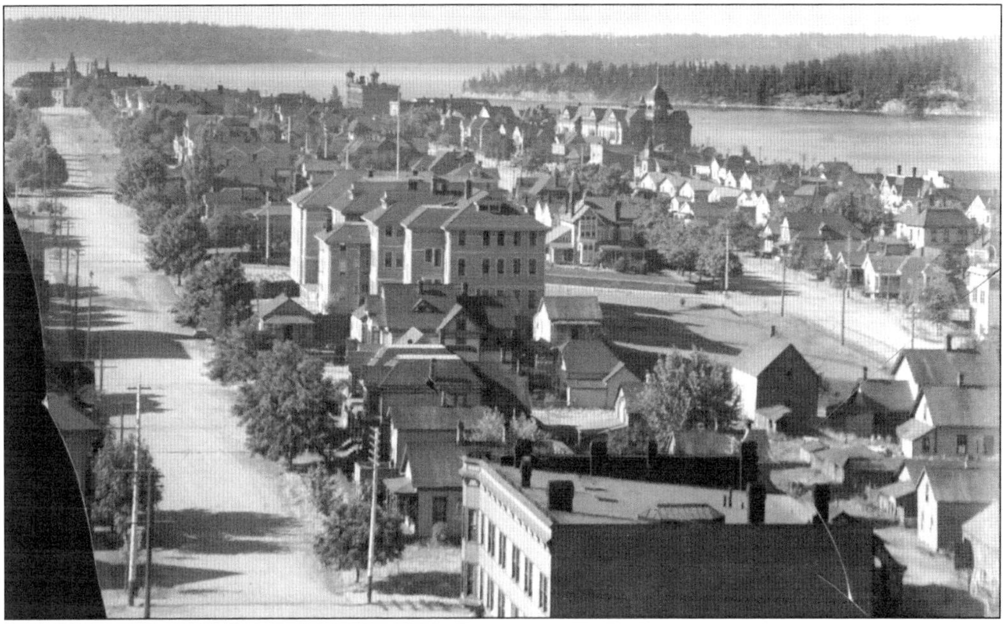

Around 1900, Tacoma photographer Paul Richards looked northward along South G Street and captured an urban landscape of apartments and houses constructed after the introduction of streetcars in the late 1880s. While the large building in the middle of the image remains unidentified, large buildings seen in the distance are, from left to right, Annie Wright Seminary, the Bonneville Hotel, and Emerson School. (Paul Richards Collection, Tacoma Historical Society.)

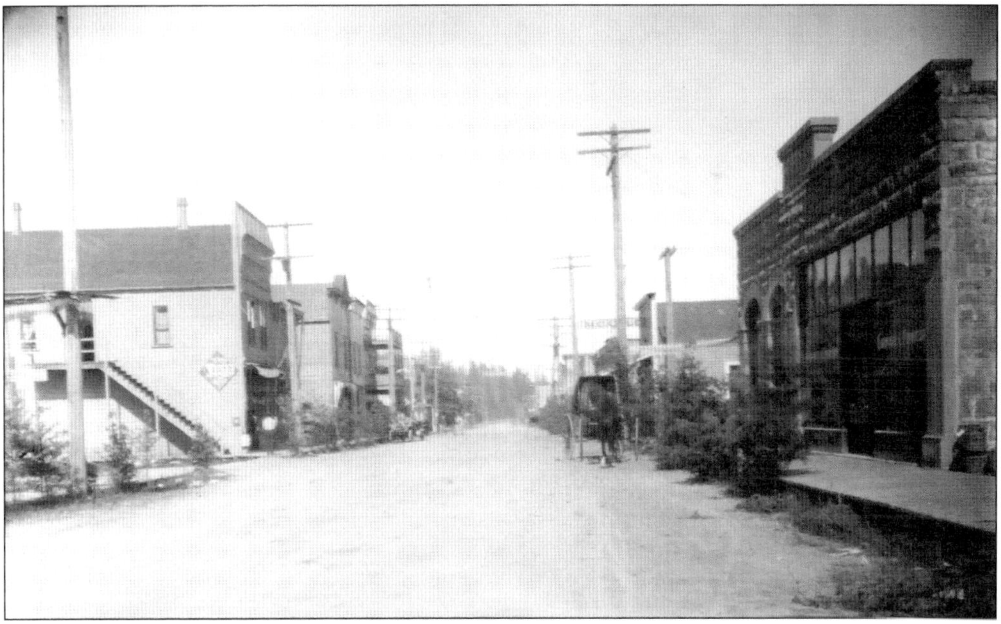

In 1908, while A.D. Browning was photographing scenes throughout the South Tacoma neighborhood, the area had become home to the workers at the Northern Pacific shops or at other manufacturing plants associated with the railroad. A commercial district along South Tacoma evolved adjacent to the industrial zone, providing local residents most of the necessities of life. (Amzie D. Browning Collection, Tacoma Public Library.)

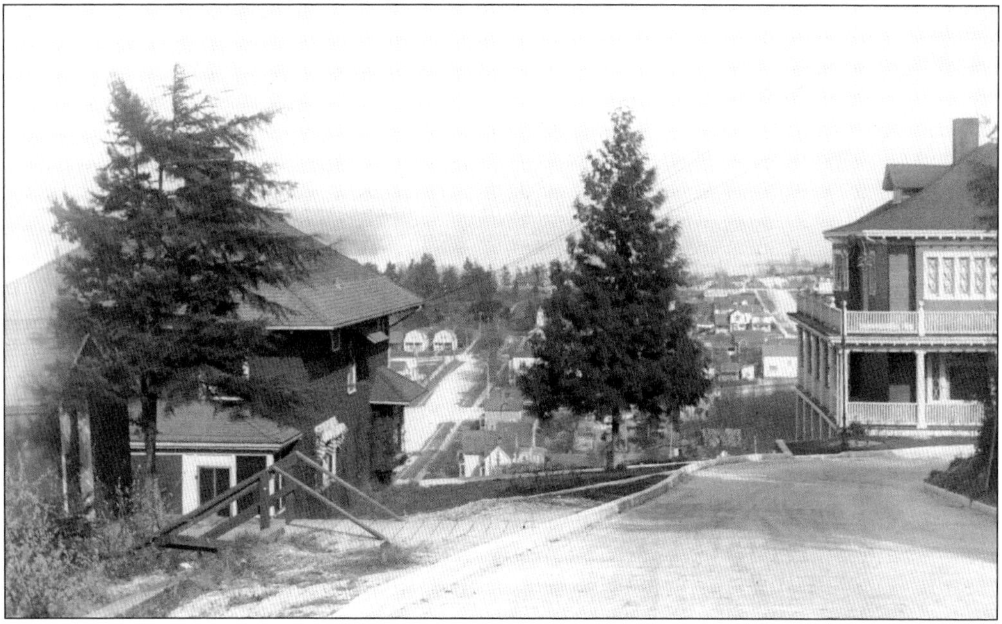

The Paul Richards house (right) on Prospect Hill's East Road was a favorite place to photograph Old Tacoma, which was located to the east below this upscale residential community. Records indicate that Richards himself took several images, including this one dating to about 1910. Even though Old Tacoma was where the city began and many old building remain, the Tacoma City Council has yet to designate the neighborhood as a historic district. (Thomas R. Stenger collection.)

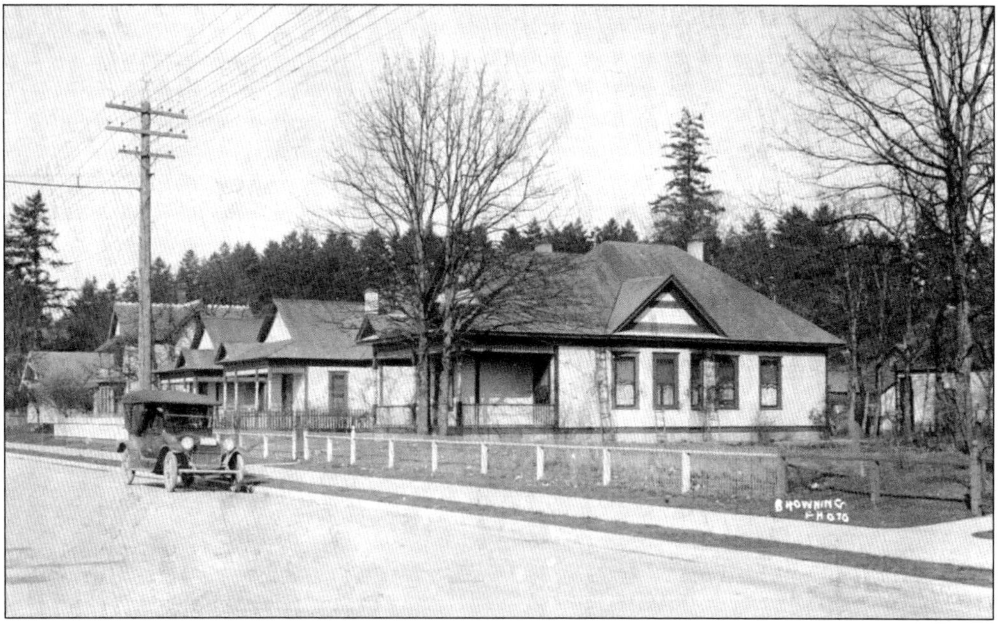

On his photographic tour of South Tacoma, A.D. Browning included residential streets in his images. This streetscape image was probably taken on either South Puget Sound Street or Warner Street east of South Tacoma Way. The trees in the background mark both Old Tacoma and Oakwood Cemeteries, the city's first. Both, along with the Pierce County cemetery located there, provide the earliest history of the region. (Amzie D. Browning Collection, Tacoma Public Library.)

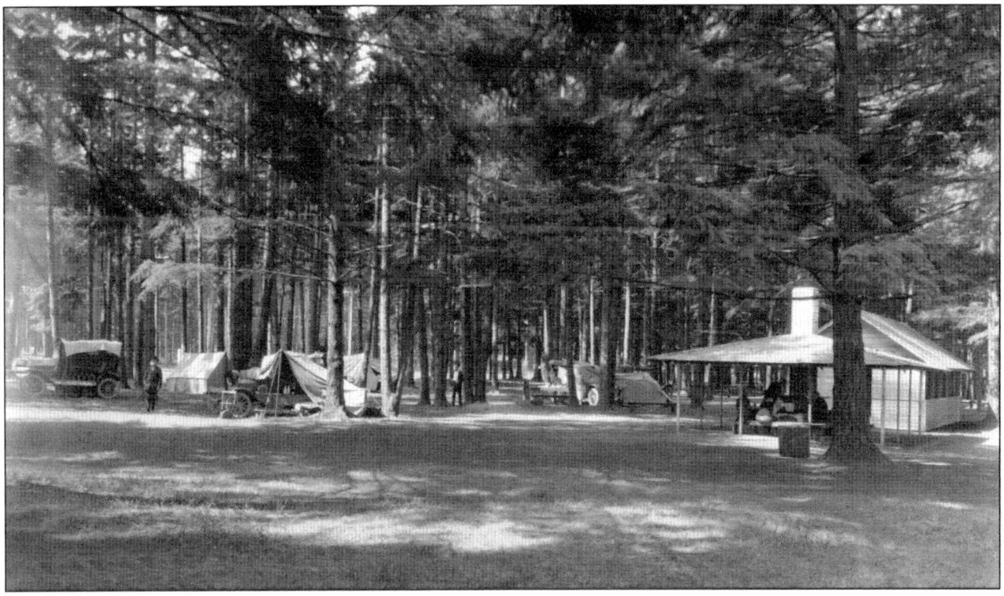

In 1915, Tacoma's Metropolitan Park District purchased land on South Sixty-Sixth and Tyler Streets. The Pacific Traction from downtown Tacoma to American Lake ran through the property, providing easy access for those wanting to get out of the city's bustle. By 1921, the year of this Marvin Boland photograph, until 1927, a part of the property became the Manitou Tourist Park for those enjoying the new fad of automobile camping.

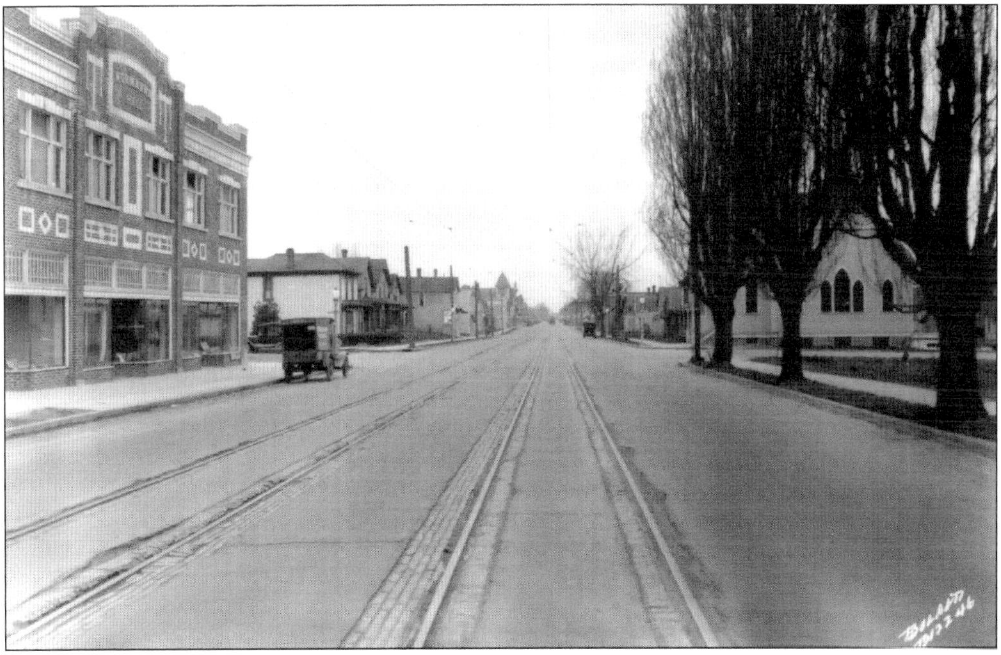

Before World War II, K Street (now Martin Luther King Jr. Way) was a focal point for early Scandinavian settlers. In 1925, Marvin Boland photographed this view looking north from South Fifteenth Street and showing the Normanna Hall (left), an ethnic center for immigrants. Behind the trees along this residential street was the Norwegian Free Lutheran Church. (Marvin D. Boland Collection, Tacoma Public Library.)

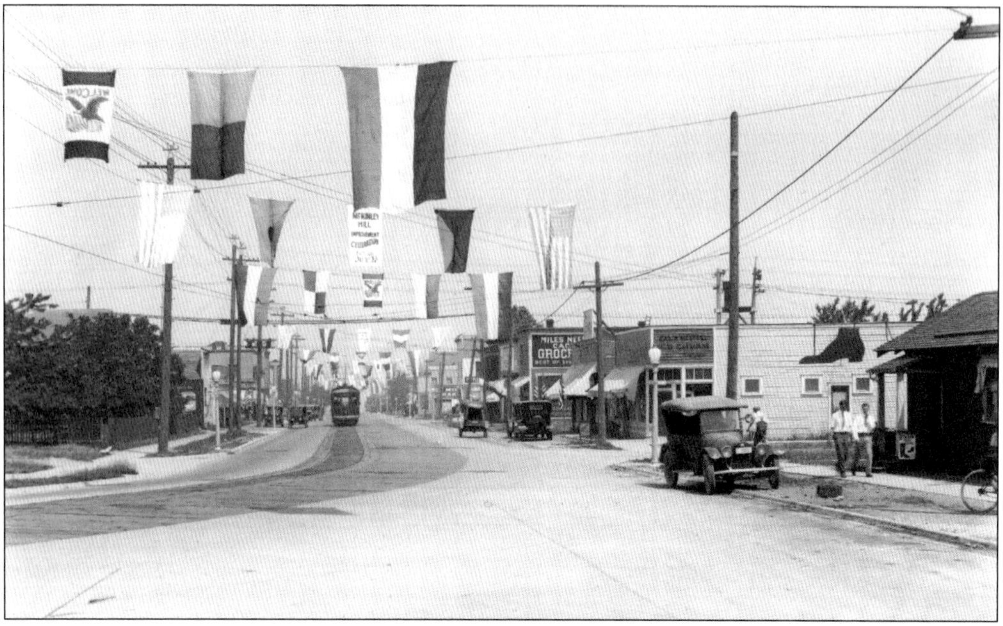

South McKinley Avenue and the park located at the northern end of this view acquired the moniker following the assassination of Pres. William McKinley in September 1901. When this photograph was taken in 1925, the McKinley Avenue Improvement club was preparing for its annual summer tradition of gaiety. Like most historic neighborhoods in Tacoma, this one was originally linked to the downtown area via streetcar. (Richards Studio, Tacoma Public Library.)

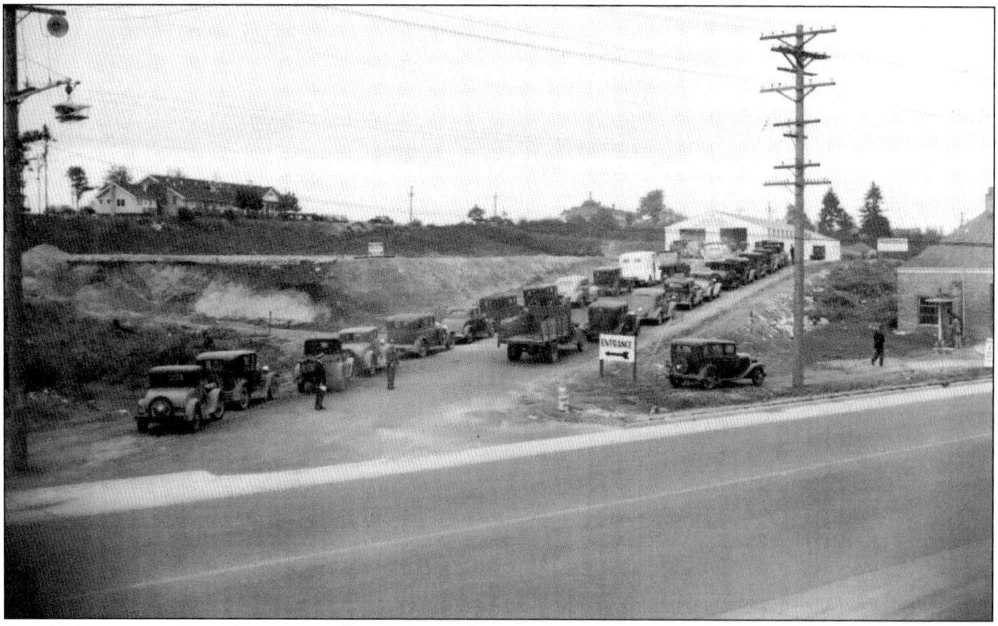

In 1939, cars are lined up to undergo a Washington State vehicle safety inspection on South Thirty-Eighth Street near South Lawrence Street. This hill was also once used for local soapbox derby competitions. The building to the left was originally Tacoma's Contagious Hospital, but at this time, it was headquarters for the New Deal Works Progress Administration. (Richards Studio, Tacoma Public Library.)

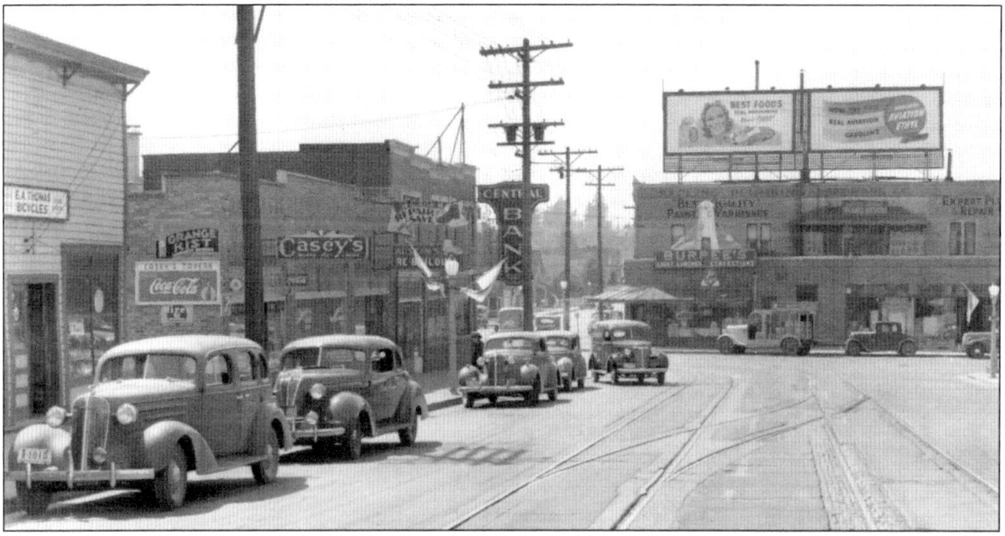

Photographer Chapin Bowen provided this street view looking west where Sixth Avenue jogs at South Pine Street sometime in 1940. This was a time when the last remaining streetcar tracks in Tacoma were removed and sold as scrap to Japanese industries. While most of the businesses shown here have not lasted the test of time, many University of Puget Sound alumni remember time spent in Casey's Tavern.

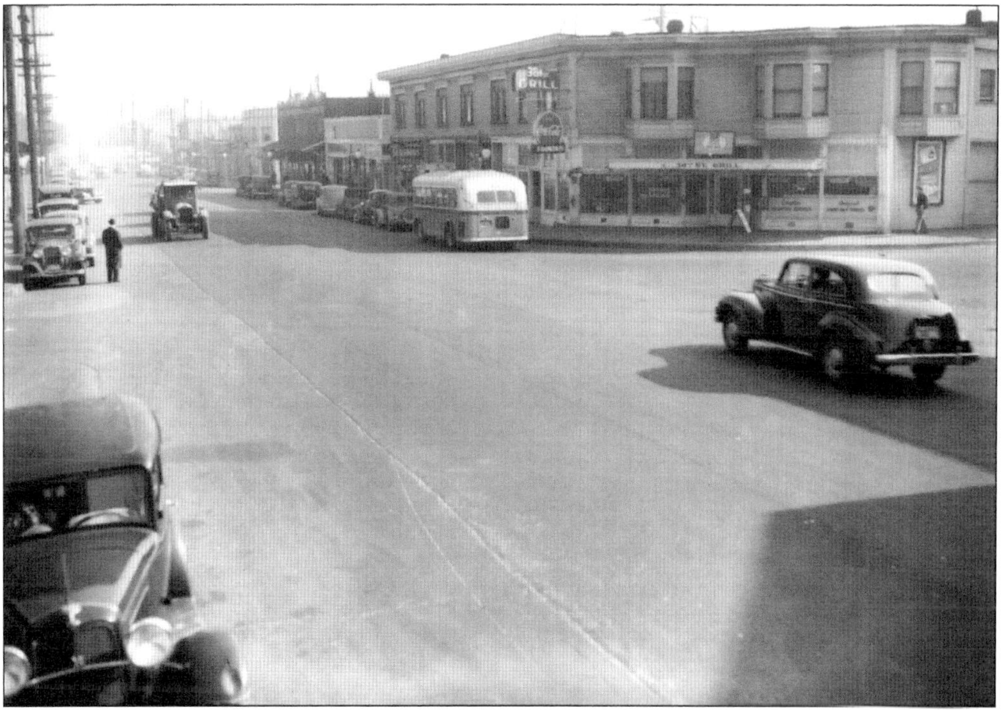
By the early months of 1941, most of Tacoma's streetcar tracks were gone, and buses ruled mass transit in the city. At the intersection of South Thirty-eighth Street and Yakima Avenue, the new paving received a photographer's attention. The bus is stopping in front of the Thirty-eighth Street Grill and Lincoln Seafoods. Lincoln High School is out of view to the left. (Richards Studio, Tacoma Public Library.)

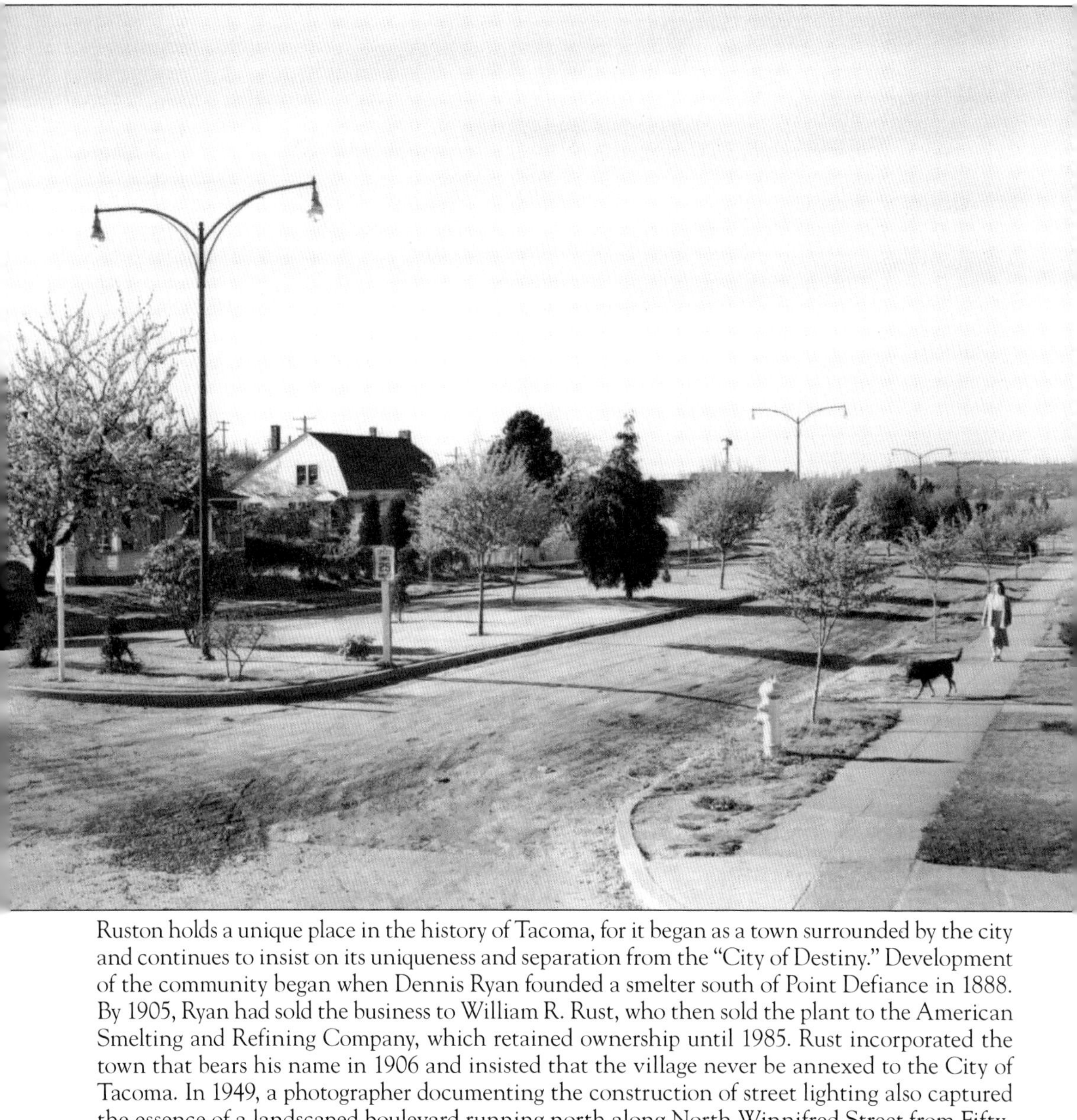

Ruston holds a unique place in the history of Tacoma, for it began as a town surrounded by the city and continues to insist on its uniqueness and separation from the "City of Destiny." Development of the community began when Dennis Ryan founded a smelter south of Point Defiance in 1888. By 1905, Ryan had sold the business to William R. Rust, who then sold the plant to the American Smelting and Refining Company, which retained ownership until 1985. Rust incorporated the town that bears his name in 1906 and insisted that the village never be annexed to the City of Tacoma. In 1949, a photographer documenting the construction of street lighting also captured the essence of a landscaped boulevard running north along North Winnifred Street from Fifty-first Street to the Point Defiance Park boundary. Such urban landscaping is rare in Tacoma, but does reflect an interest in the beautification of cities at the time Ruston was platted. (Richards Studio, Tacoma Public Library.)

Two

FIRES

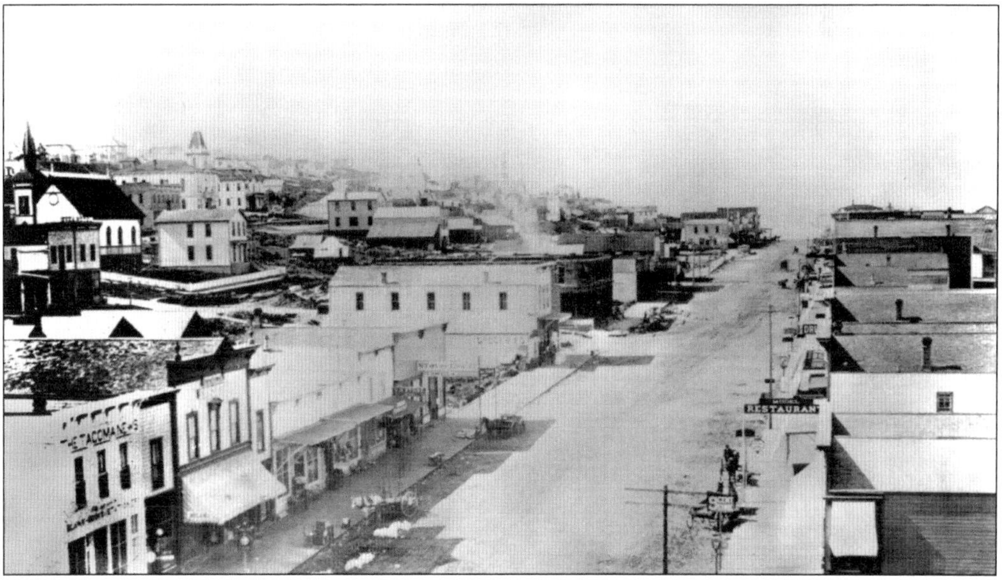

Fires by both accident and arson have caused major loss of property in Tacoma, especially during the early days when wood was the primary construction material. In the 1890s, when Tacoma citizens agreed to purchase the privately owned water and power company, the major reason why they bought it was the lack of water to fight fires. Pure drinking water was a secondary concern. Accompanying this purchase was a city ordinance mandating that all downtown commercial buildings be constructed of brick, because companies refused to insure the town. Fire also played a role in the expulsion of the Chinese from the city in late 1885. In this view, on the left side of Pacific Avenue, there is a vacant lot caused by a fire. Since a Chinese community had already developed on the hillsides west and north of this block, a debate ensued to determine if the Chinese should be allowed to expand into the empty land. Following the expulsion, fire company hoses were slashed to keep the men from fighting the fires set to burn down the Chinese residences.

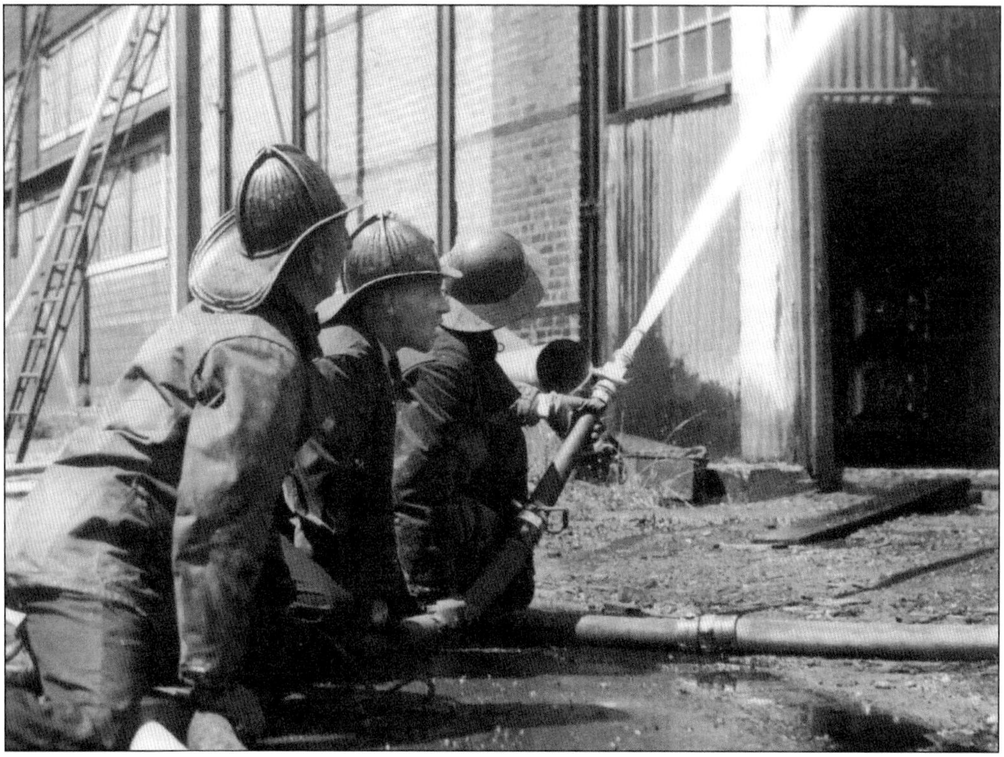

In 1889, Tacoma became the first city in Washington to replace its volunteer fire department with paid professionals. From that point in time, the firehouse has become a standard feature within the city's landscape, and many of these buildings are designated landmarks. Shown here are firemen battling the 1937 Puget Sound Manufacturing Company fire, which required eight companies to respond. (Richards Studio, Tacoma Public Library.)

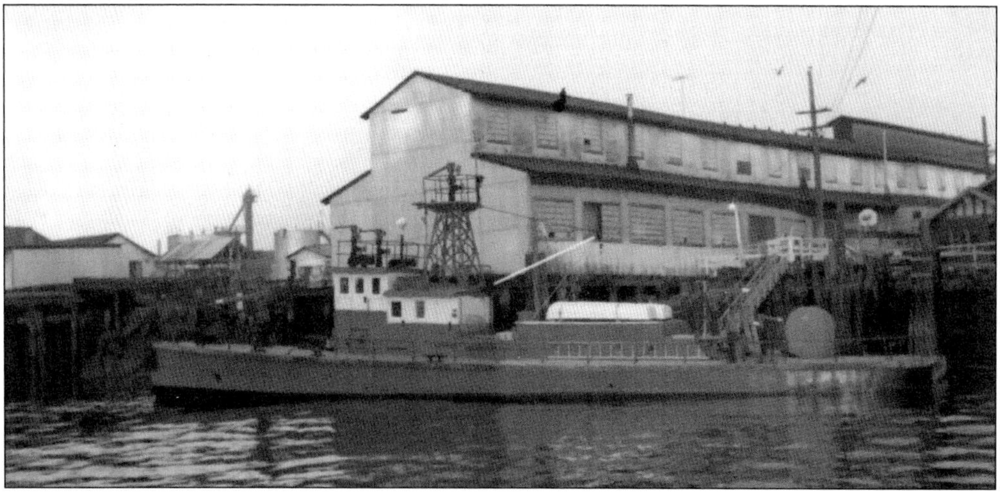

Prior to the commissioning of Tacoma's *Fireboat No. 1* in 1929, specially outfitted tugboats were used to fight shoreline fires. From this year until 1982, when it was retired from service, it became a well-known feature of the waterfront, especially when the "Big Bertha" monitor (or hose) demonstrated its power. *Fireboat No. 1* is now ashore along the Ruston Way Park and is a national landmark.

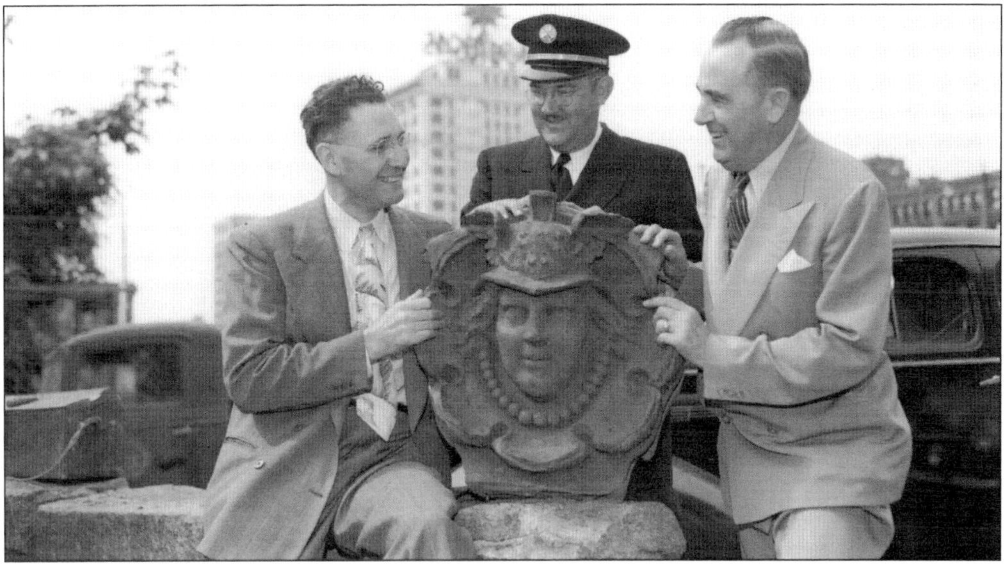

In July 1949, Tacoma fire chief Charles Eisenbacher, battalion chief Harold Fisk, and public safety commissioner Robert Temme (not specifically identified) examine a tile ornament taken from an earthquake-damaged Fire Station No. 6 at Ninth and A Streets. The three were competing over who would get the artifact. Chief Fisk won the argument by saying he planned to have it put on his grave when he died. Fisk died in 1989, but the ornament is not on his grave in Vashon Island Cemetery. (Richards Studio, Tacoma Public Library.)

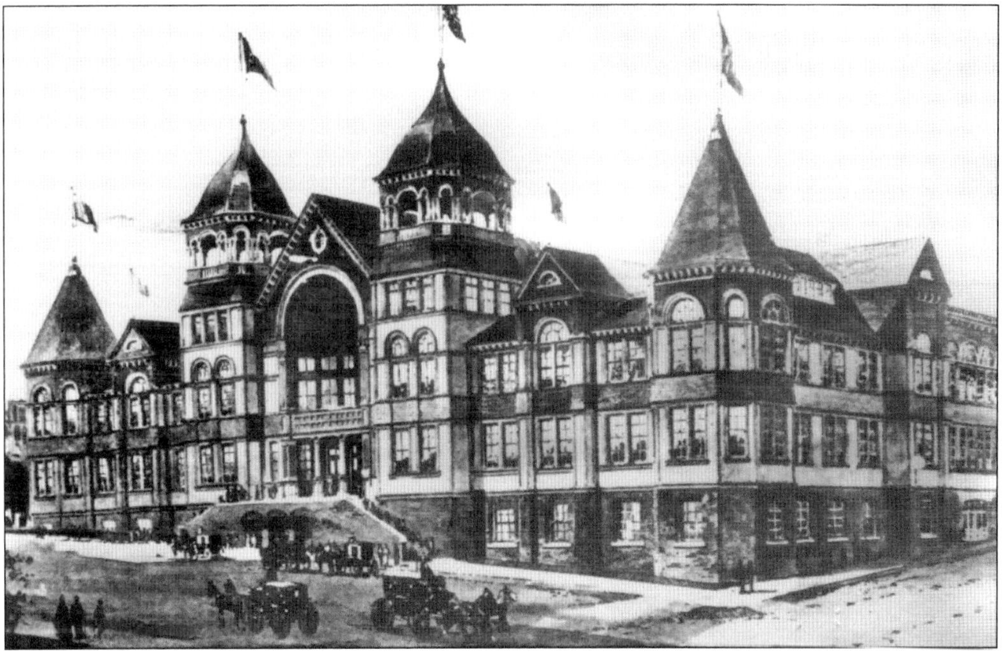

One of Tacoma's more sensational early events occurred on September 20, 1898, when the Western Washington Industrial Exposition Building was destroyed by fire six years after its dedication. Located near the present-day Annie Wright School on Tacoma Avenue North, the building was used for purposes ranging from industrial and product demonstrations to a roller-skating rink and a music hall. (Tacoma Public Library.)

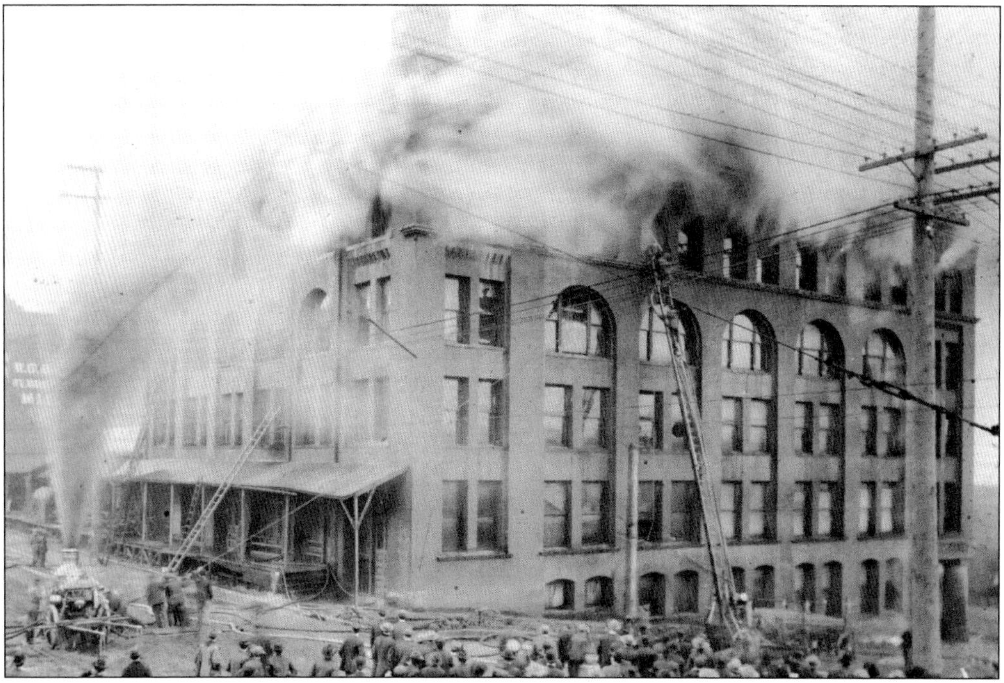

Some Tacoma fires were deadly for those fighting them. When the Davis Smith and Company Building at 1754 Pacific Avenue was engulfed in flames in 1908, one fighter was killed and another 11 men were injured. A horse-drawn hose wagon was over turned racing to the fire. The building survived and is now part of the University of Washington's Tacoma campus. (Richards Studio, Tacoma Public Library.)

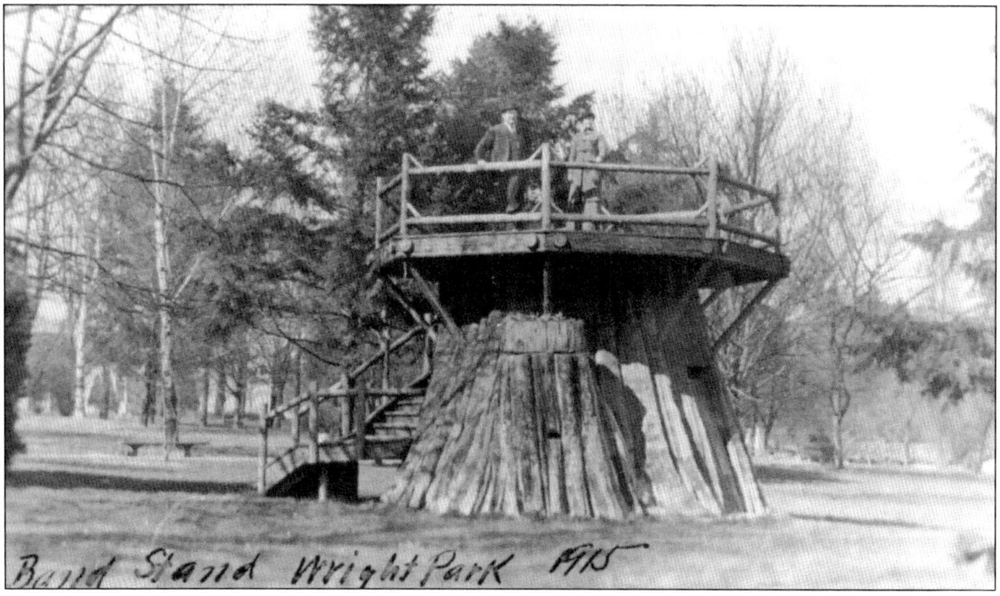

Bandstands were a common feature in parks nationwide and were used both for music and public speakers. The origins of the one located in Wright Park are unclear, but it was in operation at least by 1915. From this time until it was destroyed by fire in 1930, it was a focal point for a wide array of public entertainment. (Tacoma Public Library.)

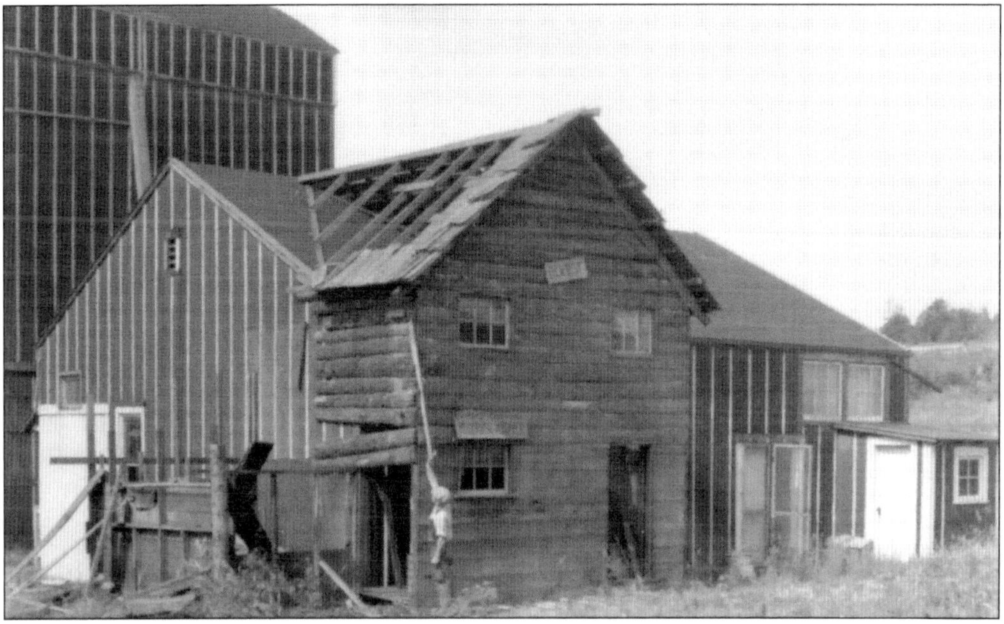

In 1924, motion picture promoters established the Weaver Pictures Studio at Titlow Beach with the hope of creating a rival company to those in Southern California. The company lasted only a few years, closing in 1928. After the structure was used a few years as a dance hall, demolition began, followed by a fire that destroyed the remaining complex; this photograph was taken just prior to its destruction. (Richards Studio, Tacoma Public Library.)

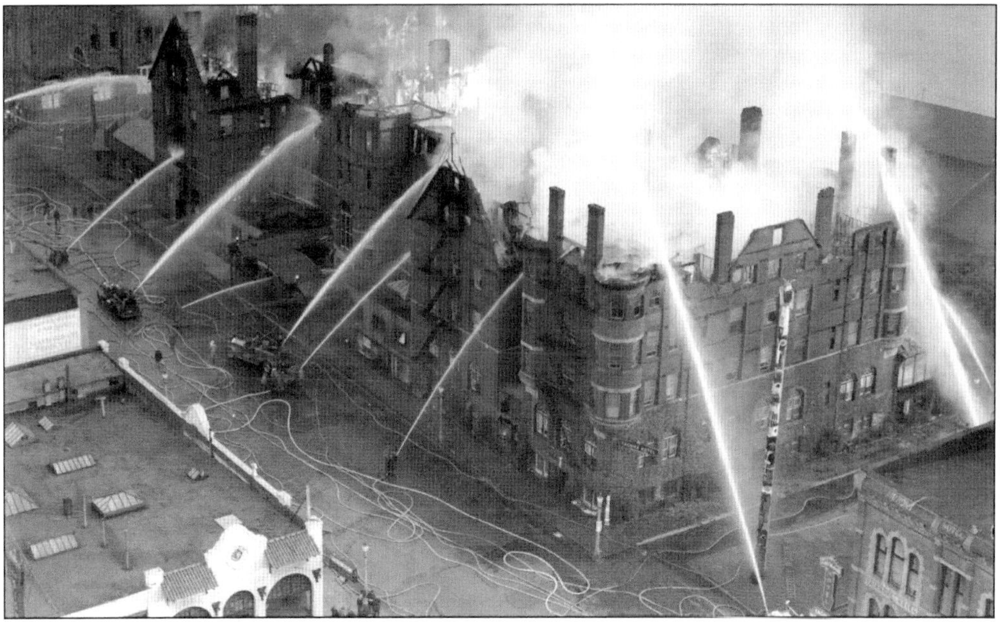

The New York architectural firm of McKim, Mead & White designed the Tacoma Hotel on A Street for the Tacoma Land Company in 1884, and stories abound about its grandeur. The hotel grew over time but was destroyed by fire on October 17, 1935—even with a fire station right across the street. The former Russell Building now occupies this location. (Richards Studio, Tacoma Public Library.)

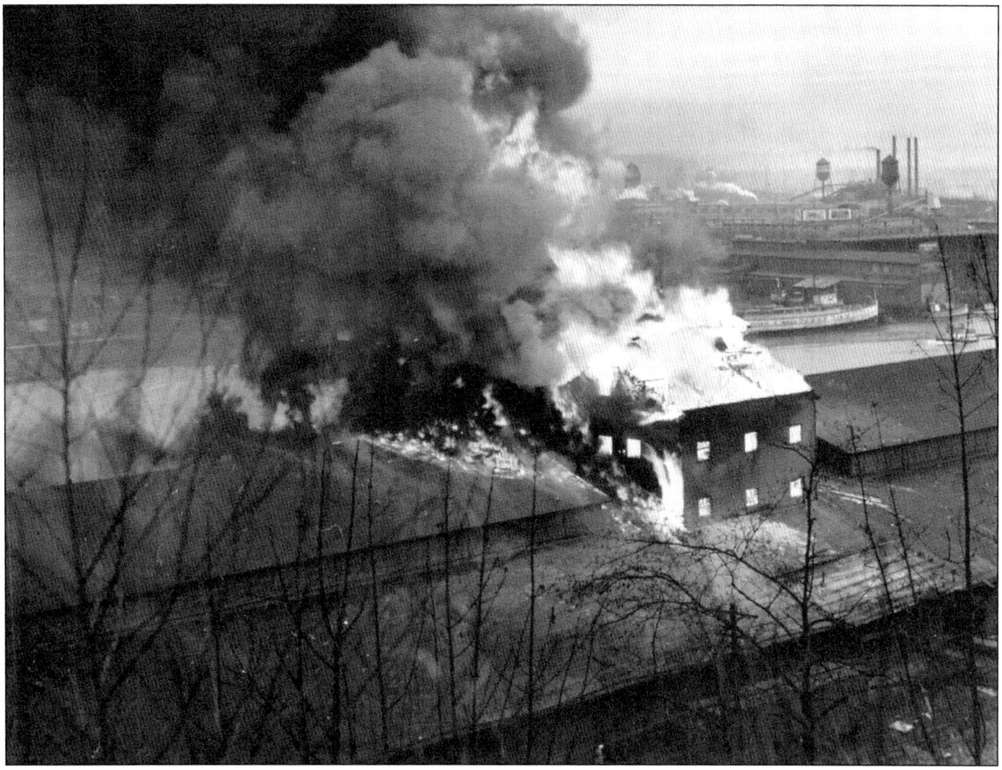

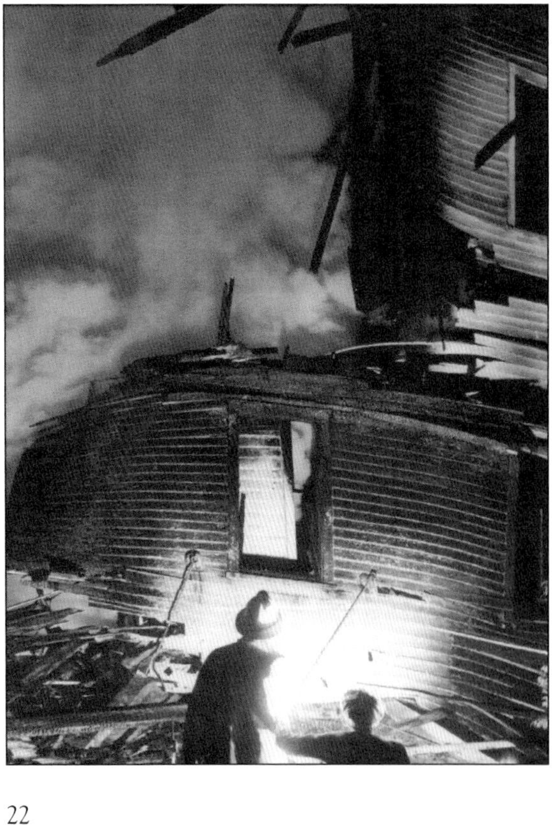

By 1900, a complex of docks stretched along the Thea Foss Waterway north from the Murray Morgan Bridge. In 1936, the London Dock housed the Waterside Milling Company's wheat warehouse when a fire, primarily fought from the shoreline by Tacoma's fireboat and local tugs, consumed it. There are no indications that the building was ever replaced. (Richards Studio, Tacoma Public Library.)

In 1928, the former Puyallup Tribal Cushman School was converted into a treatment center for tuberculosis patients. When a fire broke out in the hospital commissary in 1938, there was a lack of water pressure, which prevented firefighters from keeping the building from burning to the ground. Although most of the complex was saved, it was all demolished to construct a new hospital building on the site. (Richards Studio, Tacoma Public Library.)

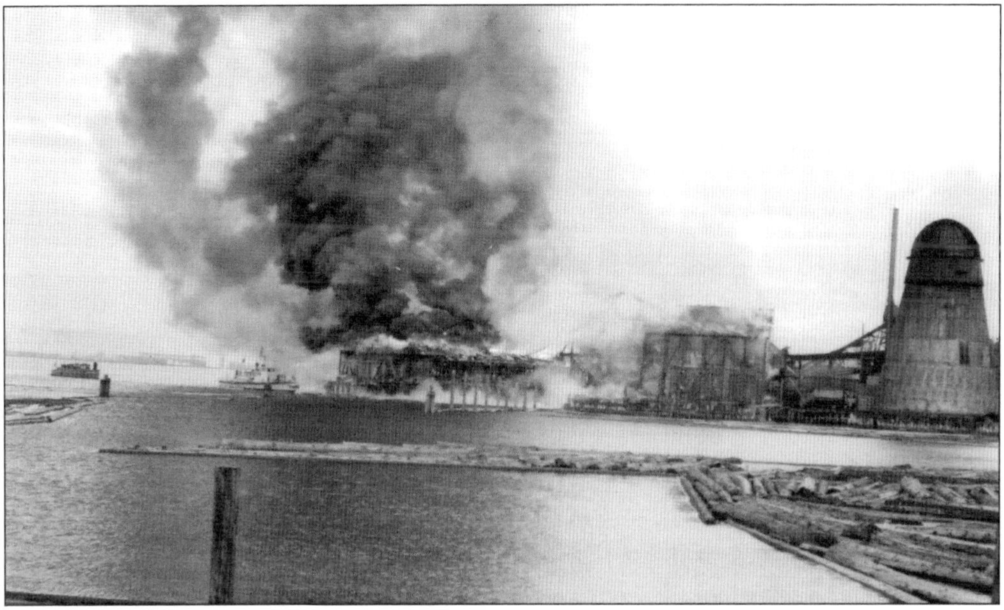

In 1925, the Henry Mill and Timber Company was founded at the foot of North Starr Street in Old Tacoma. A fire in June 1942, shown here, led to conversion of the complex into a prefabricating plant, supplying both the Army and the Navy during World War II. Sometime after 1950, business operations at the site ended; another fire that followed destroyed the plant. (Adolph Cummings photograph, courtesy of Patsy Cummings.)

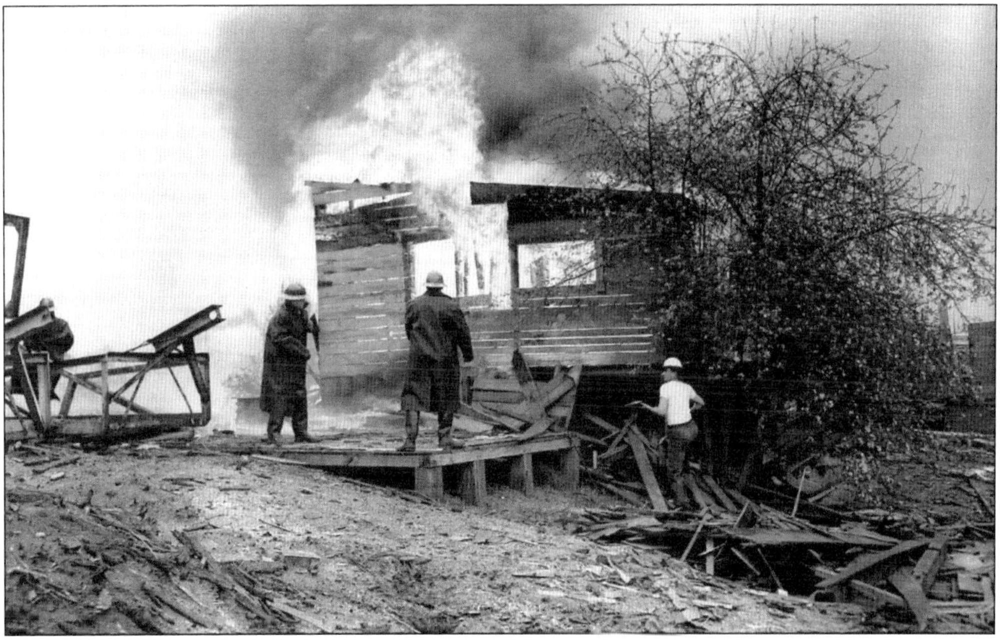

Tacoma's home for the homeless during the Great Depression was called "Hollywood on the Tideflats." It was a collection of makeshift homes grouped together on the undeveloped land east of the Port of Tacoma wharves. In April 1943, the US Coast Guard, with the help of the Tacoma Fire Department, burned down the shacks. By then, most were abandoned thanks to employment opportunities during World War II. (Richards Studio, Tacoma Public Library.)

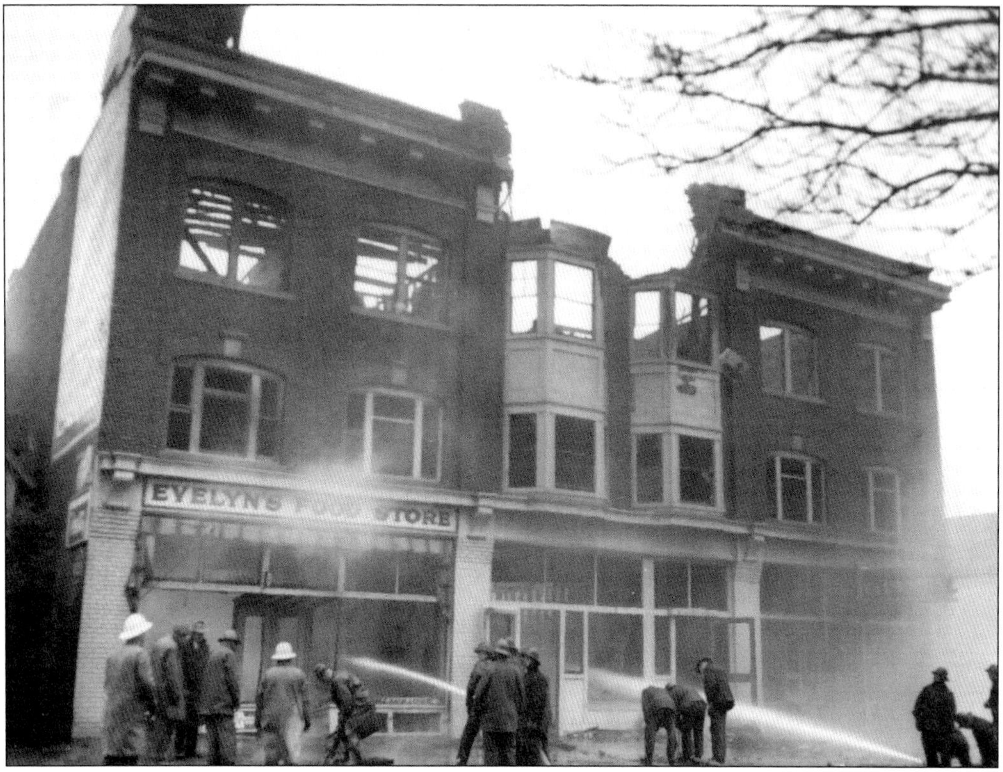

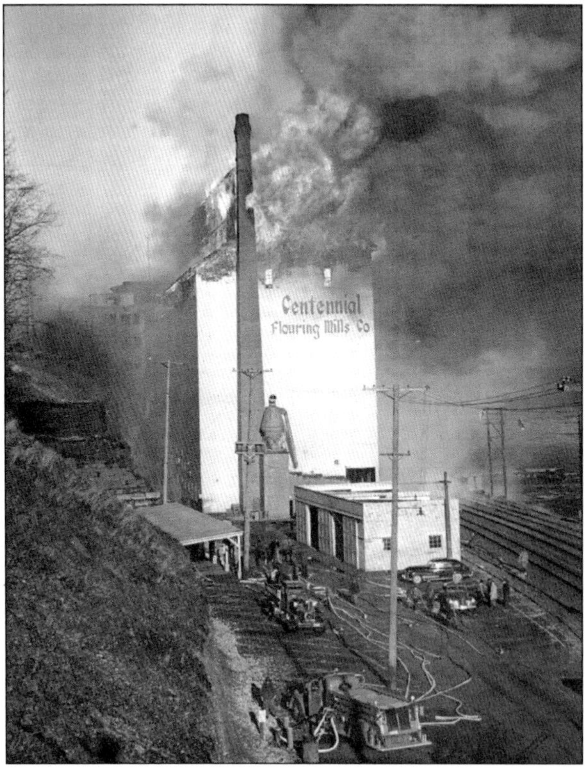

The February 17, 1945, fire at the Maefair apartments on Fawcett Avenue was one of the most deadly in Tacoma; it required an inquest to determine who was to blame for the deaths of 19 war workers, soldiers, and their families. The jury could not determine if an explosion in the candy factory in the basement contributed to the fire and deaths. The apartment house was not rebuilt. (Richards Studio, Tacoma Public Library.)

A fire broke out at the Centennial Flour Mill on the morning of January 30, 1947. The fire was the result of a malfunctioning switch, which caused flour dust in the building to ignite, setting the massive structure located on Bayside Drive (now Schuster Parkway) on fire. (Thomas R. Stenger collection.)

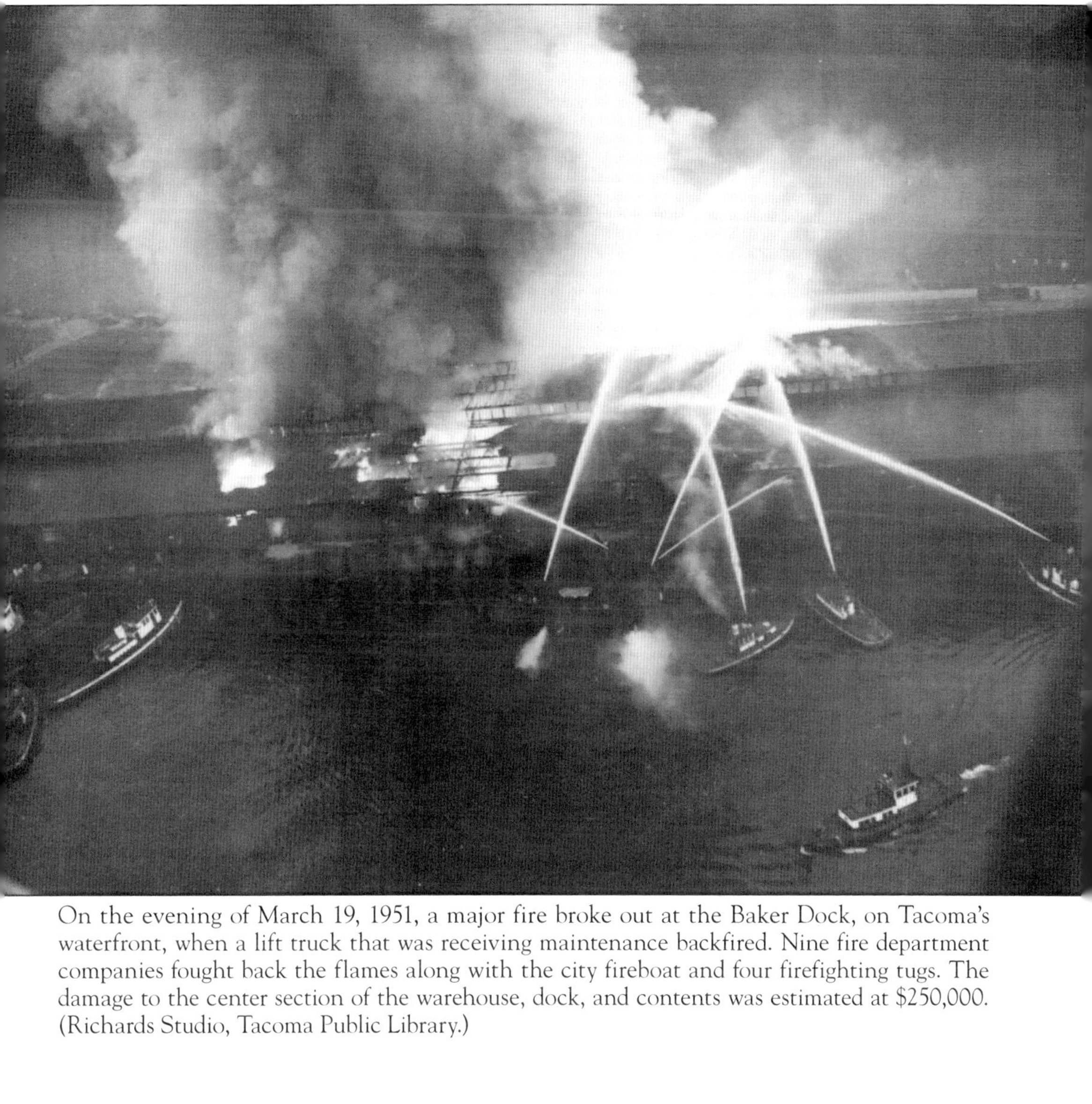

On the evening of March 19, 1951, a major fire broke out at the Baker Dock, on Tacoma's waterfront, when a lift truck that was receiving maintenance backfired. Nine fire department companies fought back the flames along with the city fireboat and four firefighting tugs. The damage to the center section of the warehouse, dock, and contents was estimated at $250,000. (Richards Studio, Tacoma Public Library.)

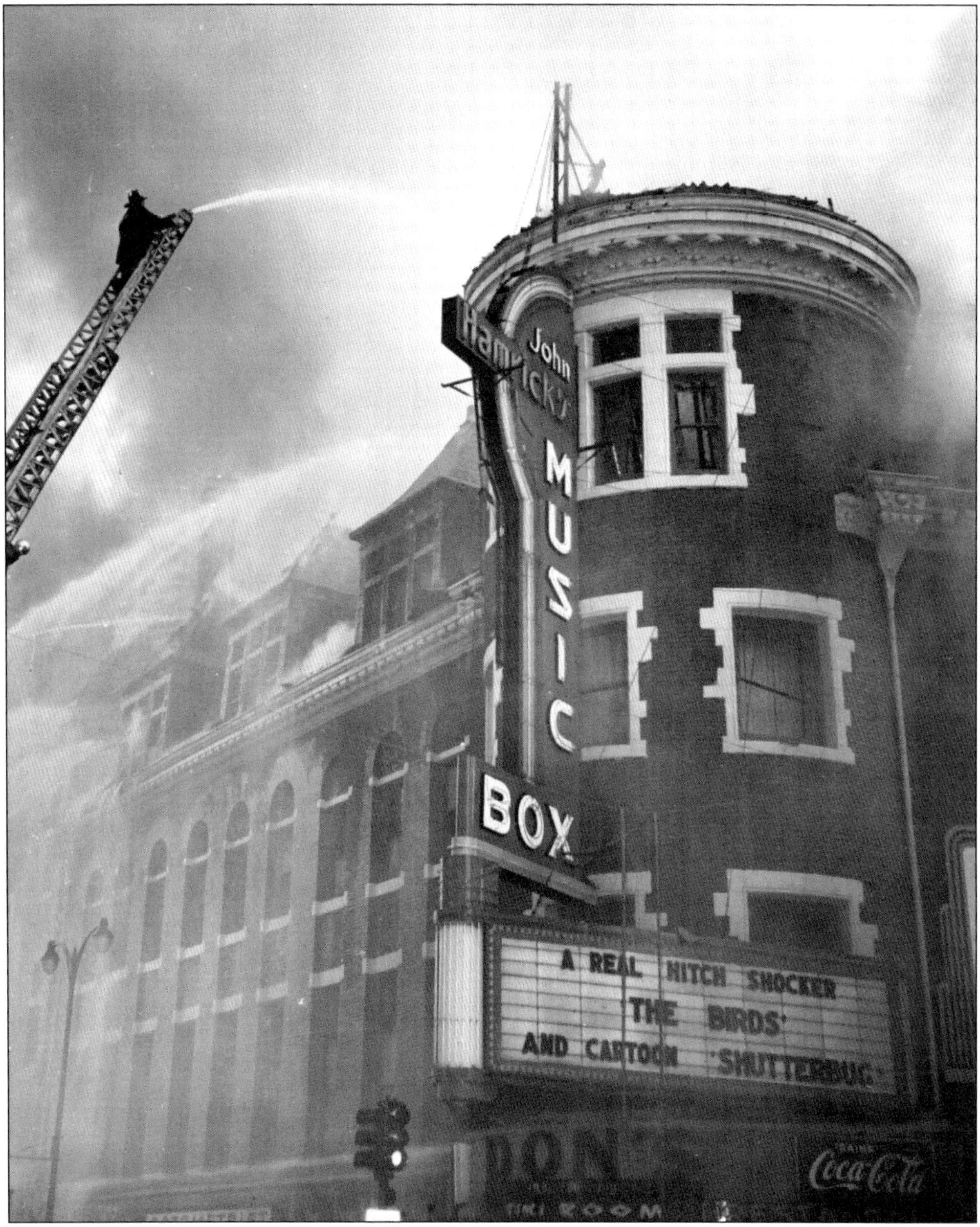

In 1874, the Tacoma Land Company constructed its office building at the corner of Ninth Street and Broadway Avenue. It was demolished to make way for the Tacoma Opera House in 1889, which became the second substantial brick building erected in Tacoma's downtown. (The Tacoma Hotel was just down the hill at Ninth and A Streets.) By the 1920s, as movies replaced vaudeville, owners of the opera house pondered tearing it down and replacing it with a high-rise hotel. Instead, owners converted the building to show movies. The name was changed first to the Broadway Theater and then later the Music Box. It was showing Hitchcock's *The Birds* in 1963 when fire destroyed the building, and no obvious attempts were made to restore it. One year later, the architectural firm of Lea, Pearson & Richards designed the Broadway Terrace Building, which remains to this day. (Richards Studio, Tacoma Public Library.)

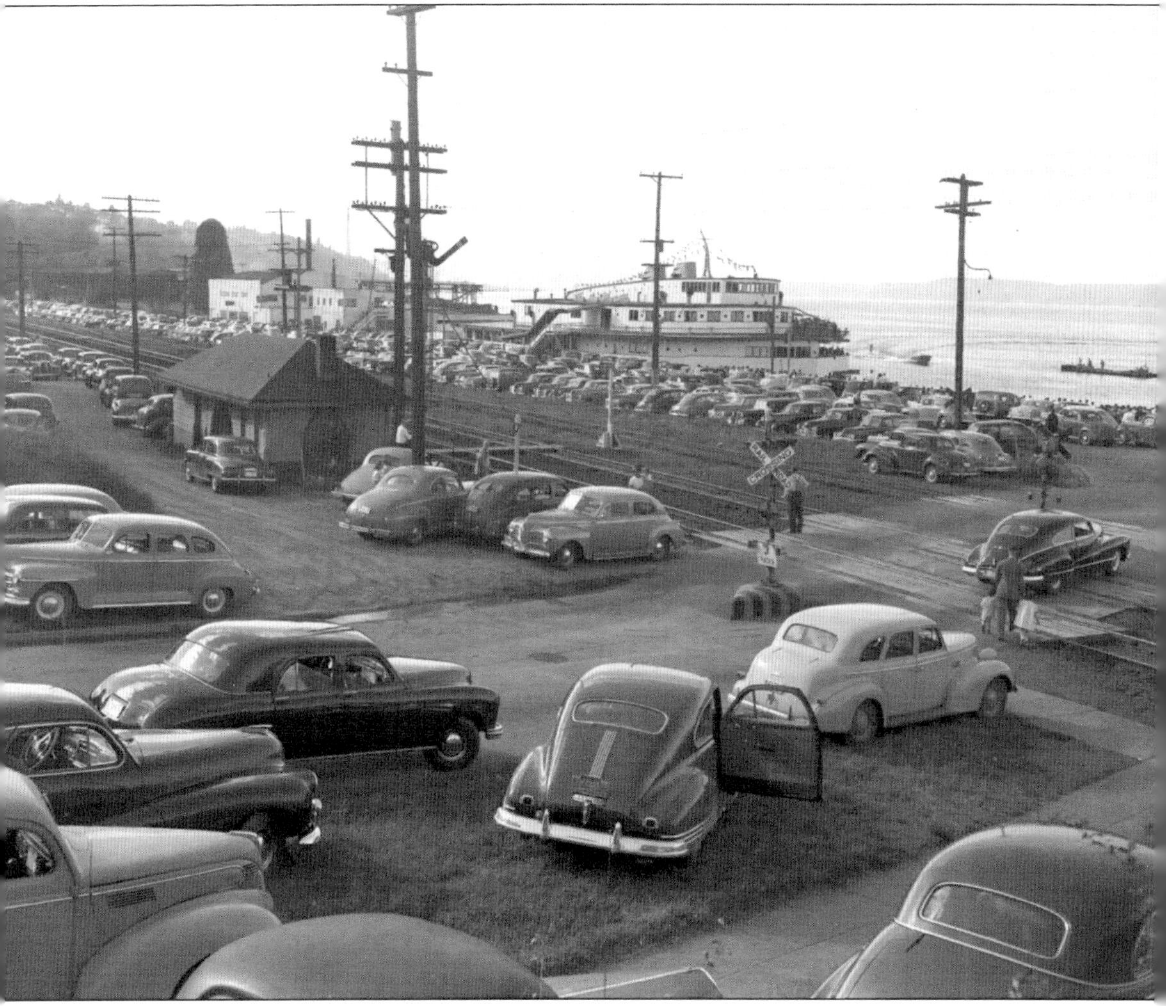

In this 1948 view taken from North McCarver Street and Ruston Way, a Richards Studio photographer was able to capture two buildings that would be destroyed by fire in the 1970s. The Tacoma Athletic Commission was one of the first owners when the Top of the Ocean (foreground) opened in 1946. While there, the organization introduced the city to the Water Carnival shown in this image. The restaurant continued under various owners until April 1977, when an arsonous fire consumed it. While there were attempts to restore the building, it was demolished later that year. The same year that the "Top" was lost, the owners of the Dickman Mill (background) had already sold the last surviving lumber company on Commencement Bay to private developers. As the new owners began dismantling the site, a fire broke out one morning in January 1979. Like the Top of the Ocean, the Dickman Lumber Company was later demolished (by 1997), and both properties became part of a lineal park bordering Commencement Bay along Ruston Way. (Richards Studio, Tacoma Public Library.)

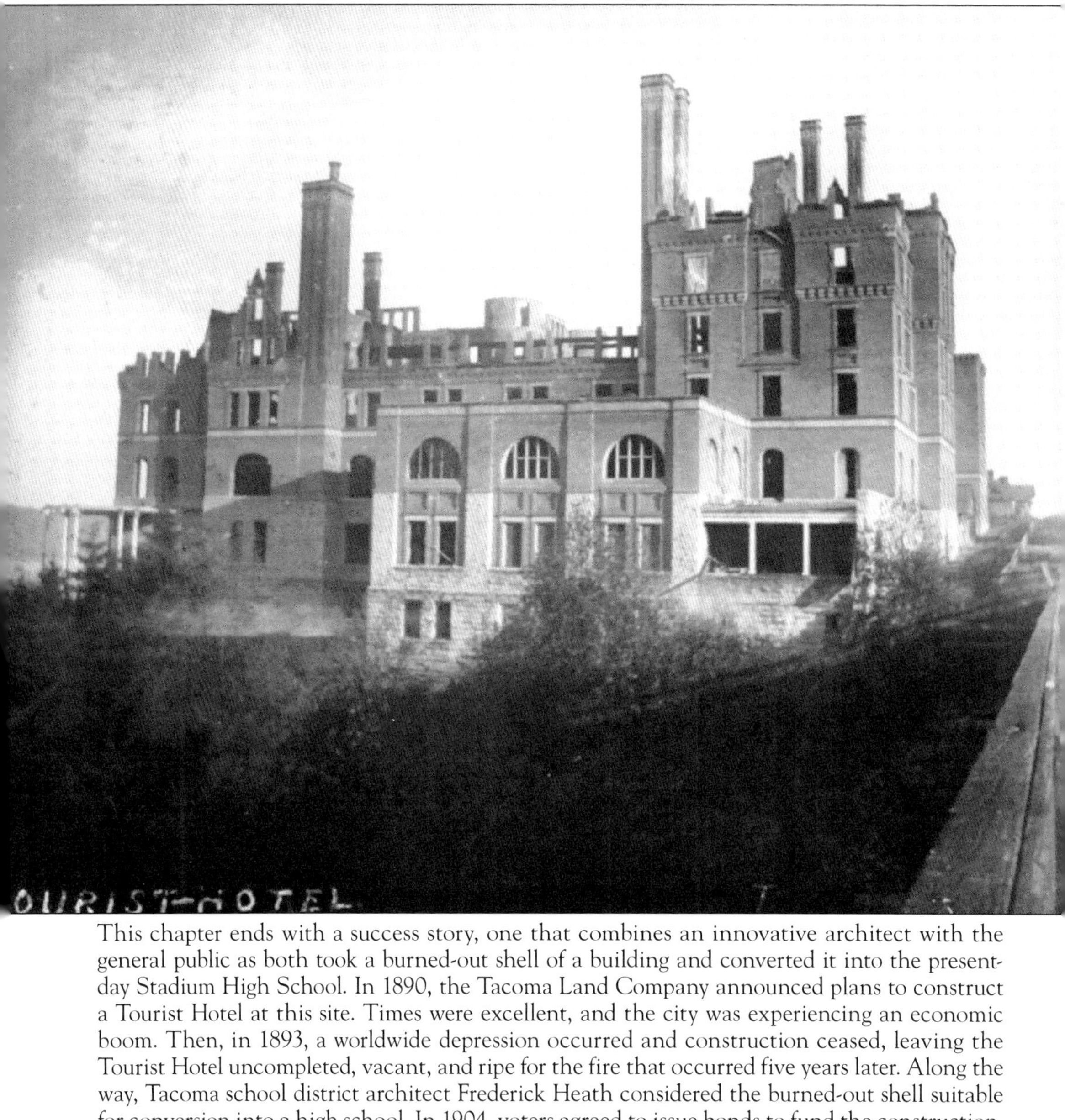

This chapter ends with a success story, one that combines an innovative architect with the general public as both took a burned-out shell of a building and converted it into the present-day Stadium High School. In 1890, the Tacoma Land Company announced plans to construct a Tourist Hotel at this site. Times were excellent, and the city was experiencing an economic boom. Then, in 1893, a worldwide depression occurred and construction ceased, leaving the Tourist Hotel uncompleted, vacant, and ripe for the fire that occurred five years later. Along the way, Tacoma school district architect Frederick Heath considered the burned-out shell suitable for conversion into a high school. In 1904, voters agreed to issue bonds to fund the construction, following as closely as possible the original plans for the Tourist Hotel, and Tacoma High School welcomed its first graduating class in September 1906. The name was changed in 1913 with the completion of Stadium Bowl. Even though there have been changes over the years, the school retains all those qualities required of its status as a Tacoma and national landmark.

Three

DISASTERS

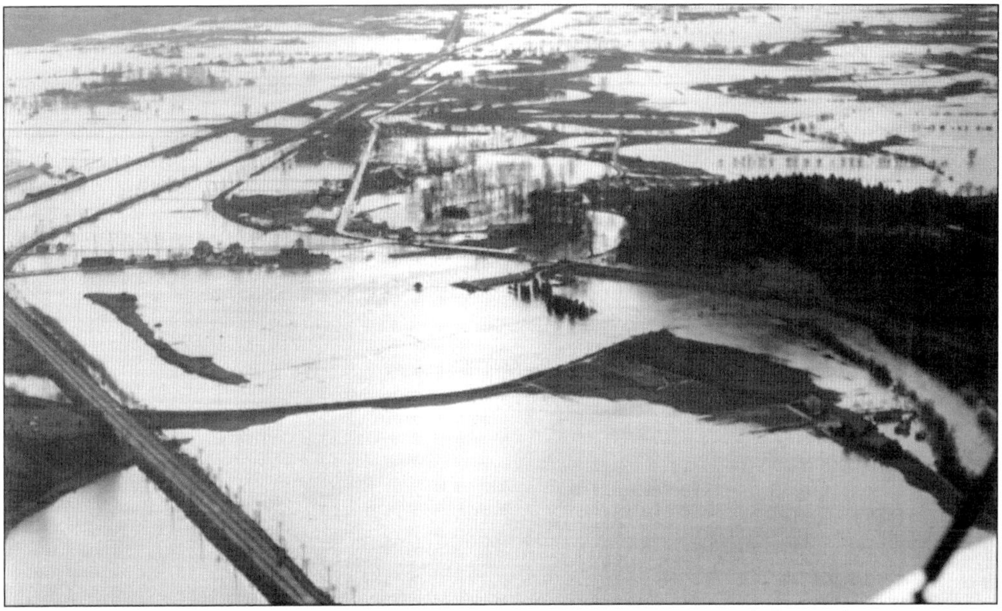

Tacoma's urban landscape has been continuously destroyed, remade, and changed in response to both natural and human-engineered disasters. This chapter provides a few examples as to how parts of the city's history vanished through floods and snowstorms, building and bridge collapses, and earthquakes. Shown here is a view looking east at the December 1933 flood. The rising Puyallup River caused the flooding. From the city's beginning, developers pondered how to tame the river and its tributaries in order to expand port facilities. The process began in the 1880s when Native American land was gradually taken from the Puyallup tribe. By the time of World War I, local businessmen—with the aid of the Army Corps of Engineers—had already started taming the upstream parts of the river through an intricate diversion of water from stream to stream that eventually affected rural and urban areas of both King and Pierce Counties. More flooding occurred, and more time was needed to complete the project. (Thomas R. Stenger collection.)

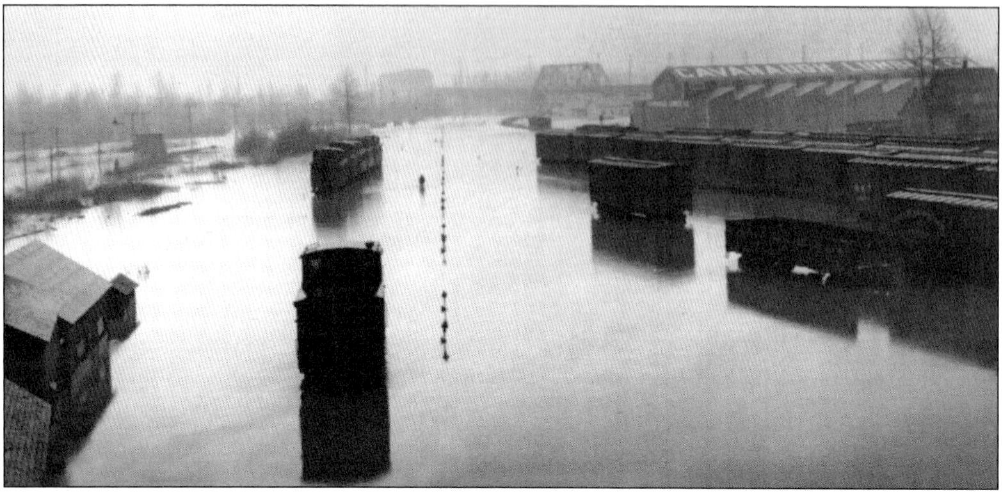

The 1933 flood wreaked havoc on railroad, shipping, and industrial facilities throughout the Puyallup River delta region. The above photograph shows the damage done to the Northern Pacific Railway freight yards at that time. Unfortunately, World War II intervened in the 1940s, and human and economic resources being used for river reconstruction were now diverted to the war effort. By 1958, however, the Puyallup River was completely diked, and a waterway was extended into Commencement Bay. The below image also shows the five bridges crossing the reconstructed river stretching from South Twenty-first Street to the Puyallup Indian Reservation. The Interstate 5 freeway bridge would eventually cross the river in the vicinity of the three bridges shown just before the bend seen in the background. An aerial photograph today would show an entirely different delta configuration, as other waterways were filled to accommodate container cargo. (Above, Thomas R. Stenger collection; below, Richards Studio, Tacoma Public Library.)

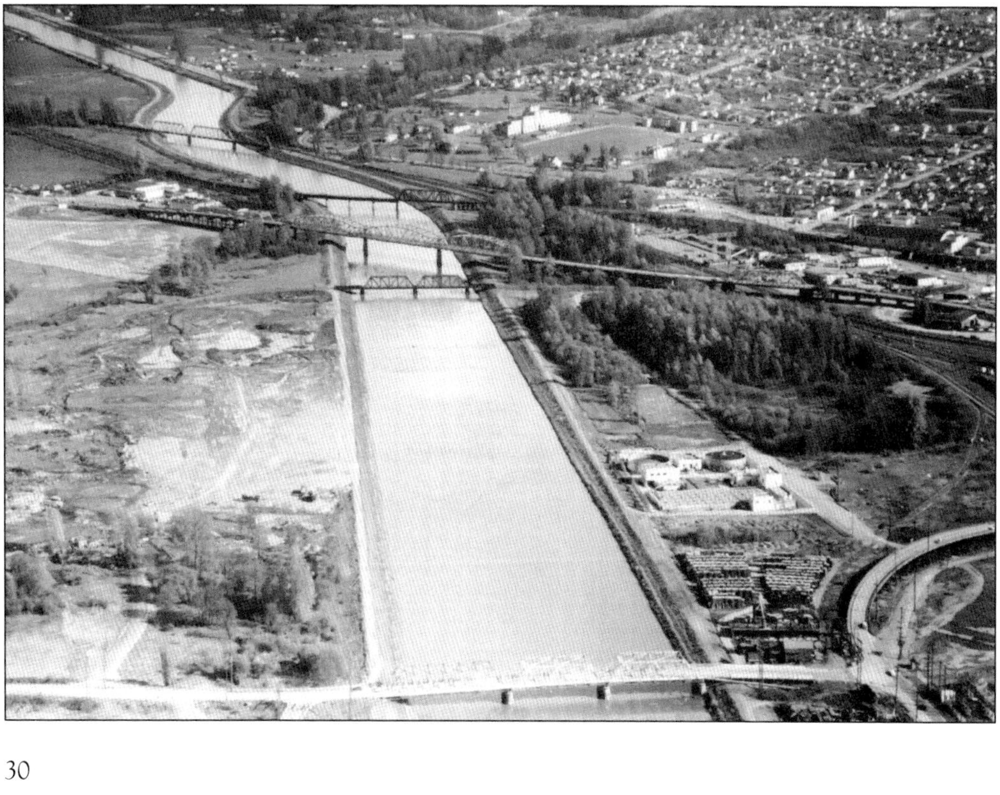

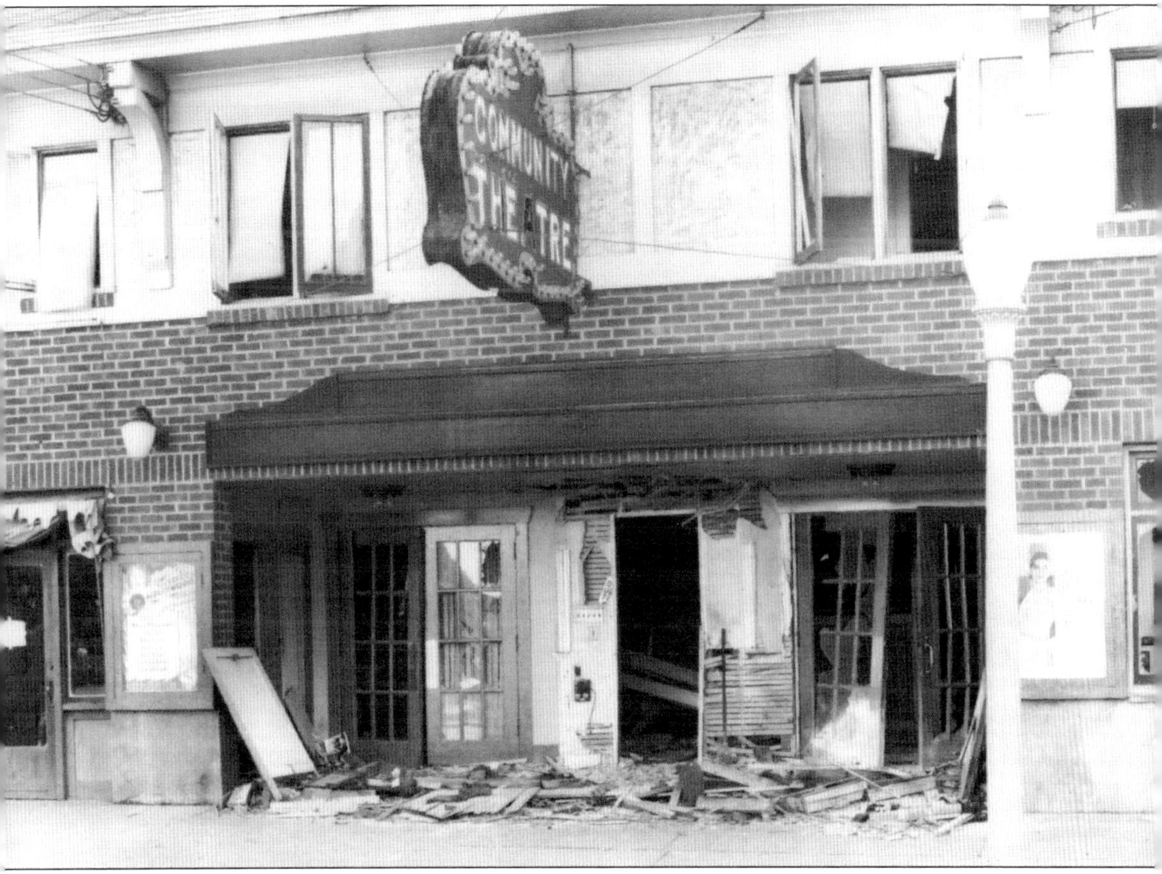

The Tacoma Public Library photograph archives yields very few images related to bombings. Most pertained to civil defense activities during World War II, as servicemen from Fort Lewis were prepared for the possibility of a city bombed by the enemy. The Korean War and the Cold War that followed gave photographers the opportunity to document bomb shelters designed to allegedly protect citizens from atomic and nuclear weapons. Prior to this time, however, there were a few instances between 1930 and 1935 when property was damaged through bombings. Two known instances were related to labor disputes. In 1930, the community theater, located at 5441 South M Street, was damaged by early-morning dynamite explosions powerful enough to hurl debris onto the stage. Three men were arrested, found guilty, and sentenced to prison for the blast. The theater was rebuilt and continued to be used for films and live concerts into the later years of the 20th century. (Tacoma Public Library.)

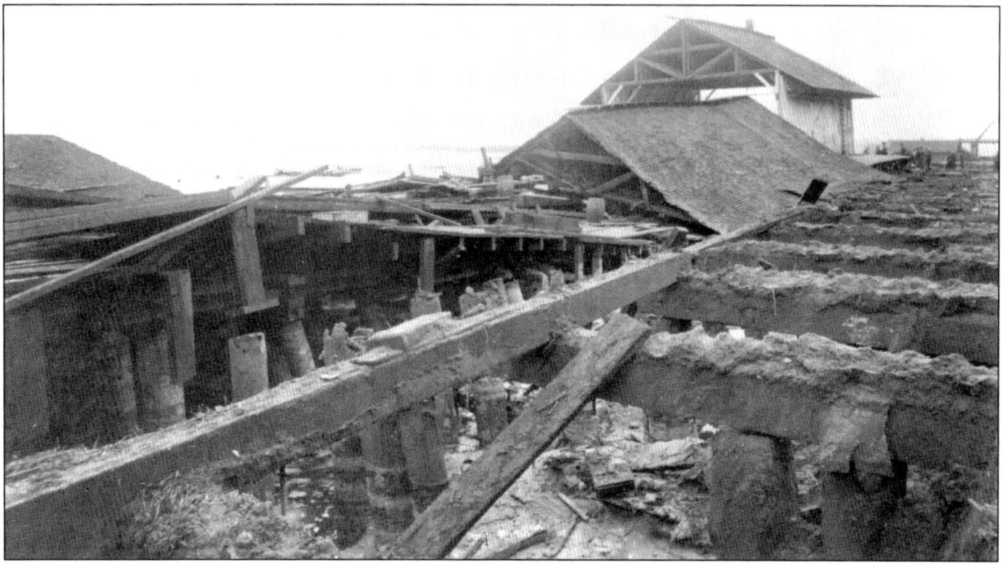

Slides into Commencement Bay from the present-day Schuster Parkway have plagued Tacomans for a long time, with most caused by poorly constructed support systems as development proceeded along the shoreline. Given the importance of this area as the city's first port, repairs were usually quick, using newer technologies each time. One of the first structural collapses occurred at the Northern Pacific Railroad wharf in 1894.

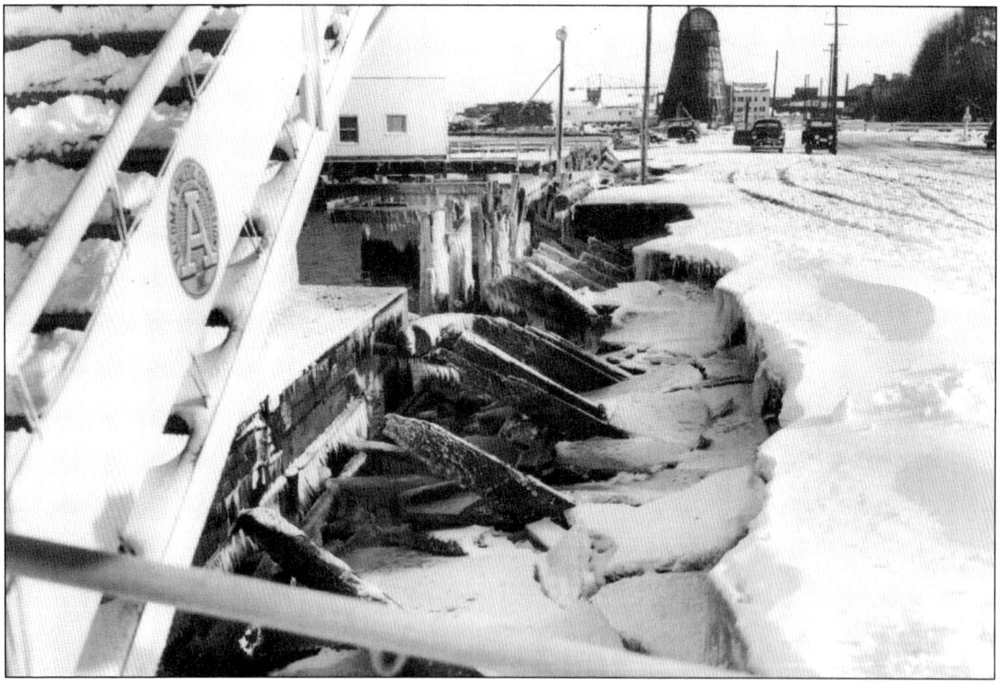

Snowstorms could be equally damaging to the shoreline. In this instance, it was a January 1950 blizzard that brought five-foot snowdrifts, icy weather, and a million dollars worth of damage to property in Tacoma. The storm damaged the bulkhead of the Top of the Ocean located at the foot of North McCarver Street. It, along with the Henry Mill shown in the background, later became a victim of fire. (Richards Studio, Tacoma Public Library.)

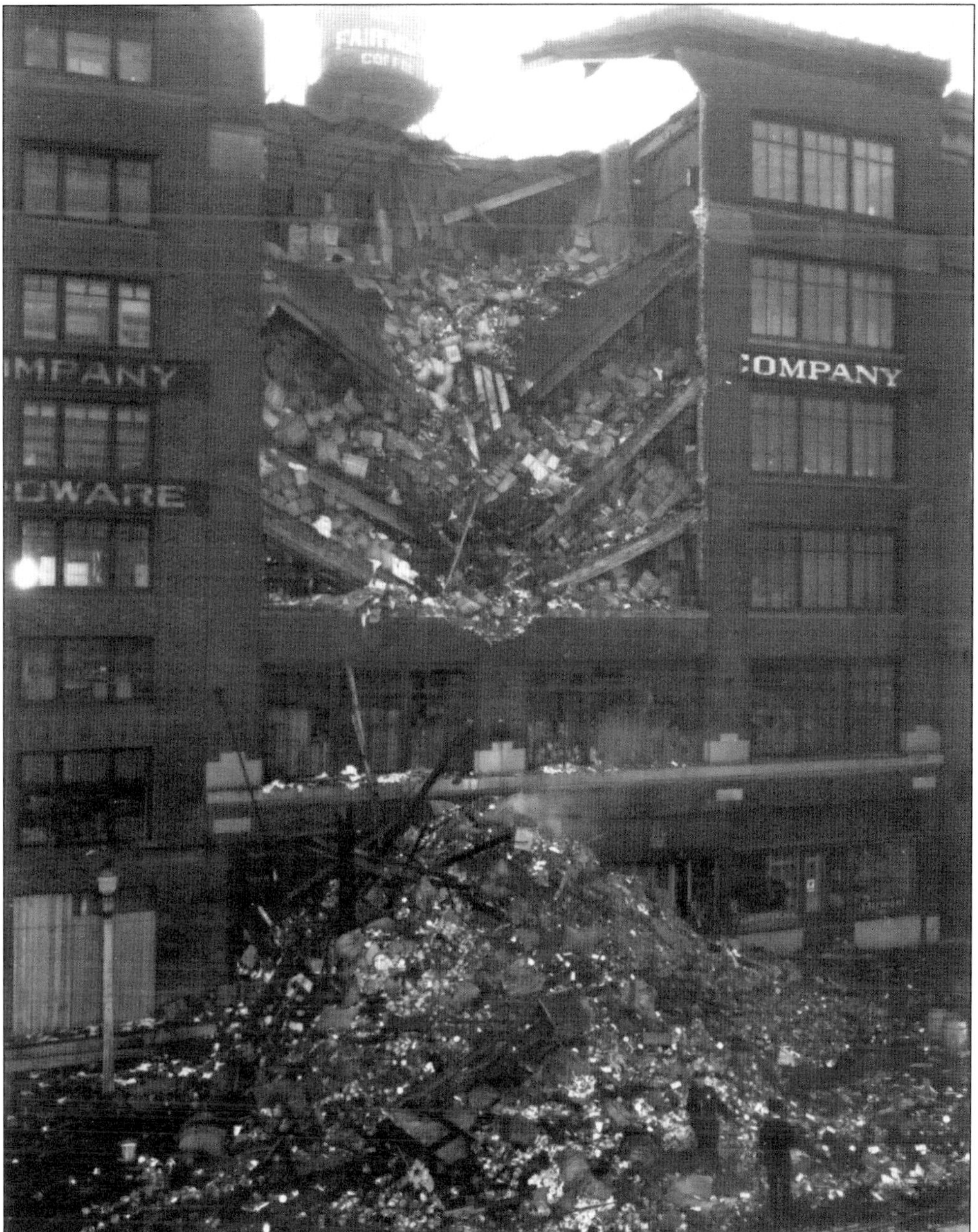

Architect Frederick Heath designed the Love-Johnson (Tacoma Grocery Company) Building at 2108 Pacific Avenue in 1906, and it became a part of the warehouse district located south of Tacoma's business district. In October 1934, its fire system sprinklers broke and flooded the entire structure, leading ultimately to its collapse. Of particular interest in this view is the water tower constructed for the Tacoma Grocery Company in 1915; it was probably a partial cause of the collapse. As firefighting improved through the decades, such structures were no longer needed and have gradually becoming a part of vanishing Tacoma. The grocery building was subsequently rebuilt and, in 1949, reinforced with concrete. Buildings located to the north of here are now part of the University of Washington Tacoma. (Richards Studio, Tacoma Public Library.)

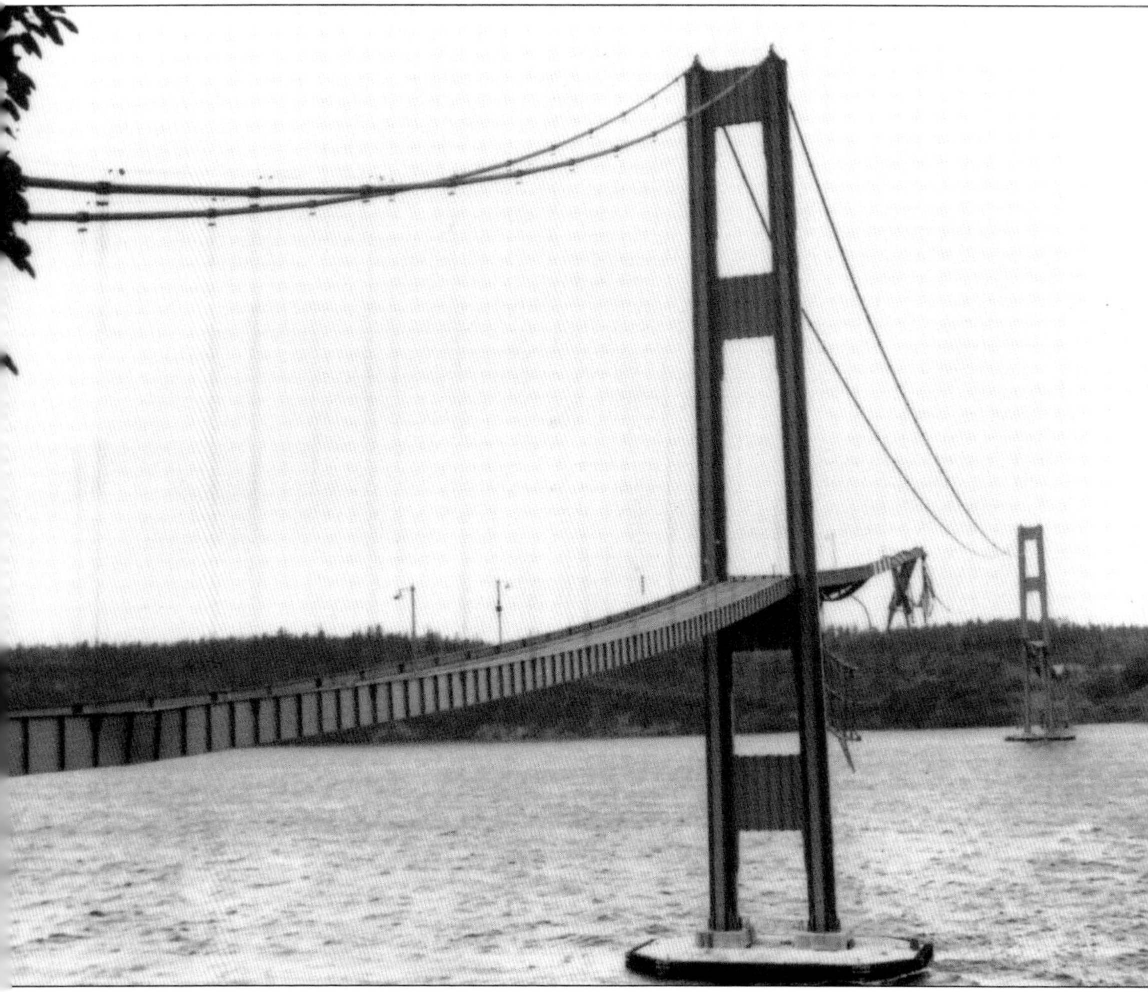

"Galloping Gertie"—Tacoma's first Narrows Bridge—became a national celebrity when it collapsed into Puget Sound on November 7, 1940, four months after it was dedicated. The underwater remnants are now in the National Register of Historic Places, while new bridges constructed in 1950 and 2007 connect Tacoma to the Gig Harbor Peninsula and other suburban points beyond. (Richards Studio, Tacoma Public Library.)

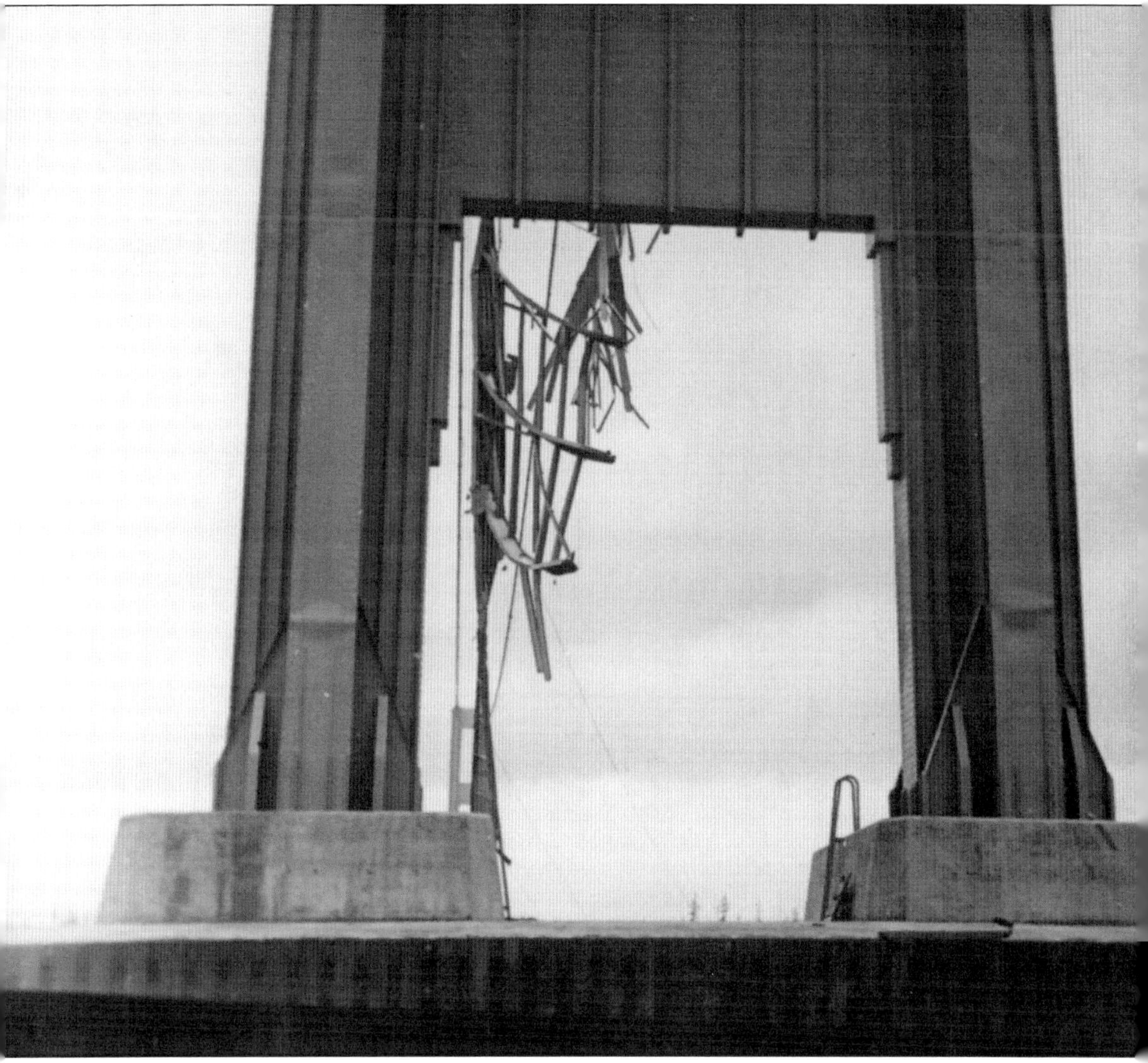

Once the bridge collapsed, it became an attraction for amateur and professional photographers alike, with some more adventurous than others out to capture the daring shot. One such Tacoman was Adolph Cummings, an engineer who purchased land along Commencement Bay for his boat repair business. After his death in 1987, his land was sold to the Metropolitan Park District for park purposes. (Adolph Cummings photograph, courtesy of Patsy Cummings.)

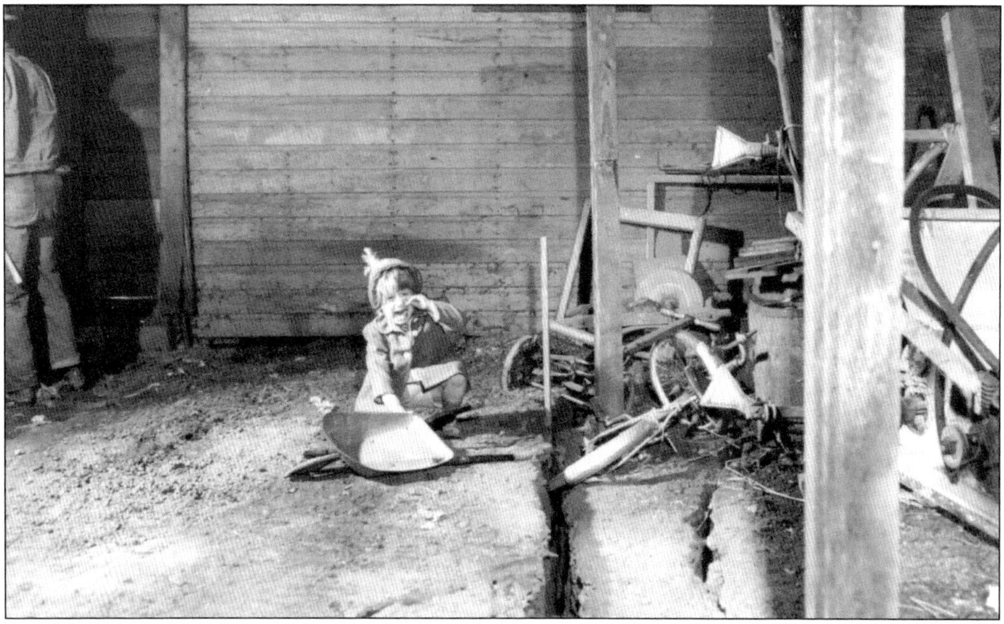

At approximately noon on April 13, 1949, the region experienced one of the worst earthquake disasters in its history, causing millions of dollars of damage throughout Puget Sound. The location of this Richards Studio photograph of a little girl is unknown, but the image does show the damage done by the earthquake. (Richards Studio, Tacoma Public Library.)

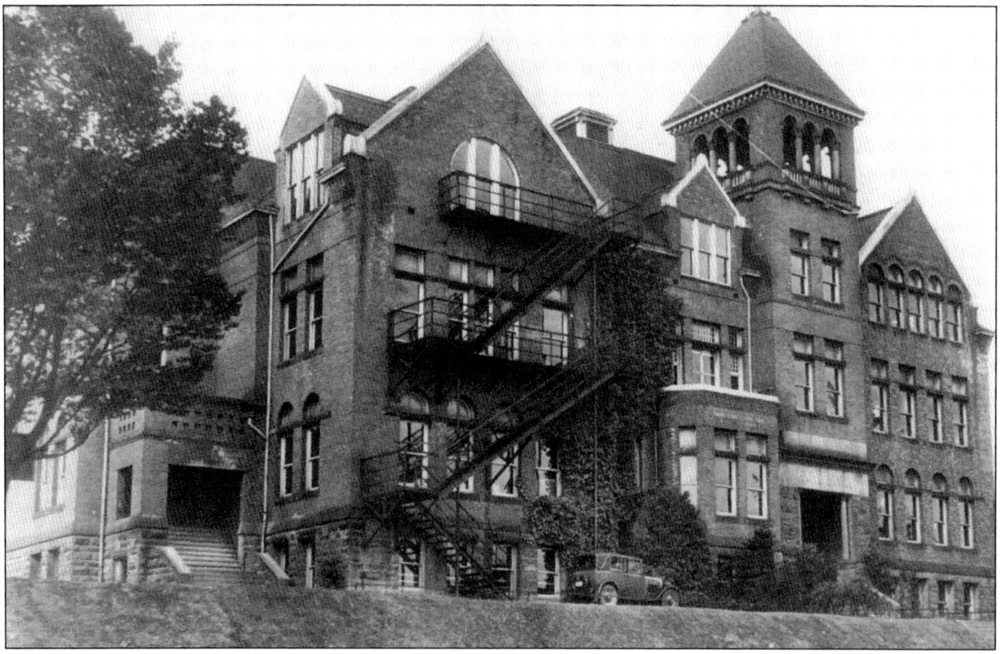

In 1892, the Tacoma architectural firm of Bullard and Hayward designed Lowell School, located at 1210 North Yakima Avenue. Named to honor James Russell Lowell, an American Romantic poet and diplomat who had died the year before, the school was located south of Old Tacoma and educated many children living in the north end. It was one of several Tacoma schools that did not survive the earthquake.

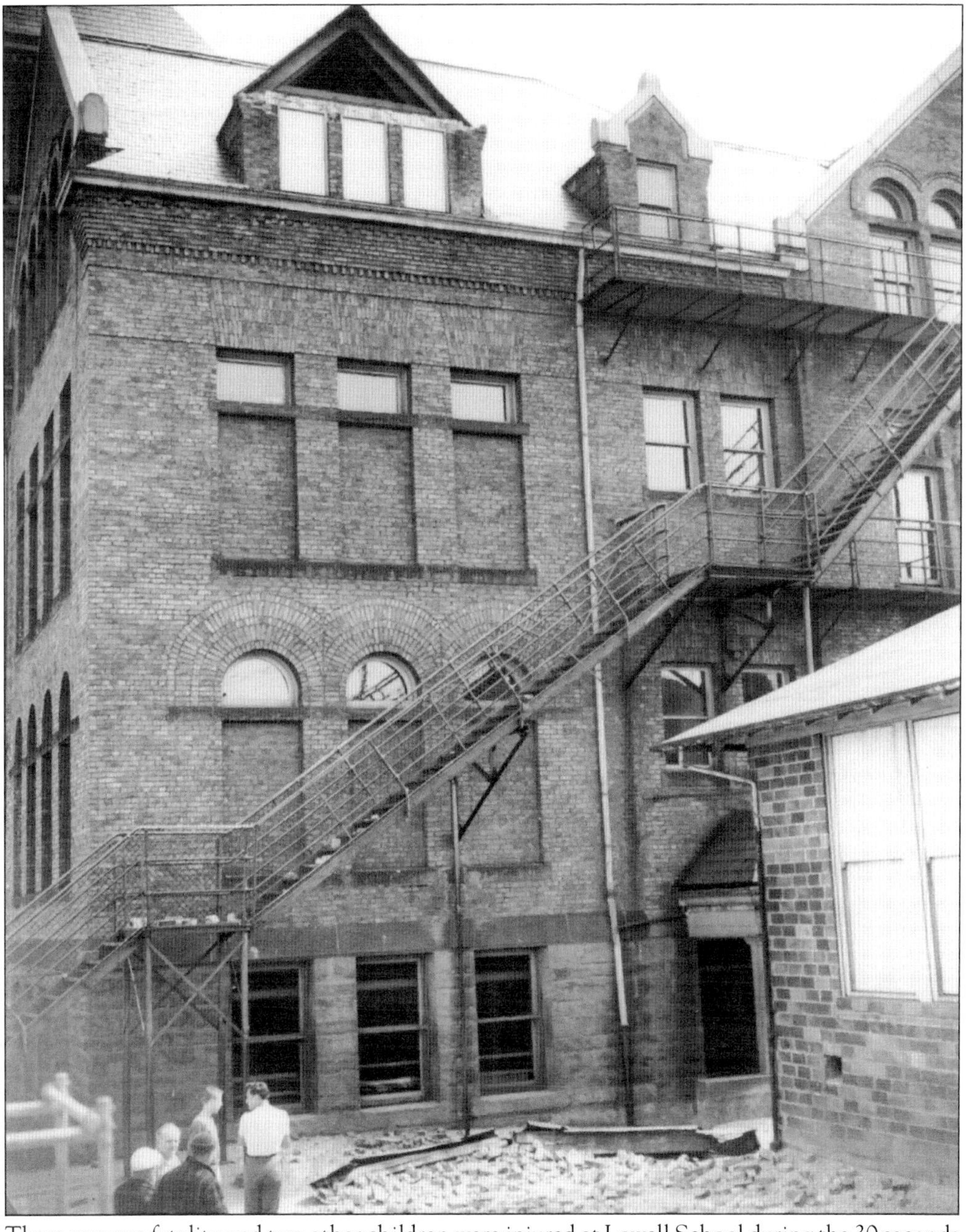

There was one fatality and two other children were injured at Lowell School during the 30 seconds of shaking that occurred that day. Marvin Klegman was killed by a falling chimney as he left the school for duty as a safety patrolman. In 2003, a sculpture of the lad, designed by Tacoma artist Larry Anderson, was placed above the present-day playground on North Yakima Street to honor his courage. (Richards Studio, Tacoma Public Library.)

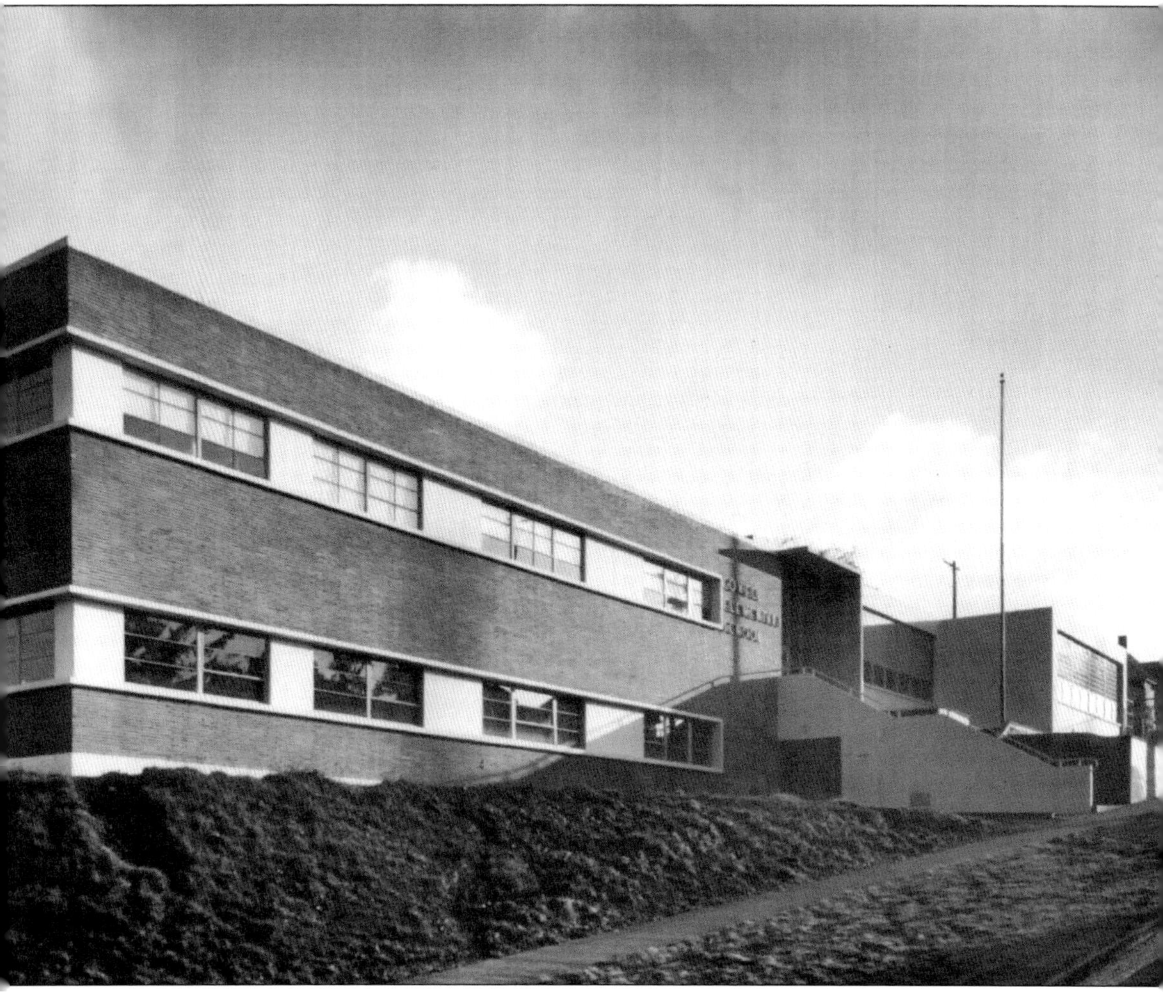

The damaged Lowell school was demolished in 1949 and replaced by a modern, earthquake-safe one, designed by the Tacoma architectural firm of Lance, McGuire & Muri. The new building was dedicated in November 1951, two months before this photograph was taken. While there have been some changes, the school appears today as it did in the 1950s. (Richards Studio, Tacoma Public Library.)

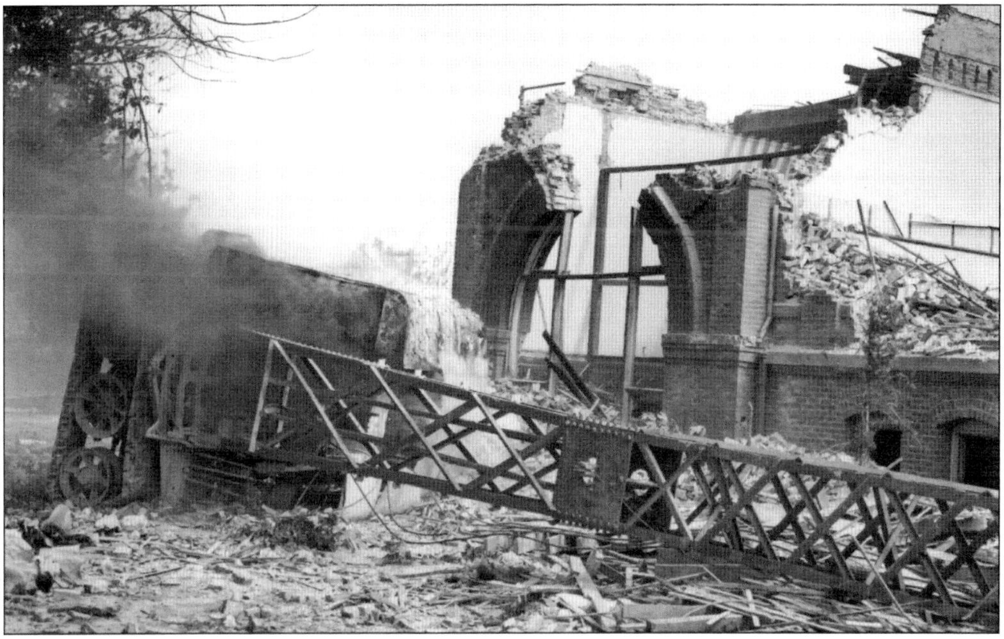

The Walt Whitman School was dedicated in March 1892 to honor one the American poet and essayist who had died that same month and year. Located at 1211 South Fortieth Street, it became one of three schools condemned as unsafe following the 1949 earthquake. It was demolished (above) the following year, while the Tacoma architectural firm of Lea, Pearson & Richards began plans for a new earthquake-proof building located a block east of the original school (below). This photograph below was taken a month after its dedication. From this time forward, professional engineers have regularly checked the stability of Tacoma's school buildings to make sure future earthquakes do not destroy human life. This practice is somewhat controversial because some feel it has led to an unnecessary loss of historic school buildings. Whitman, along with other schools, was placed in the Tacoma Register of Historic Places in 2010. (Both, Richards Studio, Tacoma Public Library.)

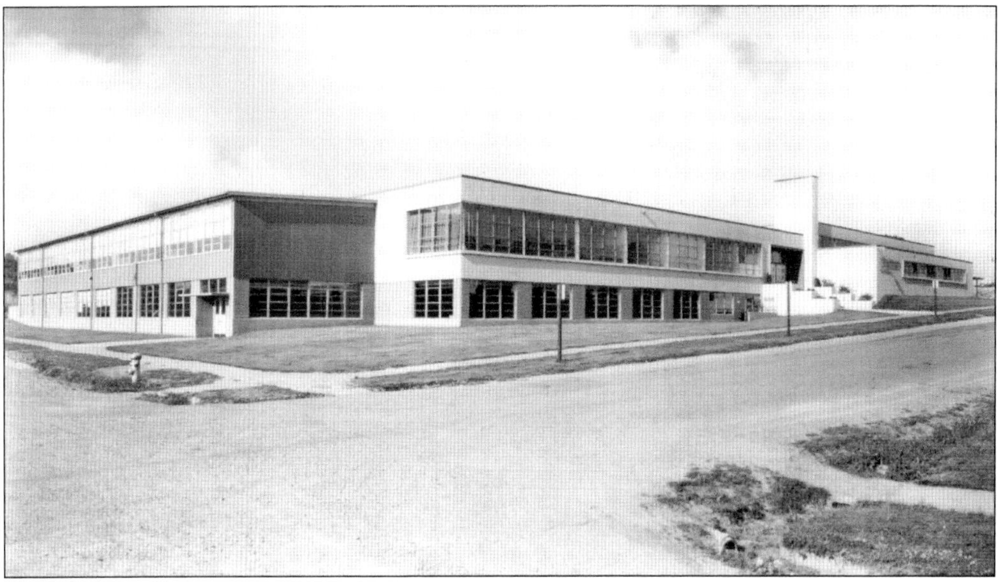

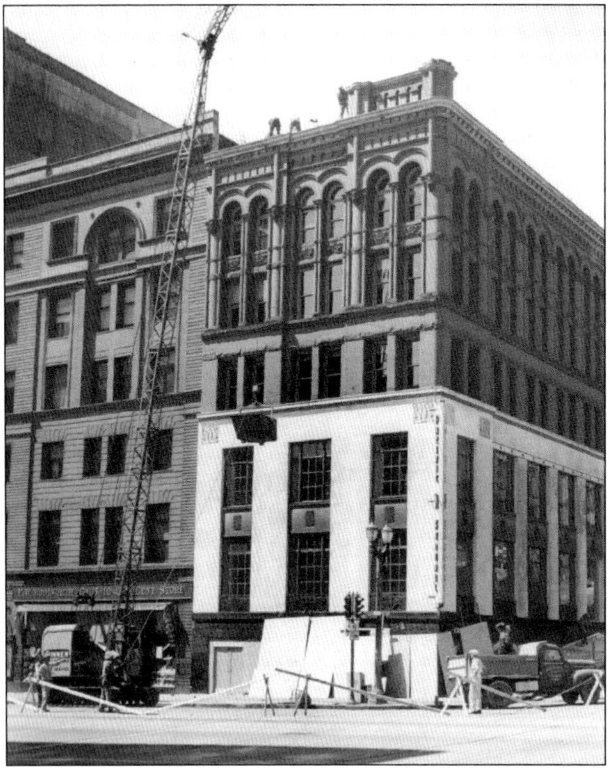

The 7.1-magnitude 1949 earthquake was the first major earthquake in Puget Sound since the earliest settlements began. Most of the damage affected downtown brick buildings, especially chimneys and architectural roof details, such as cornices. Tacoma officials immediately began ordering the removal of much of the terra-cotta decorations that made the downtown historically unique. One structure affected as such is the Pacific First Federal Building at 1102 Pacific Avenue (left), which was later demolished and replaced with a modern bank. At 960 Pacific Avenue (below), the large iconic boot advertising the Regal Shoe Store was removed from the roof. Both of these removals occurred within weeks of the earthquake. (Both, Richards Studio, Tacoma Public Library.)

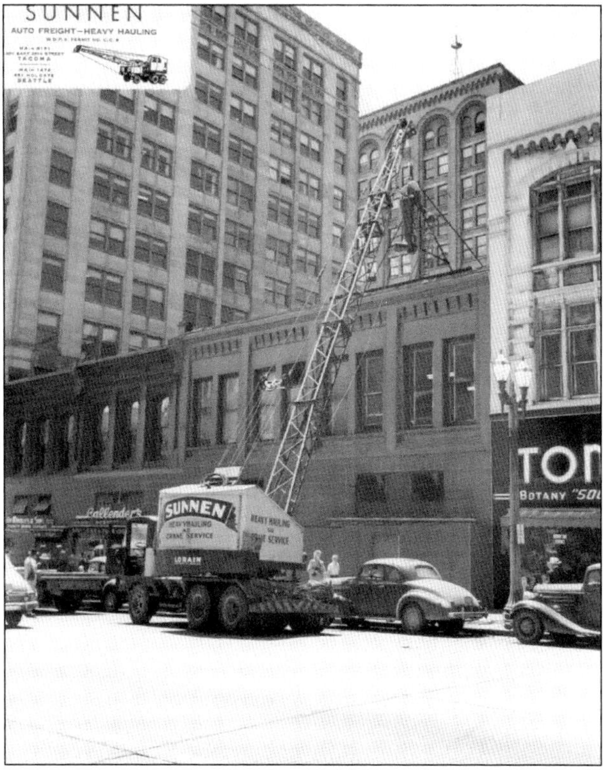

Four

TRANSPORTATION

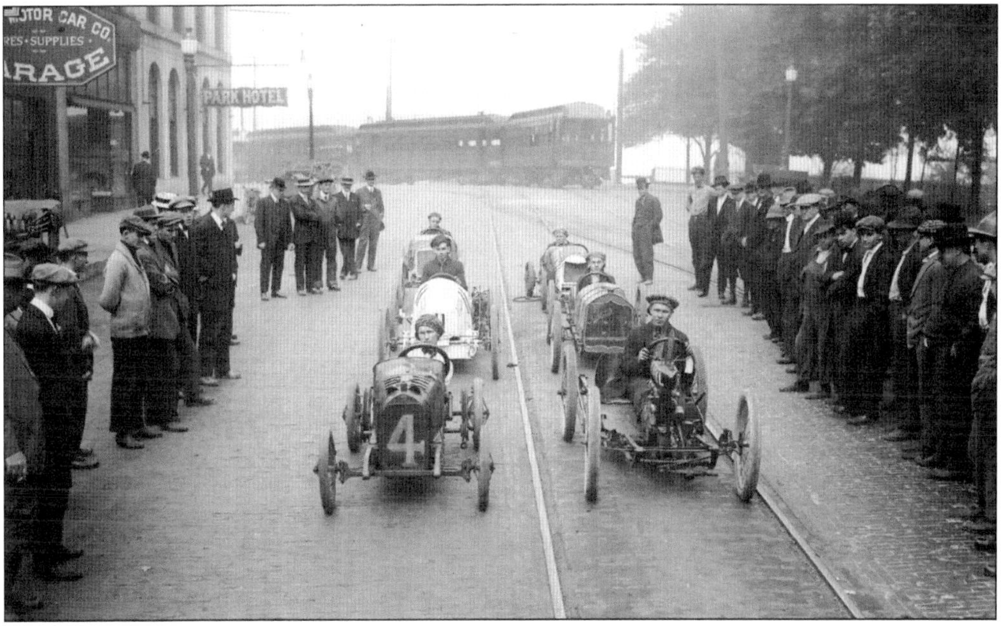

In September 1914, a group of California-based junior racers on the way to the Tacoma Speedway poses on A Street near Fireman's Park (left). A Seattle-Tacoma Interurban Railway train is leaving its station and can be seen in the background. On the left, one can see the business sign for J.F. Hickey's Motor Car Company and Garage. From the brick street to the park and the buildings along the street, nothing remains today as seen in this view. Indeed, most of the business block on the left is now a parking garage. This points to the truism that changes in the modes of transportation and the technologies that fueled them are the major causes why cities have vanished, been altered, and redeveloped over time. Fireman's Park was completely demolished to make way for Interstate 705. While the park was rebuilt, the new lacks the charm of the old. (Speedway Collection, Tacoma Public Library.)

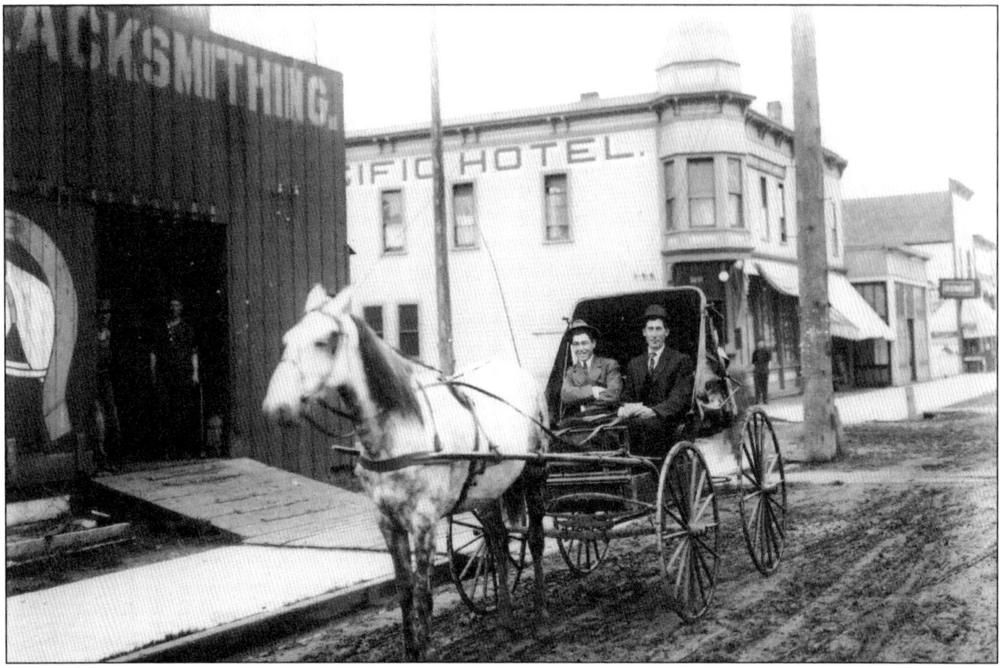

Traveling on foot and by horse led to small, unconnected communities in the Tacoma area. For example, it took the streetcar to ultimately tie South Tacoma, shown here, to Tacoma. In 1908, A.D. Browning photographed this horse and buggy posed in front of a blacksmith shop. Chances are that when the first automobile arrived in South Tacoma, the shop became a service station. (Amzie D. Browning Collection, Tacoma Public Library.)

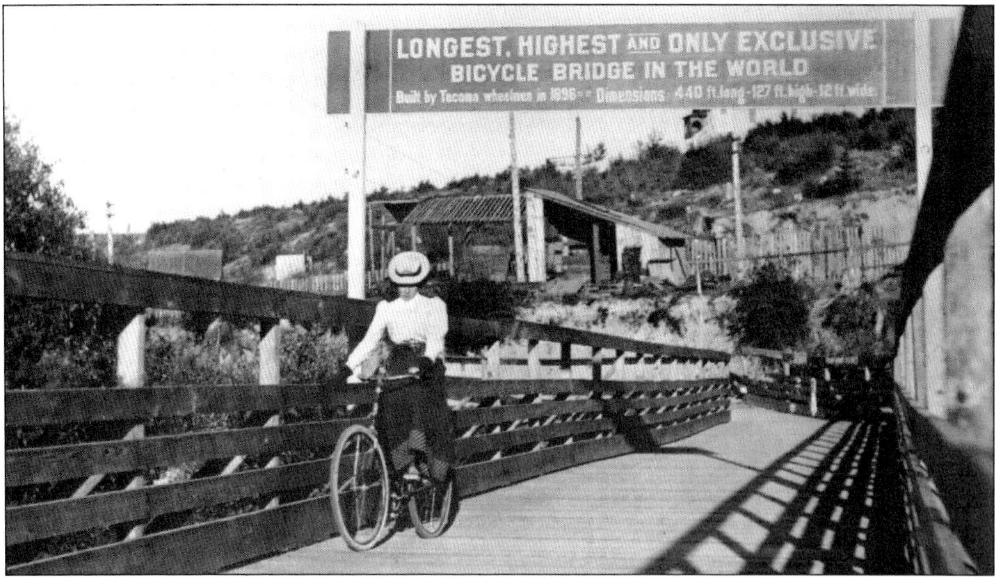

Bicycle riding became a fad in Tacoma in 1888 when the Tacoma Wheelmen's Bicycle Club was formed for those riding the penny-farthings. By 1896, bicycles designed for women expanded those enjoying the ride, and the club constructed a bridge across Galliher Gulch (near present-day Holy Rosary Church). At this time, riding was more of a hobby than a major form of nonpolluting transportation. (Richards Studio, Tacoma Public Library.)

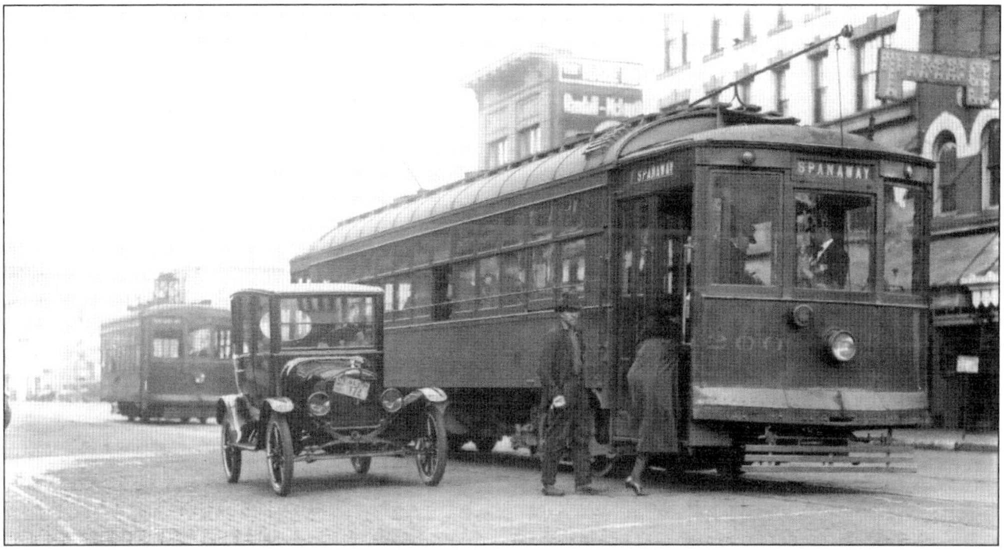

Streetcars transformed the city as various lines radiated outward from the downtown. Most ventured into undeveloped territory, where housing developments followed. These were Tacoma's first suburbs, places like present-day Stadium, Manitou, Proctor, and South Tacoma. Each suburban neighborhood had its own commercial district, schools, and churches—all buildings that later city-dwellers hoped to preserve, especially after the automobile came upon the scene to transform, once again, the urban environment. In the above view, taken in 1921, streetcar riders are delivered to their trolley by automobile. A decade later, the streetcar itself would be replaced by motorbuses. In 1908, the same year that A.D. Browning photographed the horse and buggy shown earlier, he captured a streetcar station in South Tacoma, seen below, where people have gathered to wait for their adventure to downtown Tacoma. (Both, Amzie D. Browning Collection, Tacoma Public Library.)

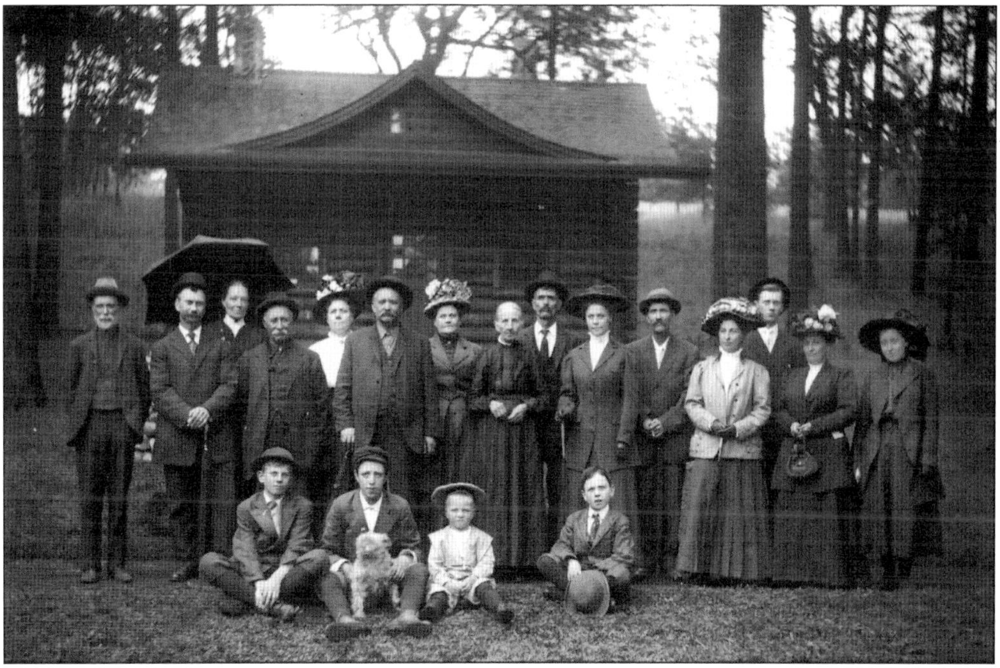

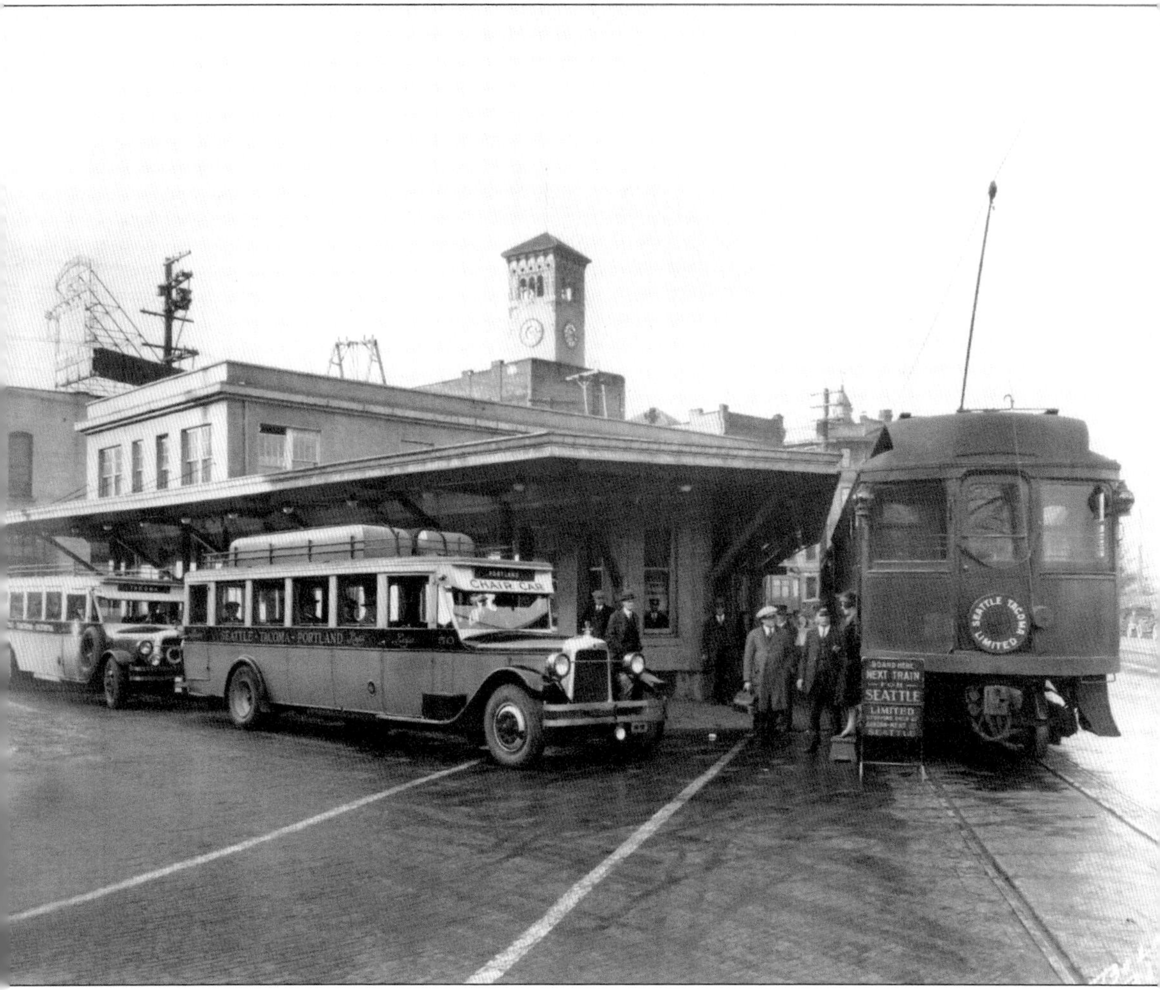

Prior to 1902, when the Seattle-Tacoma Interurban Railway was launched, travel between the two cities was by passenger steamers of the so-called Mosquito Fleet. The boats and wharves created a unique form of shoreline urban landscape throughout Puget Sound, one that would prove useful when automobiles replaced all earlier forms of public and private transportation. The interurban, owned by the Puget Sound Electric Railway Company, ran between Tacoma and Seattle from 1902 to 1928 along rights-of-way that would expand commercial development later used by businesses catering to the automobile. One notable example is the present-day Pacific Avenue (and later Interstate 5) between Tacoma and Fife. By 1925, the Tacoma interurban depot at the corner of A and South Eighth Streets was a shared facility for both buses and trains. The Tacoma depot, shown here, remains, although its awning has been removed. (Marvin D. Boland Collection, Tacoma Public Library.)

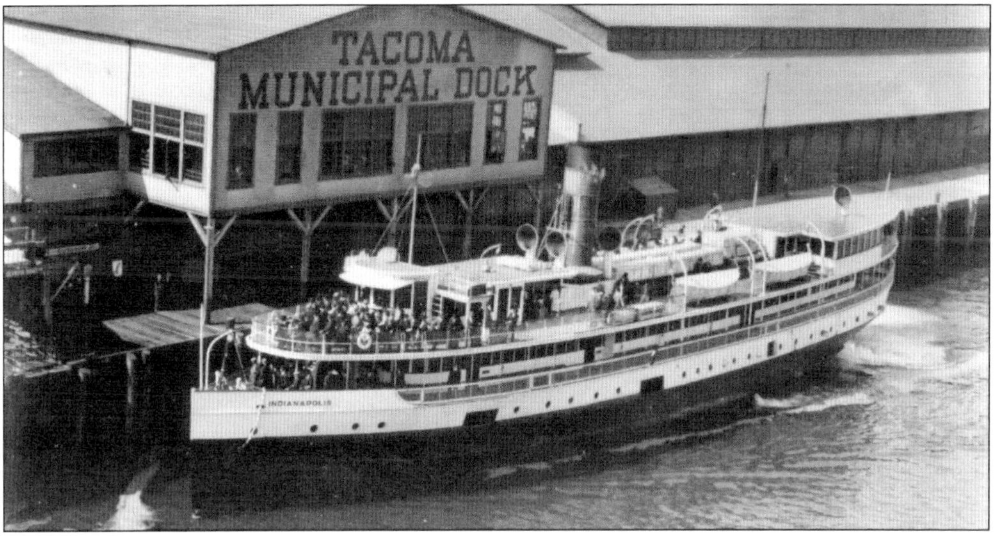

It was not until 1911 that the city had a dock it could call its own. Situated below the present-day Murray Morgan Bridge, the Tacoma Municipal Dock served as a focal point for all public waterborne passenger transportation until automobiles arrived en masse in the 1920s. Above, the steamer *Indianapolis* is ready to disembark in 1930 for its route between Tacoma and Seattle. Below, passengers are waiting to board the *Kalakala* for its last ferry ride across the Narrows in 1940. In 2002, Tacoma tore down the municipal dock in a classic case of "demolition by neglect." The public jury is still out about the future of the *Kalakala*, still sitting on Tacoma's shoreline. (Below, Richards Studio, Tacoma Public Library.)

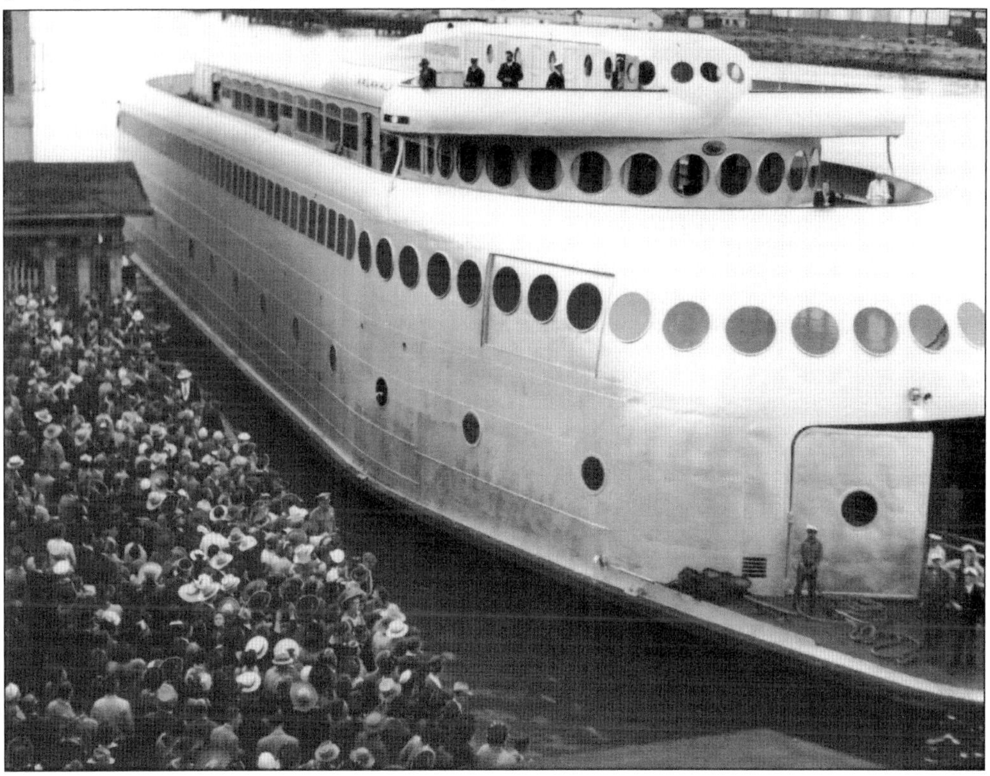

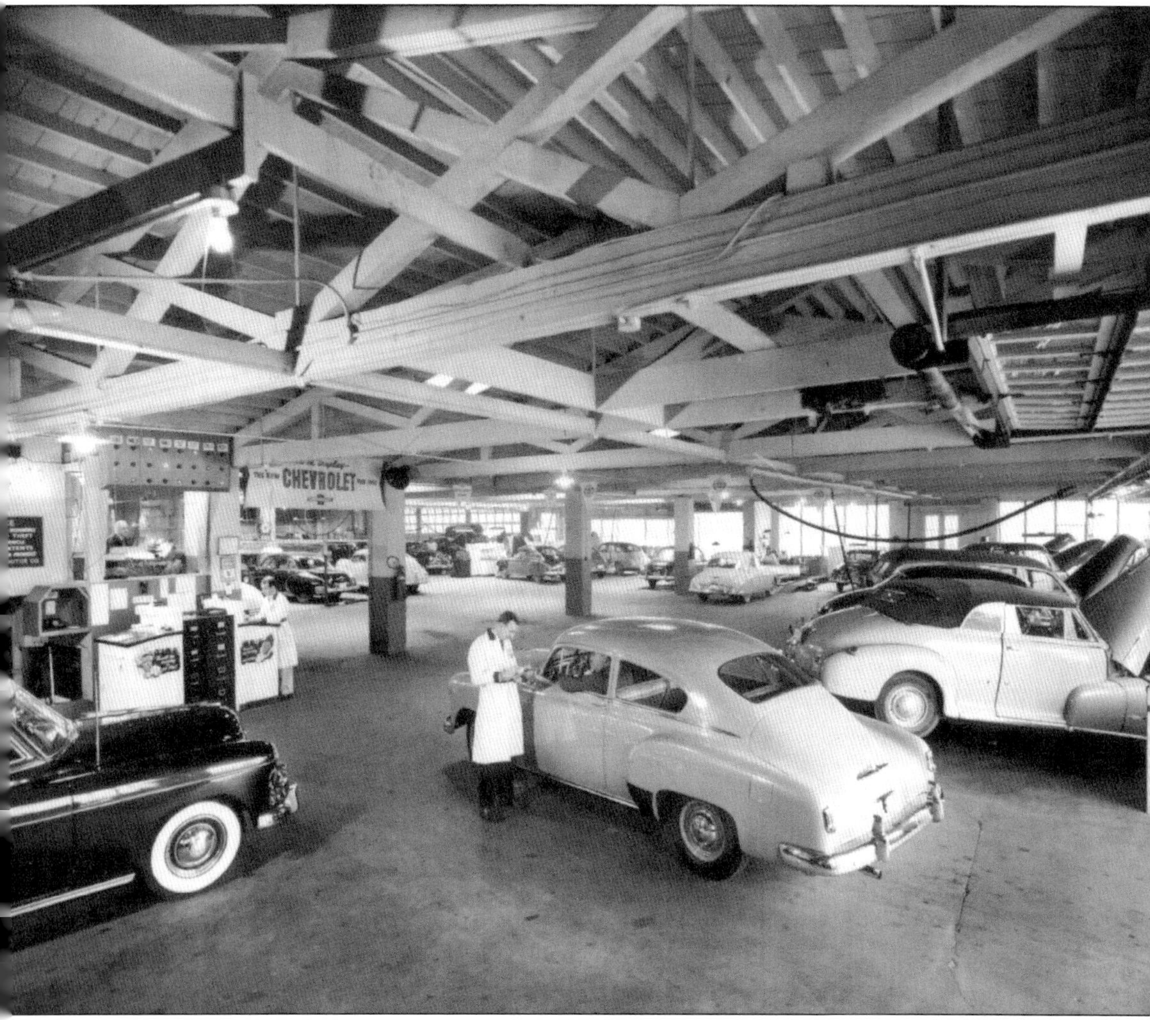

Of all the known modes of transportation, from horse to steam and electricity, nothing altered the urban environment more than the automobile. The gas-driven vehicle arrived in Tacoma prior to World War I, and its influence has continued to the present day. City directory classified listings begin with businesses that not only make cars but also sell them. From this evolved the car dealerships, service and parking garages, car rentals, and used car sales. Downtown buildings constructed for one purpose were converted to sell or store automobiles. New buildings were designed specifically for the sale and maintenance of the new vehicles. And in some instances, as shown here in this 1951 view of the South Tacoma Motor Company, former liveries (or blacksmith shops) were converted to accommodate this new form of transportation. In addition, the automobile was the force that expanded Tacoma farther outward from the central business district to the point where new suburbs formed and, in some instances, became cities themselves, thus threatening the very life of the older city. (Richards Studio, Tacoma Public Library.)

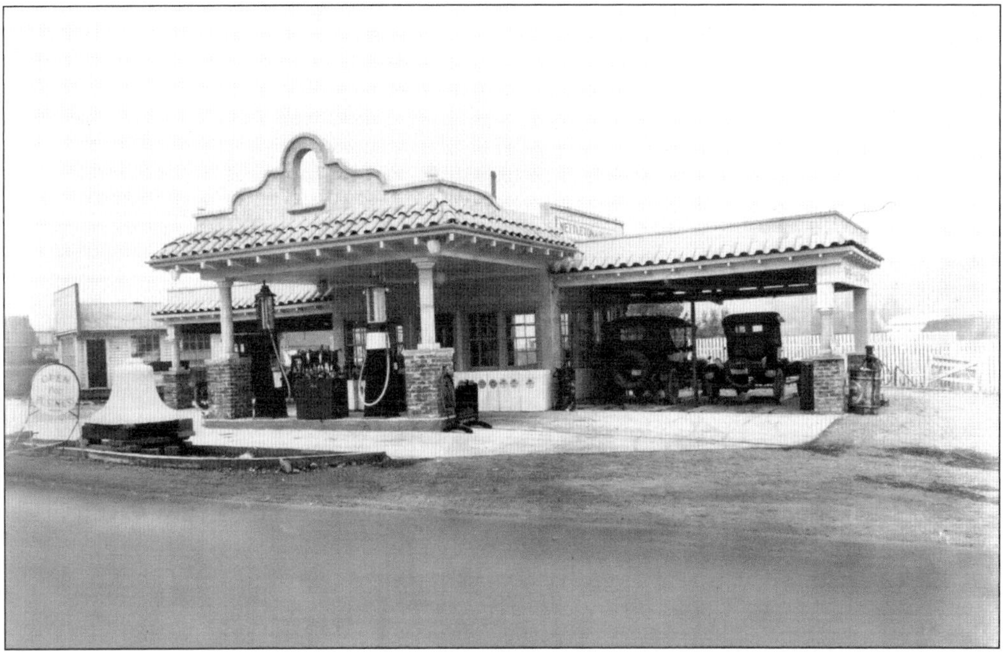

Before major oil companies emerged with standardized designs for service stations, each entrepreneur was at liberty to create an architectural motif that the owner assumed would lure the most traffic. Designs ranged from the Mission style to those influenced by Tudor or Art Deco styles. Given time and industrial influences, it is rare to see such unique examples of the service station. They are all lost.

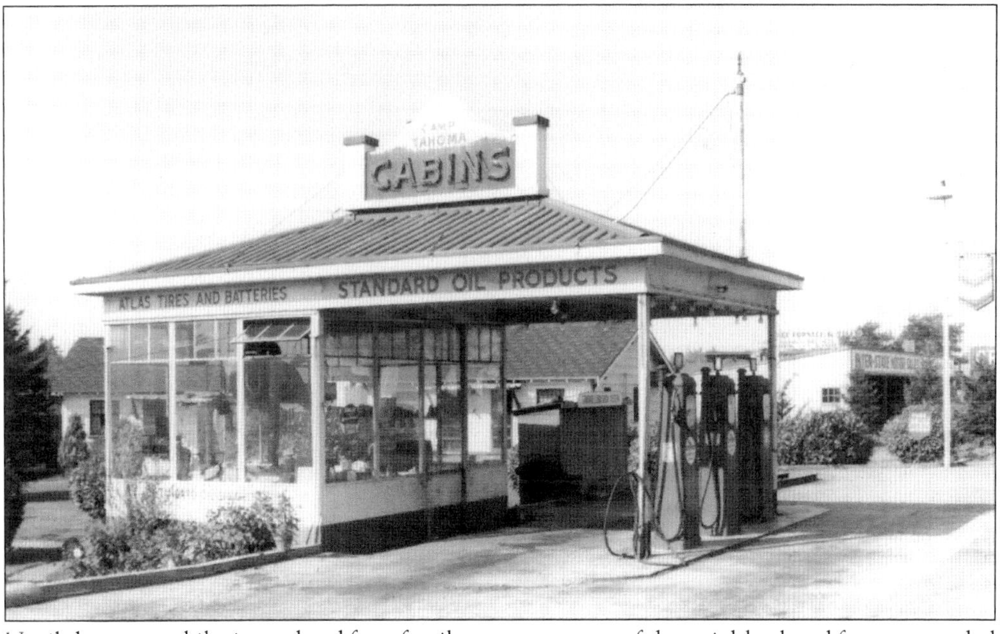

Until the automobile, it was hard for a family to venture out of the neighborhood for an extended stay away from home. Auto courts such as the Camp Tahoma Auto Camp, shown here in 1945, enabled a family to escape the city. This site now contains a large warehouse surrounded by a parking lot. (Richards Studio, Tacoma Public Library.)

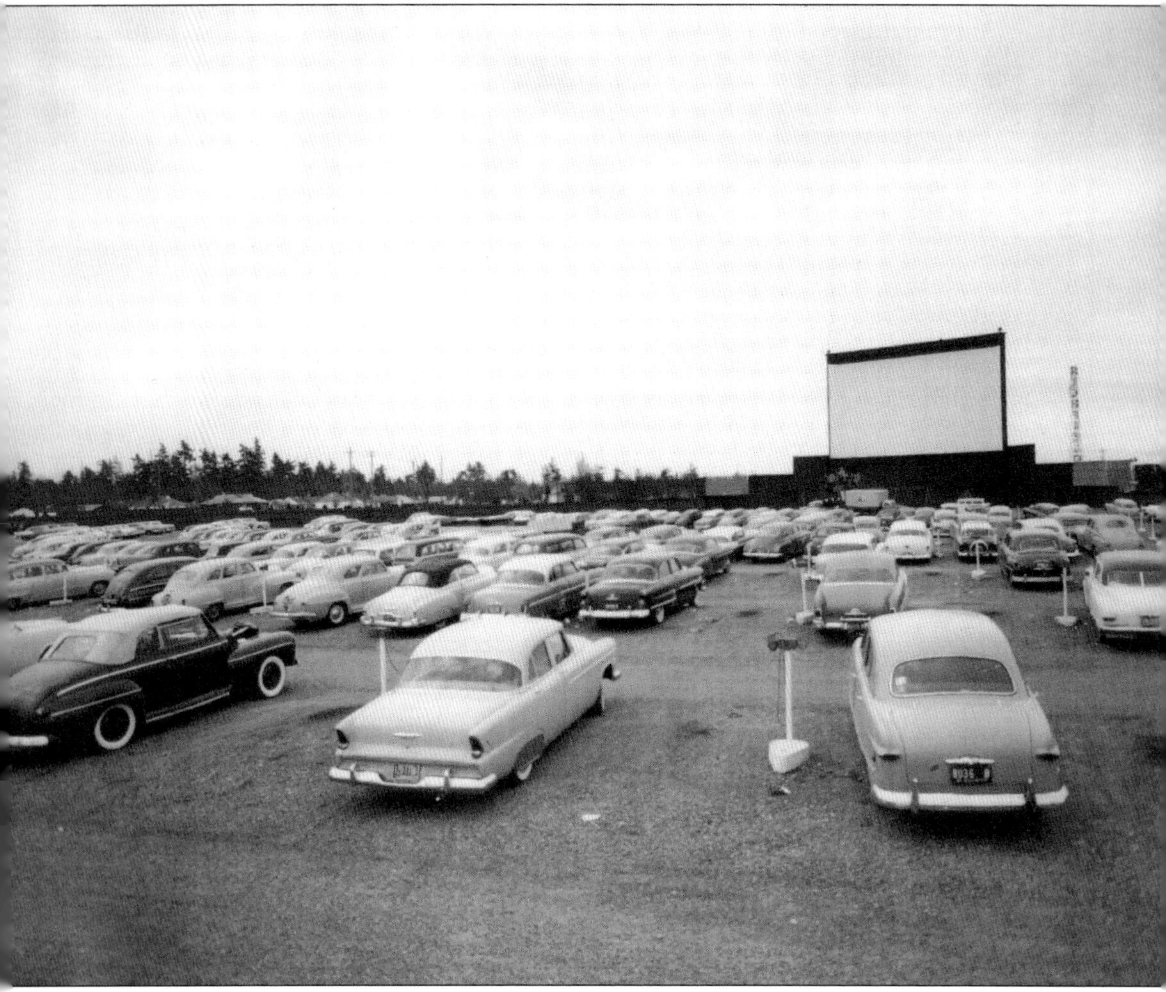

For many, especially women and young people, the automobile meant liberty and a new culture that included the drive-in theater. In addition to showing movies, drive-ins also hosted other events. In this 1957 view of the Star-Lite Drive-in Theater in South Tacoma, families gathered to participate in a sunrise service on Easter Sunday. The Star-Lite was one of two drive-ins built locally following World War II. The other was located on Pearl Street in West Tacoma. The demise of this unique form of entertainment occurred because of the real estate market; owners realized that building housing and commercial developments on the site could make more money than selling movie tickets. This transformation can be seen on Pearl Street near its entrance ramps to State Route 16, where the Auto View once stood. (Richards Studio, Tacoma Public Library.)

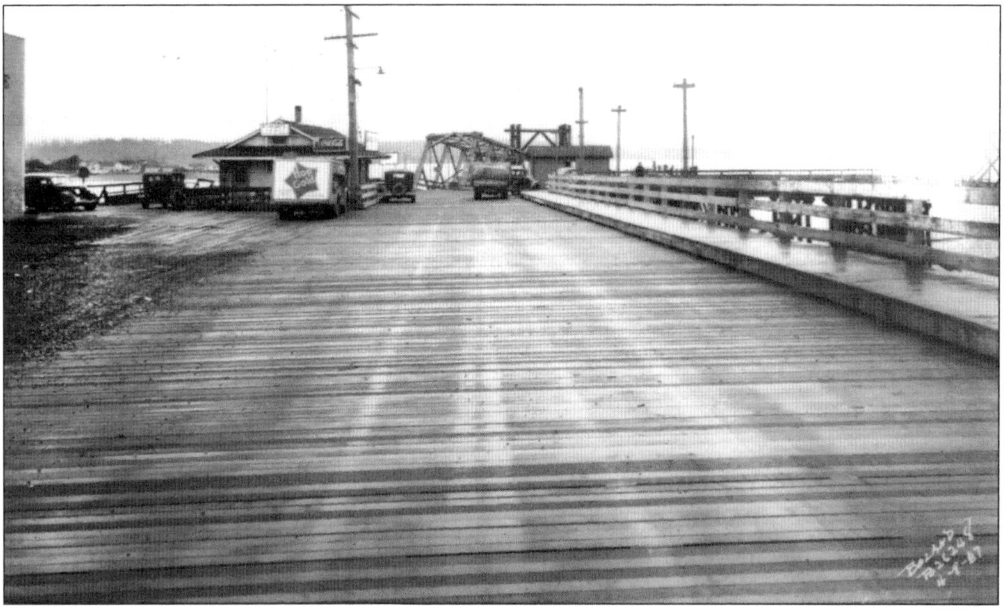

Since the confined space of the Tacoma Municipal Dock did not allow conversion into slips for automobile ferries, other locations along the shoreline served the need. The end of Sixth Avenue was such a place. Here, automobiles would embark for various shoreline destinations throughout lower Puget Sound, as this 1937 photograph documents. The slip was left to ruin following the completion of the second Narrows Bridge in 1950. (Marvin D. Boland Collection, Tacoma Public Library.)

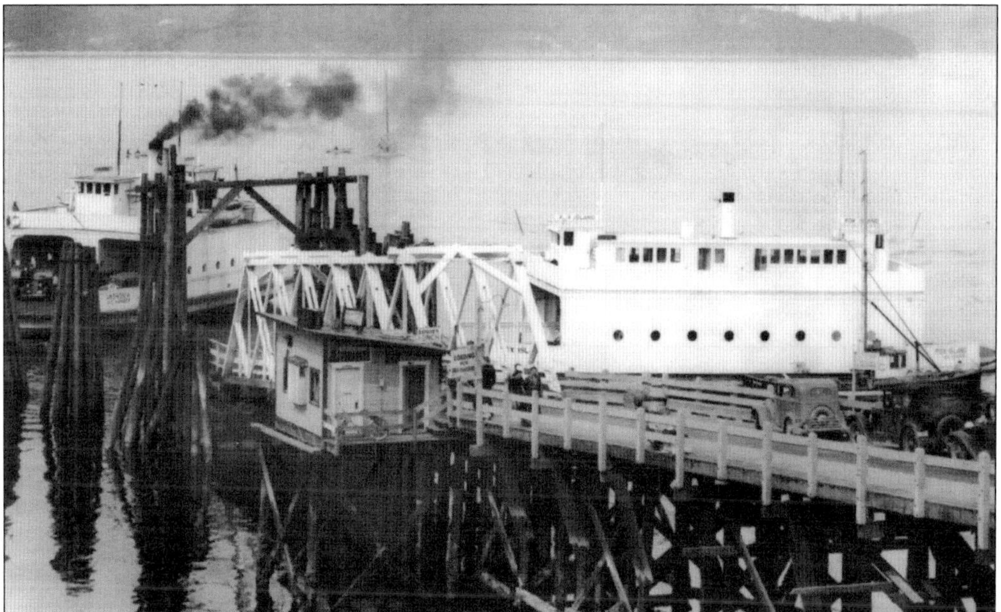

Unlike the Sixth Avenue ferry, the one at Point Defiance is still in operation, taking travelers from Tacoma to Vashon Island. In 1937, when this photograph was taken, the ferries were part of the Washington Navigation Company operations, headed by Mitchell Skansie. Ferries left here to Gig Harbor and Fox Island. (Richards Studio, Tacoma Public Library.)

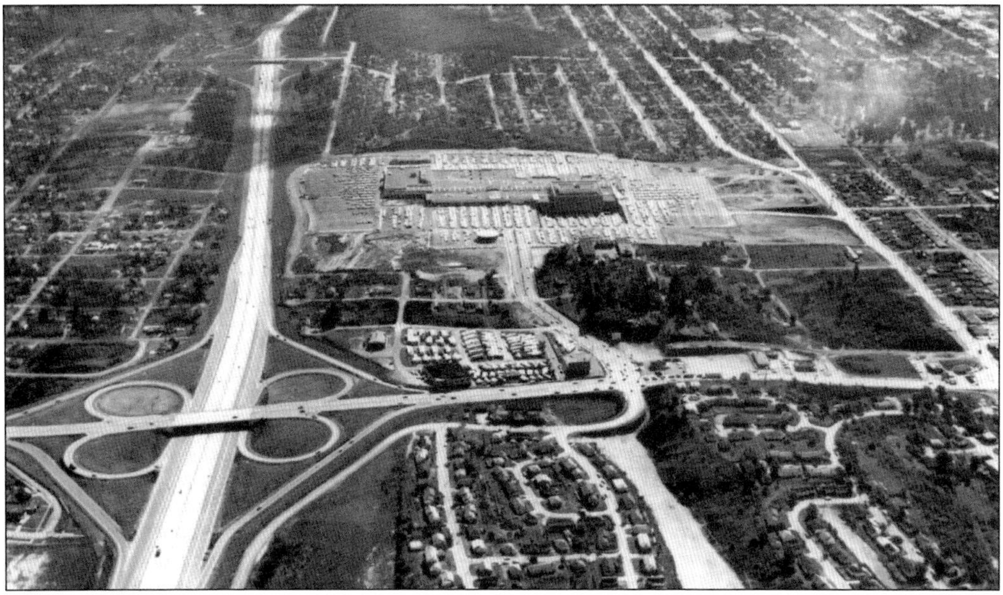

Freeway development expanded the impact of the automobile throughout the region, which included additional housing developments and damage to the historic urban fabric of Tacoma. Even today, freeway construction is still altering the landscape of Tacoma. The image above, taken in 1966, shows the South Thirty-eighth Street interchange leading to the Tacoma Mall, which had its grand opening the year before. These dual developments signaled the end of the city's historic downtown, as more shoppers were lured to a place where there was plenty of parking and no rain to slog through as one moved from store to store. Below, the camera is pointed eastward, showing the city center interchange just prior to its opening in 1968. As the freeway expanded its right-of-way, more and more of the housing shown here was demolished or moved. (Both, Richards Studio, Tacoma Public Library.)

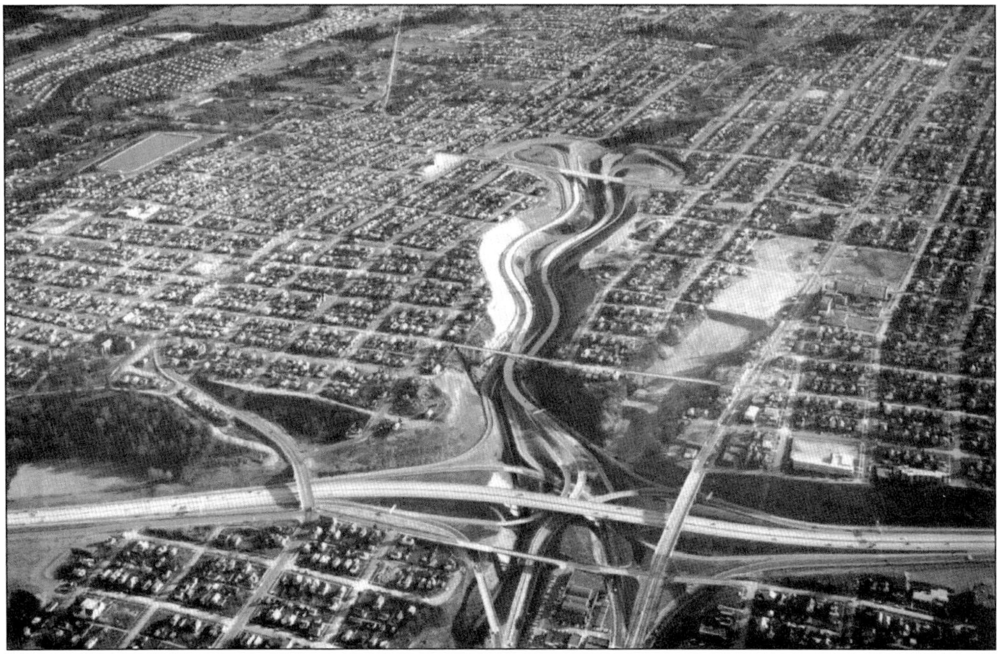

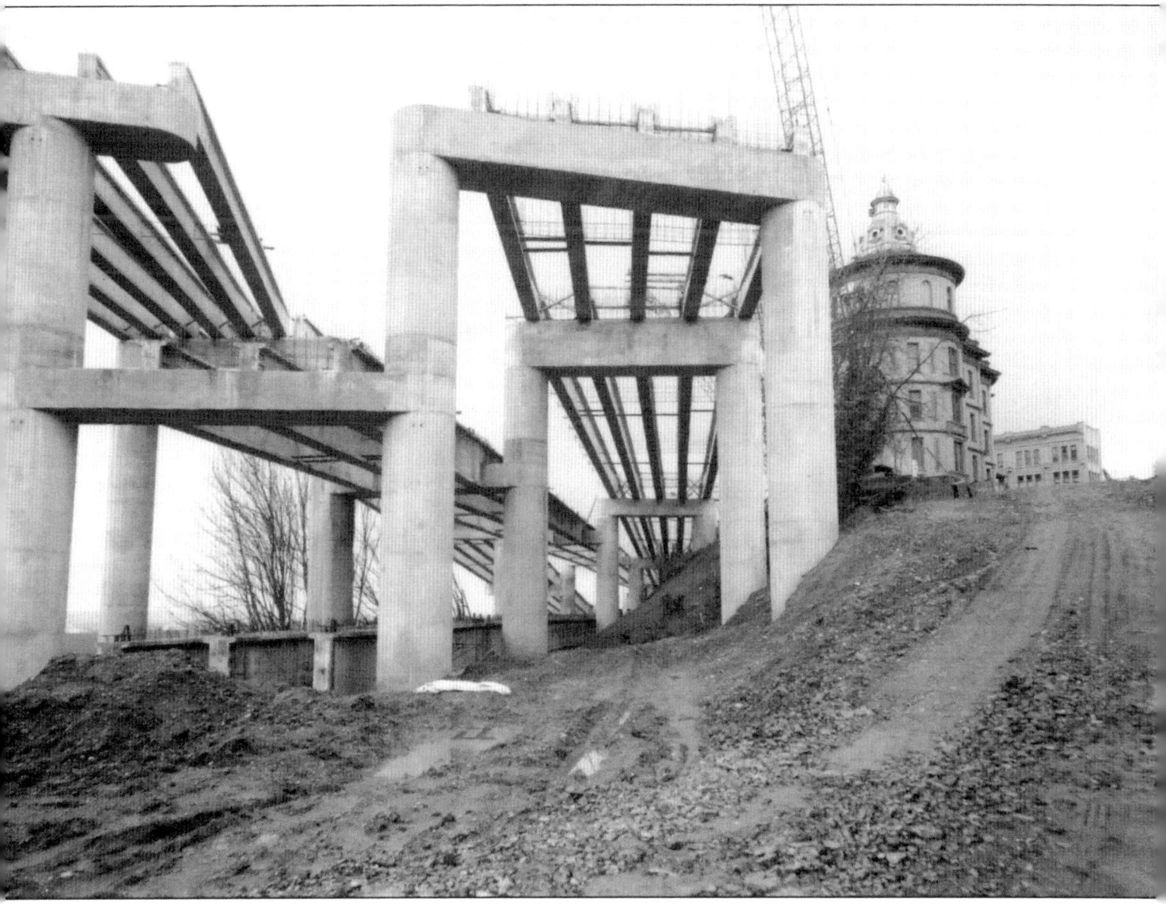

Tacoma greeted the prospect of urban renewal following the Korean War with plans designed to accommodate the automobile regardless of what impact the endeavor had on the historic downtown. This image, taken by Ron Karabaich around 1974, epitomizes the reason why a public outcry resulted and the Tacoma City Council agreed to create a landmarks preservation commission. Here, the Tacoma spur meets the Northern Pacific Headquarters Building at the northern end of Pacific Avenue. The plans originally called for the demolition of both the Northern Pacific Headquarters Building (left) and the old city hall not seen in this view. Tacoma architect Alan Liddle, whose office building is in the background of this view, was instrumental in changing the city's opinion by showing how older buildings are a crucial element in Tacoma's downtown. Both buildings shown here have survived the test of time.

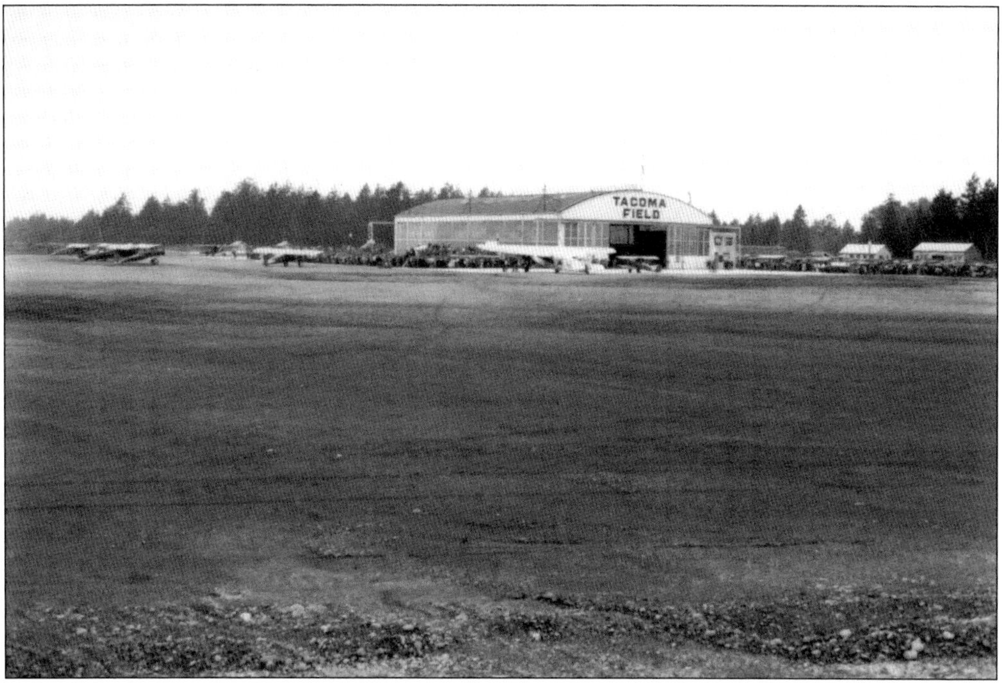

In February 1940, the Tacoma Flying Service was one of three aeronautical firms with headquarters at Mueller-Harkins Airport in what is now Lakewood. In 1940, the Tacoma Flying Service had a contract with the federal government under the civilian pilot program, established by the Civil Aeronautics Authority, to train new pilots. There was one airfield within the city of Tacoma. Known as Oswald's, it was located near the present-day Tacoma Community College. The site of this airfield is now a commercial node at the intersection of South Mildred and Nineteenth Streets. (Above, Tacoma Public Library; below, Richards Studio, Tacoma Public Library.)

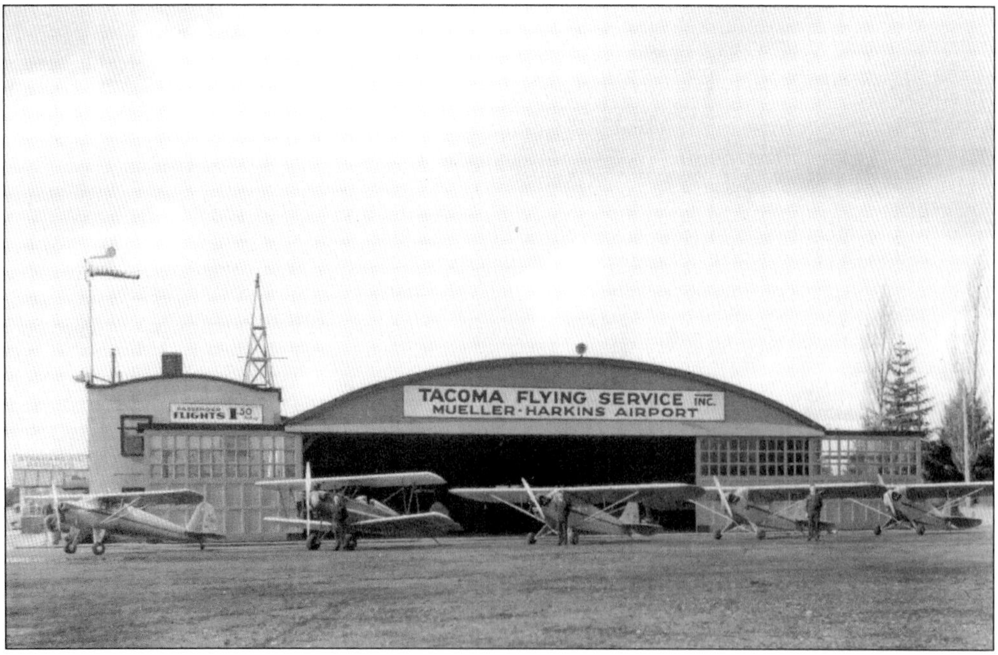

Five

DEVELOPMENT

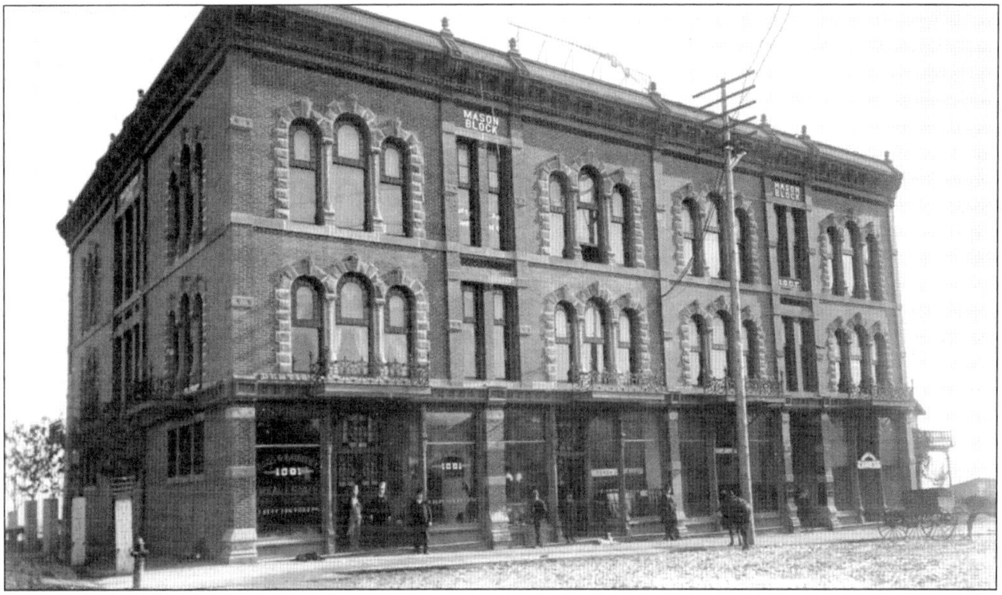

Sometime in the 1930s, modernist architect and planner Le Corbusier was quoted as admiring "a city which will be replaced by another city." Nick Paumgarten, when recounting the event in the *New Yorker*, went on to say that, in New York City, the replacement of the urban landscape is "inevitable and even exhilarating," especially "in the way that neighborhoods flourish, wilt, mutate, and bloom again." The same can be said for Tacoma, where it is possible to observe several generations of buildings appearing on a single site over long periods of time. This chapter is devoted to a few examples of the phenomenon, beginning with the Uhlman Block located near South Ninth and A Streets. Designed by Tacoma architects Pickles and Sutton and constructed in 1889, it survived until 1951; the businesses housed there included a market, butcher shop, and hotel. When looking at a changing landscape in this matter, it is up to the viewer to determine if the vanished part of urban scene is a loss or a manifestation of change.

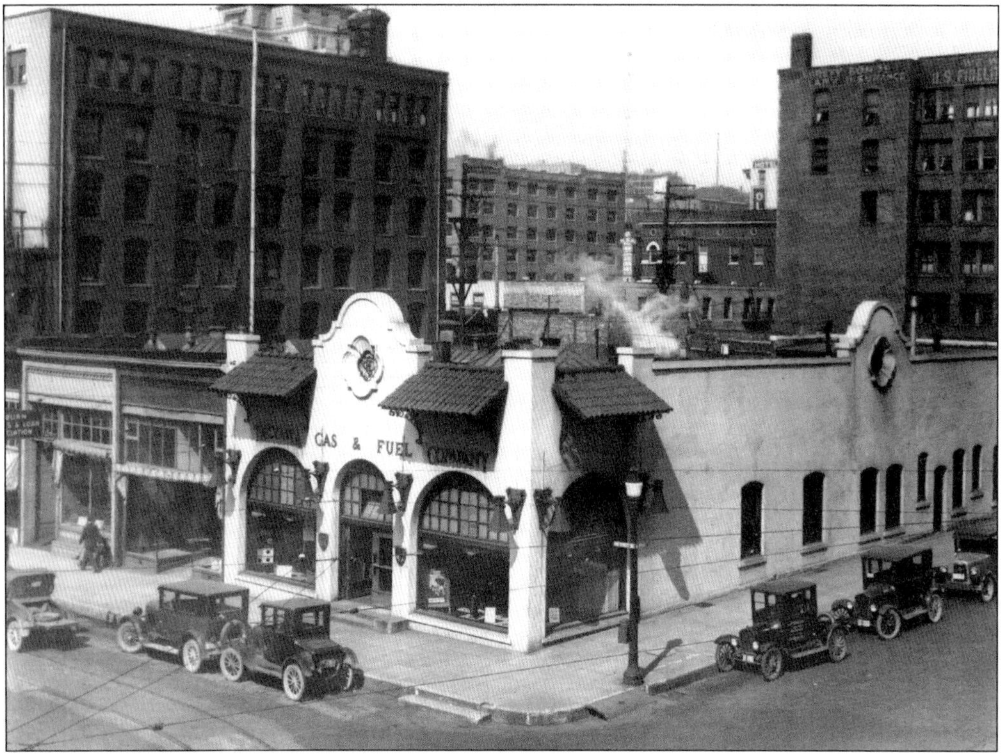

Luther Twitchell designed the Tacoma Gas Building (above) in 1910. Located a block away from the Uhlman Block, this building also housed a military store in 1918. In 1956, the architectural firm of Lea, Pearson & Richards designed a new building for the same site as the gas company. The aluminum-and-glass structure has modernist influences and black granite trim. The building became home of the Tacoma Savings and Loan Association (below) and still stands. (Above, William Trueblood Collection, Tacoma Public Library.)

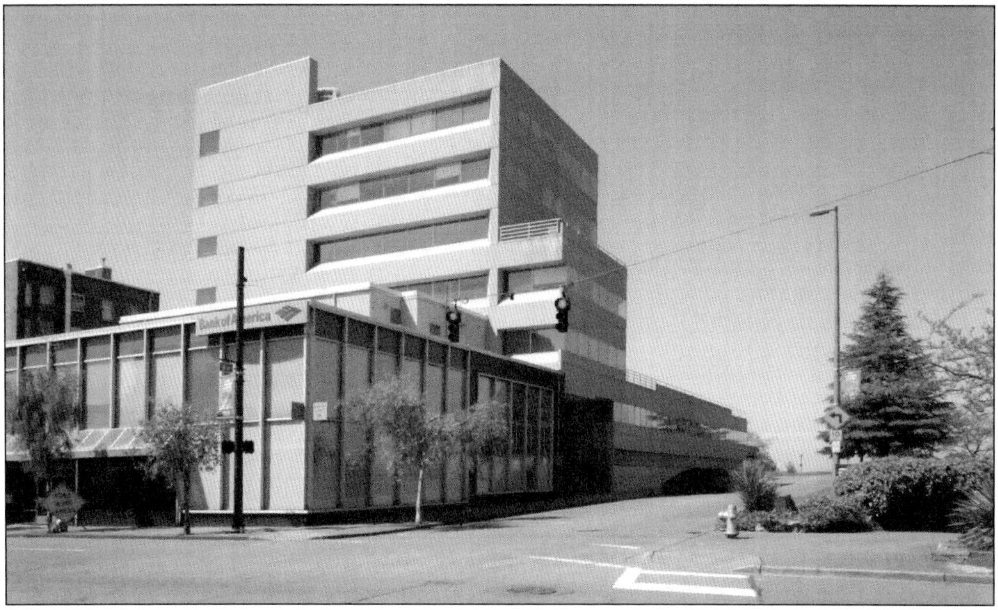

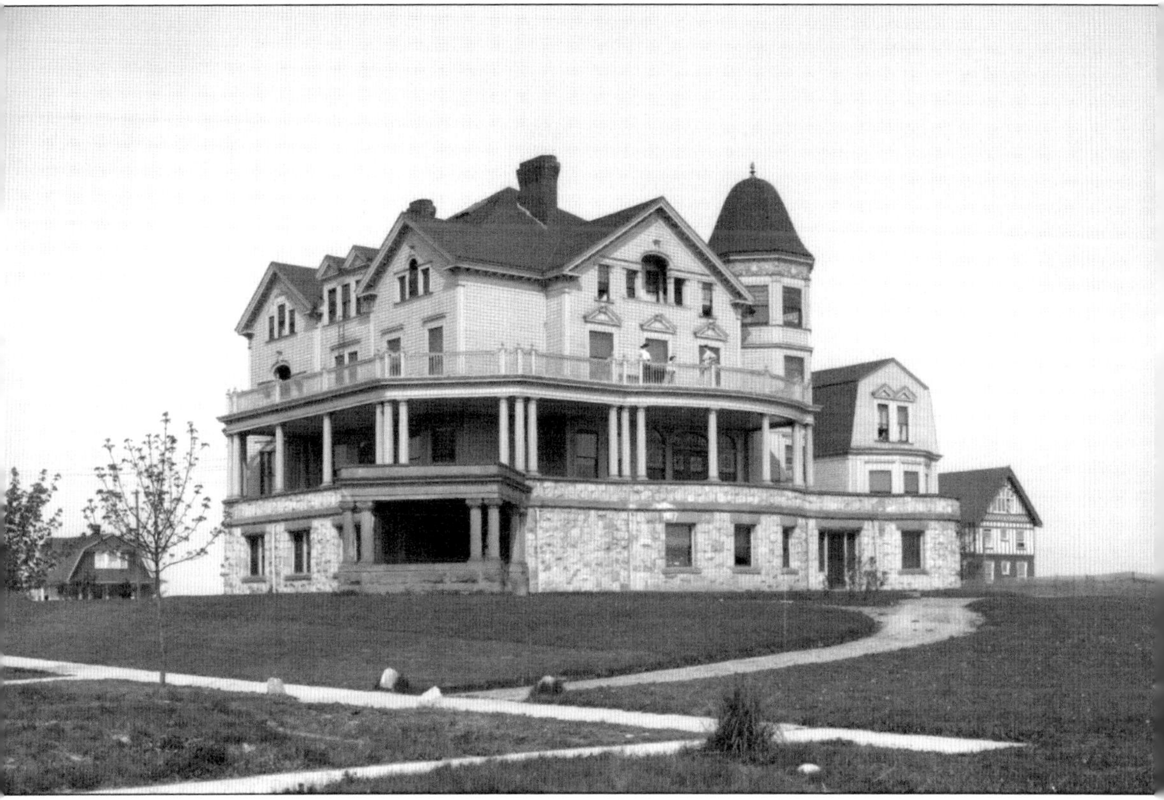

In 1889, Allen C. Mason announced in his *Every Sunday* newspaper that he planned to build his family home on North Stevens and Forty-third Streets. According to Mason's granddaughter, he was encouraged to build at this site located within his residential development. When the 1893 financial collapse and depression forced Mason to sell his house, it was acquired by Whitworth College, an academy originally founded in Sumner, a town located to the east of Tacoma. The school remained here until moving to Spokane in 1913.

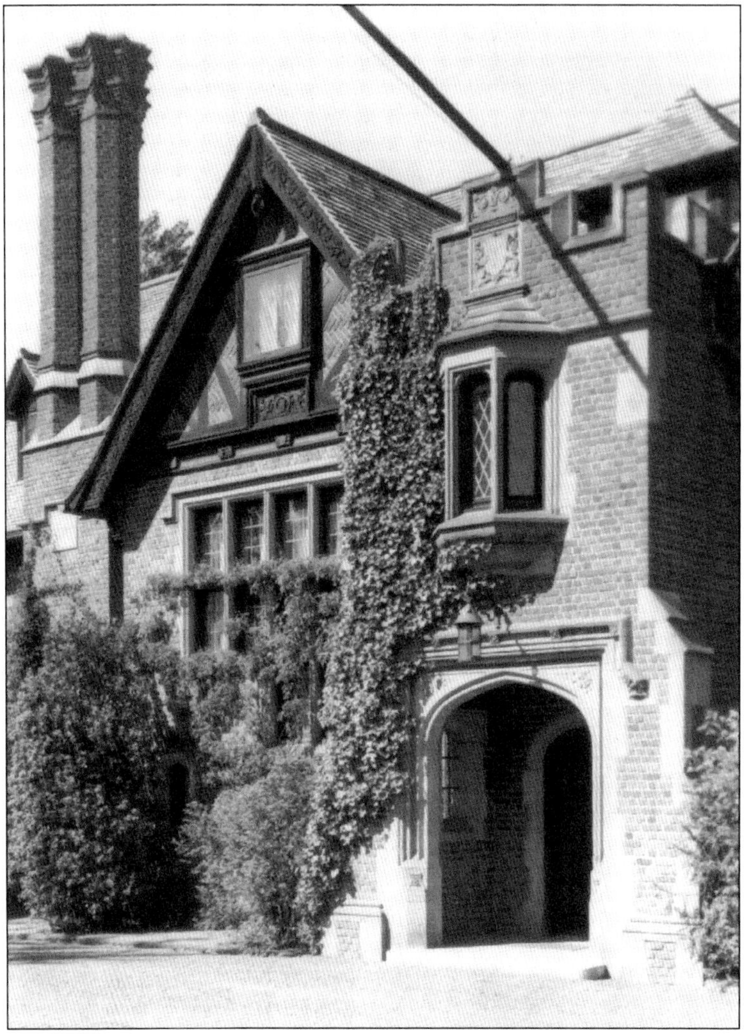

Lumber magnate John P. Weyerhaeuser purchased the property in 1920 and destroyed the Mason house so as to construct Haddaway Hall, designed by a Cleveland, Ohio, architectural firm. Some of the Mason and Whitworth College grounds were retained in the new landscaping plan developed by Olmsted Brothers. The building is a registered historic property now owned by the Northwest Baptist Seminary. (Richards Studio, Tacoma Public Library.)

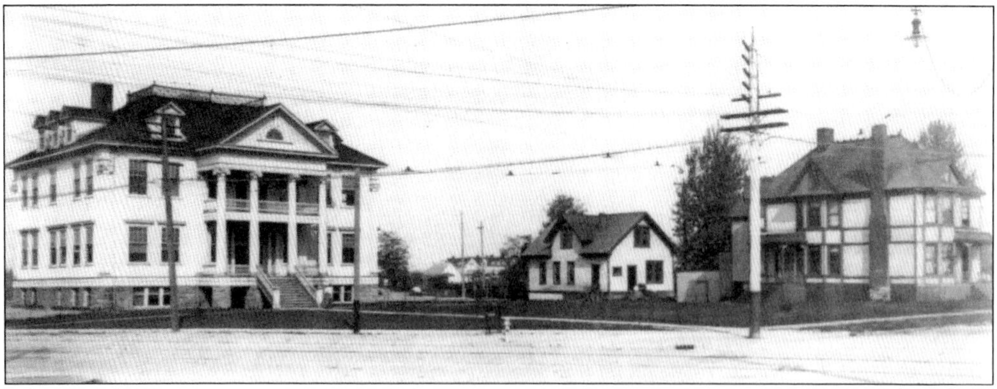

The Methodist Episcopal Church established what is today's University of Puget Sound in 1888. After various temporary locations in Tacoma, the school settled on a site at 602 North Sprague Avenue. Tacoma architect George Bullard designed the classroom building in 1903, with residential structures placed along Sixth Avenue. (Richards Studio, Tacoma Public Library.)

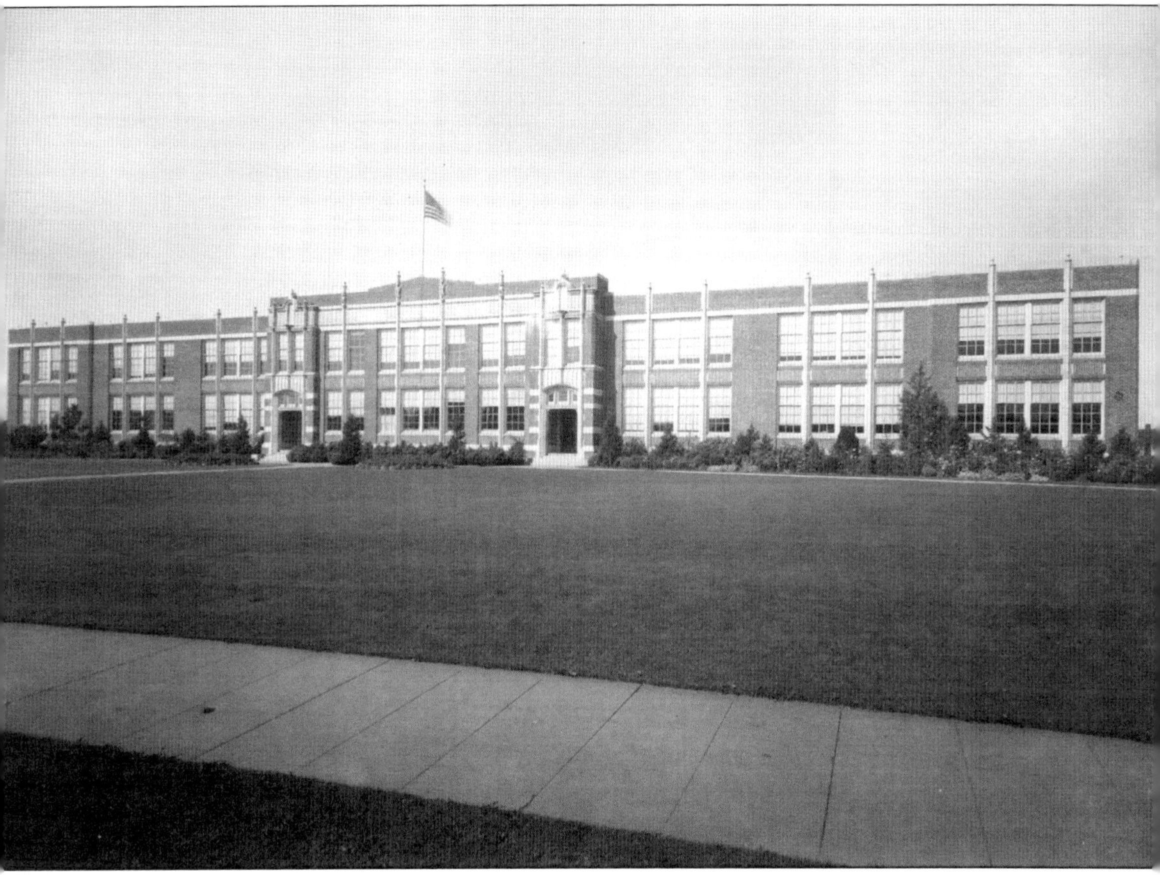

By the 1920s, the college had moved to its new campus on Warner Street while the Tacoma School District was expanding its system to include intermediate schools. The former site of the University of Puget Sound was deemed an ideal location for a new school. Designed by Roland Borhek in 1924, Jason Lee Middle School was completed in 1924 as one of six new schools.

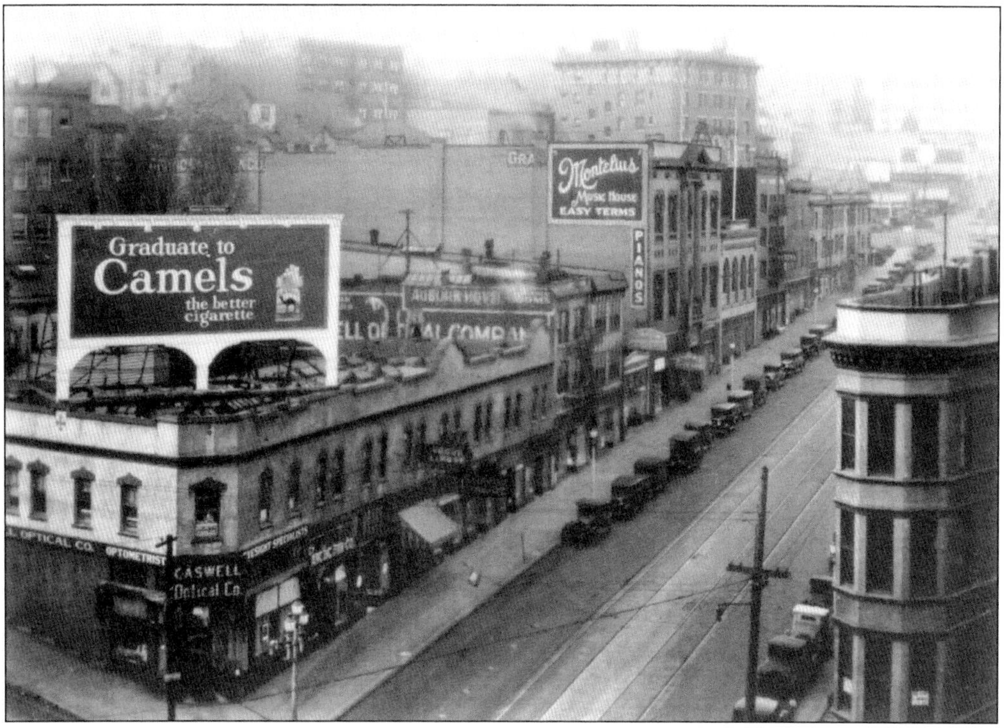

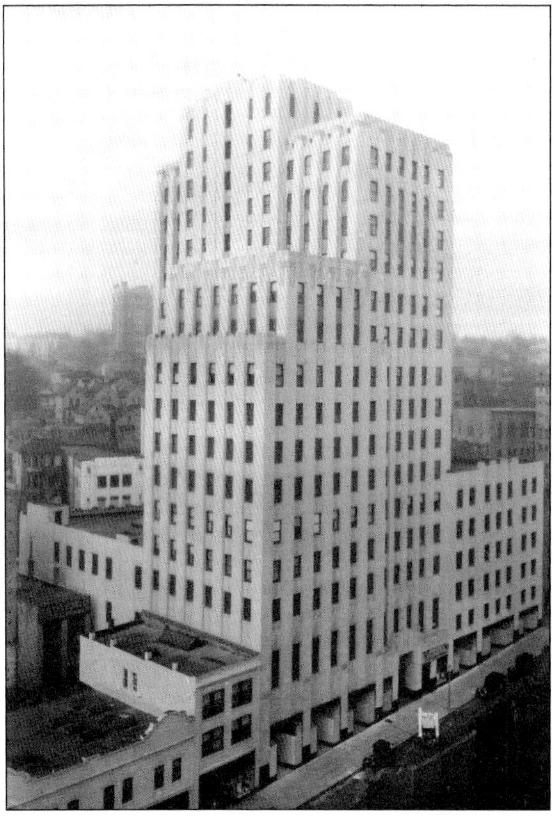

With the exception of the Caswell Building on the corner, this northward view along St. Helens Avenue from South Ninth Street, taken around 1930, shows an urban landscape about to be changed. The building midway down the block was the Masonic temple; Pres. Theodore Roosevelt dedicated its cornerstone in 1903. Adjacent to it, Conrad Hoska had his funeral home.

Overnight, the Medical Arts Building, also known as the Rhodes Medical Arts Tower, rose on the site. Designed by the architect John Graham Sr., it was a multipurpose facility, including everything from doctors' and dentists' offices to a hospital. In 1977, the City of Tacoma purchased the building and converted it into a municipal building. It is a registered landmark.

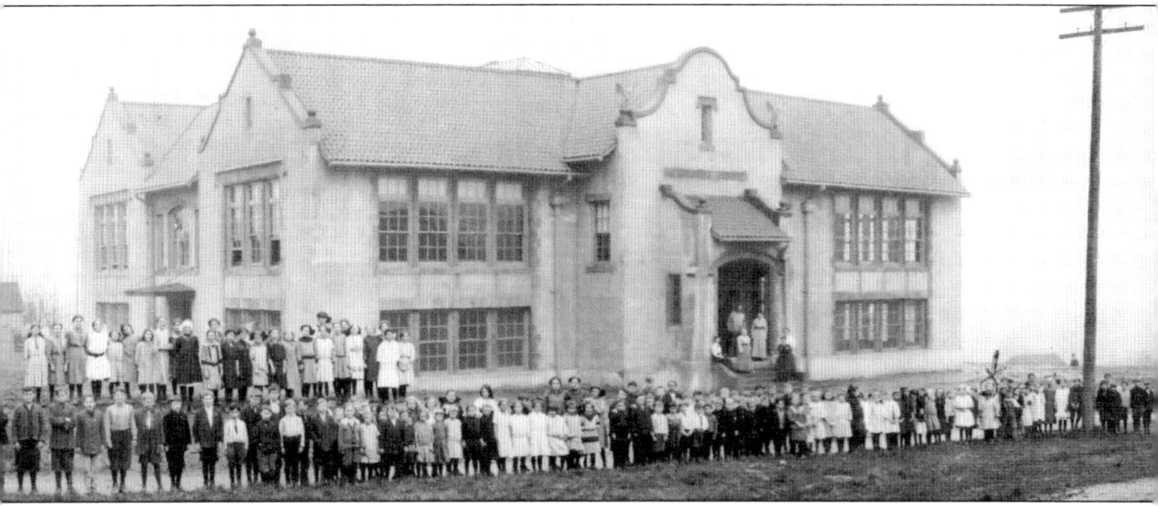

The Hawthorne School at 519 East Twenty-eighth Street, shown here in 1913, was one of the first schools in Tacoma's east side. Its proximity to the Puyallup Indian Reservation meant that Native American children received their education here; and for some time, Hawthorne was the tribe's Chief Leschi School. The building was demolished in 1981. (Tacoma Public Library.)

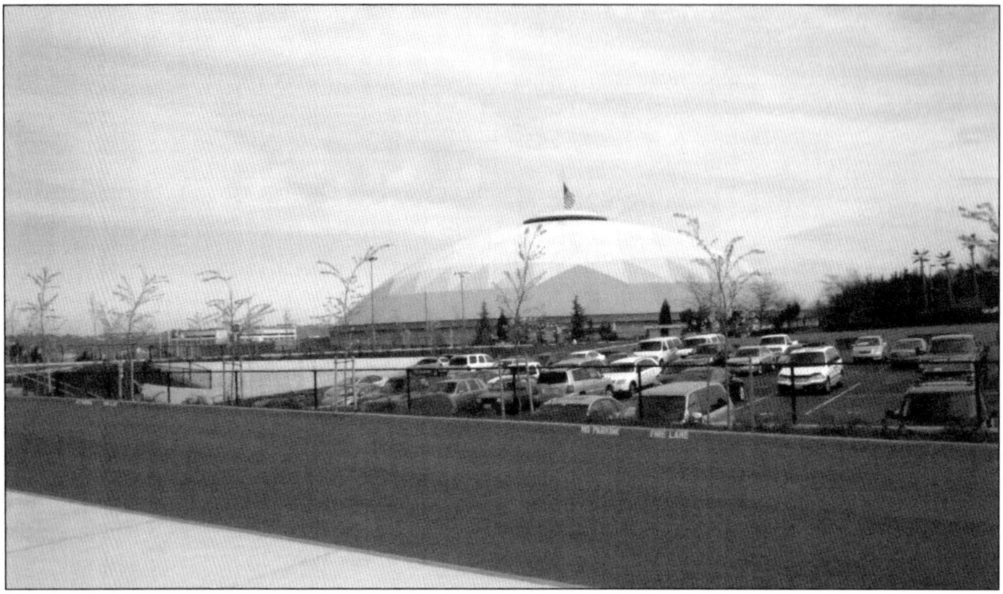

Construction began on the Tacoma Dome in 1981 following the destruction of Hawthorne School and many houses in the neighborhood. Some of the homeowners who had to move had already been displaced once due to prior freeway construction. The facility opened two years later, with a rodeo first and then a David Bowie concert.

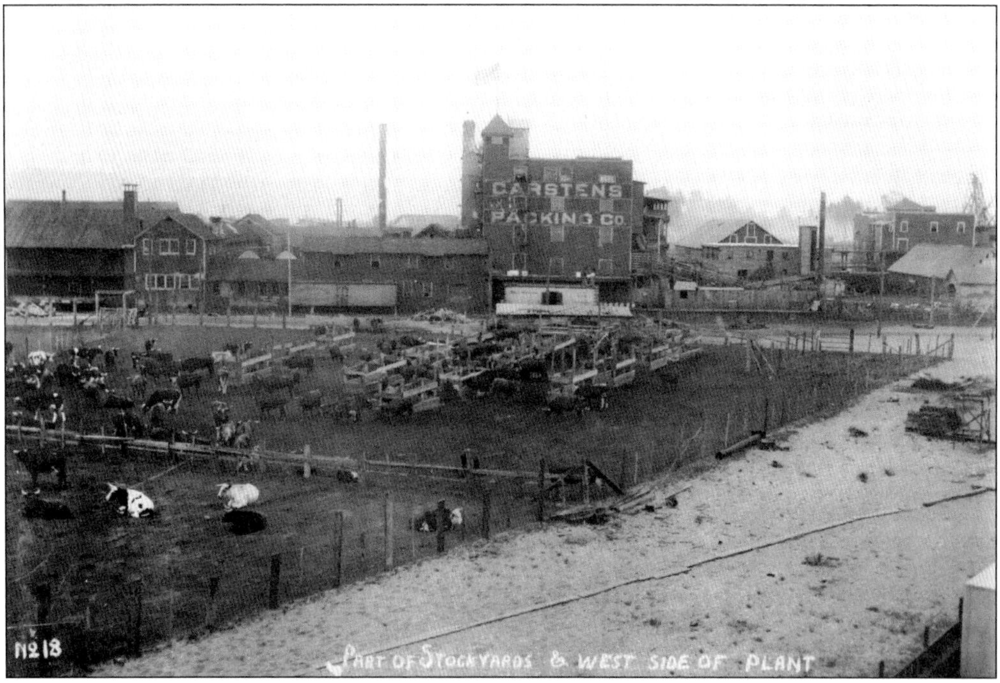

Tacoma, like Chicago, had its stockyards, although not as large. This view, taken in 1909, shows the Carstens Packing Company plant located on the tidal flats on East J Street. Thomas A. Carstens settled in Tacoma in 1903, and the business continued until the 1950s, when the plant was sold to Hygrade Food Products. By the 1980s, the plant was no longer there. (Carstens Collection, Tacoma Public Library.)

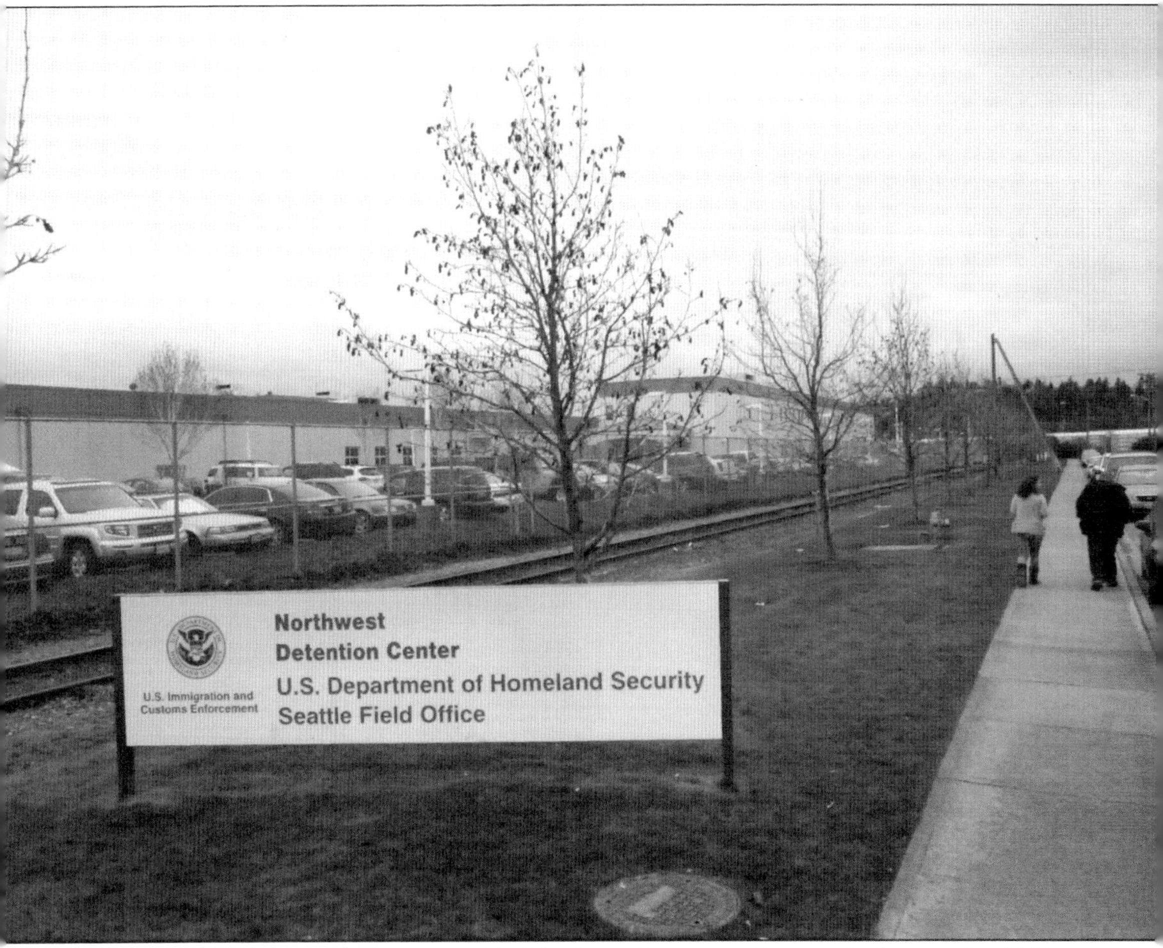

The stockyard site became the location of the Northwest Detention Center, which opened in 1994. By 2012, the facility was viewed as a contract detention facility where "problematic" immigrants are kept while determining whether or not they can remain in the United States.

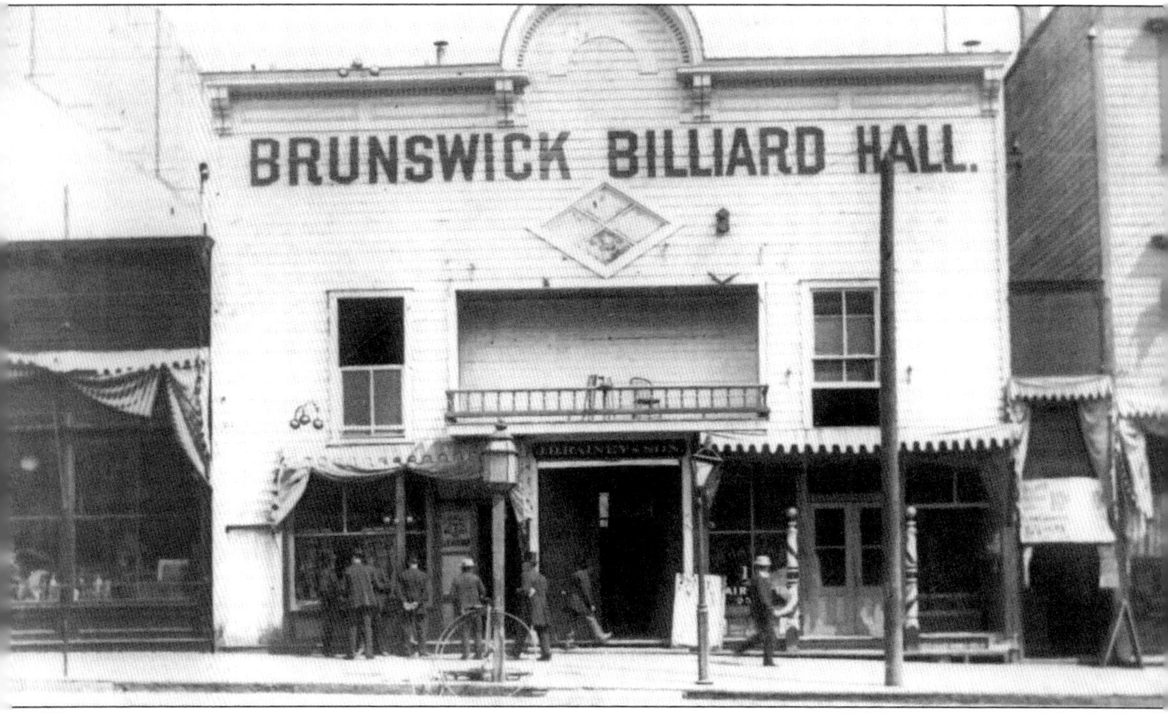

Seen here is the Brunswick Billiard Hall located at 1011 Pacific Avenue. Built in 1882, it opened as the Alpha Opera House, but was not as sophisticated as the name implies. In 1885, anti-Chinese agitators met here. In 1890, the police raided and closed down the facility because of risqué entertainment. In 1892, the billiard hall was demolished and replaced with the Henry S. Harmon Building. From that time until 1924, when it was demolished, this structure was used as restaurants, a hotel, and for automatic baseball games. The building replacing the restaurant, shown in the next photograph, has stood the test of time. (Arthur French Collection, Tacoma Public Library.)

By 1928, business owners along Pacific Avenue were transforming the area into a banking center; and in October of that year—and one year before the stock market crash ultimately led to a worldwide depression—the Bank of California opened its doors on the former site of the Alpha Opera House. The building is still there. (Chapin Bowen Collection, Tacoma Public Library.)

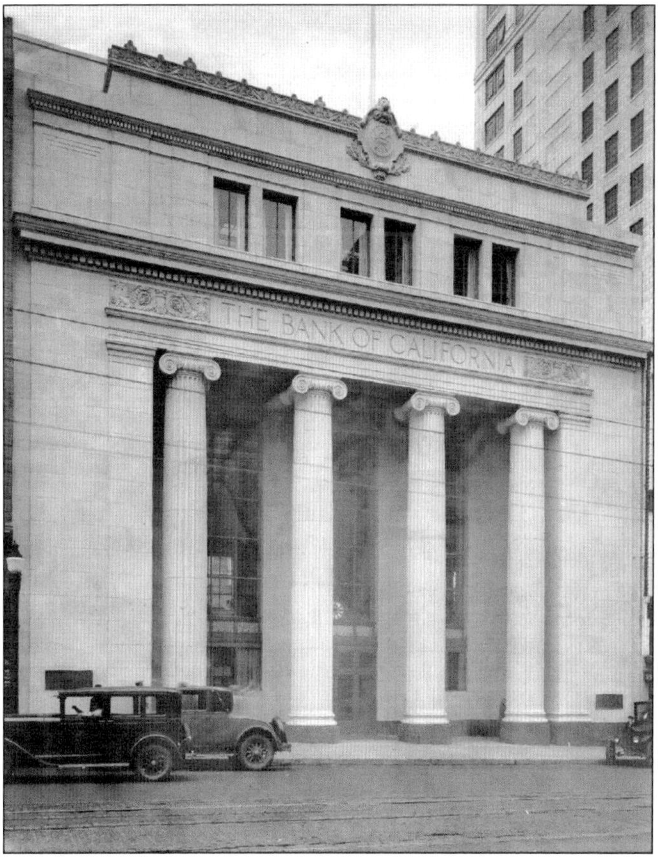

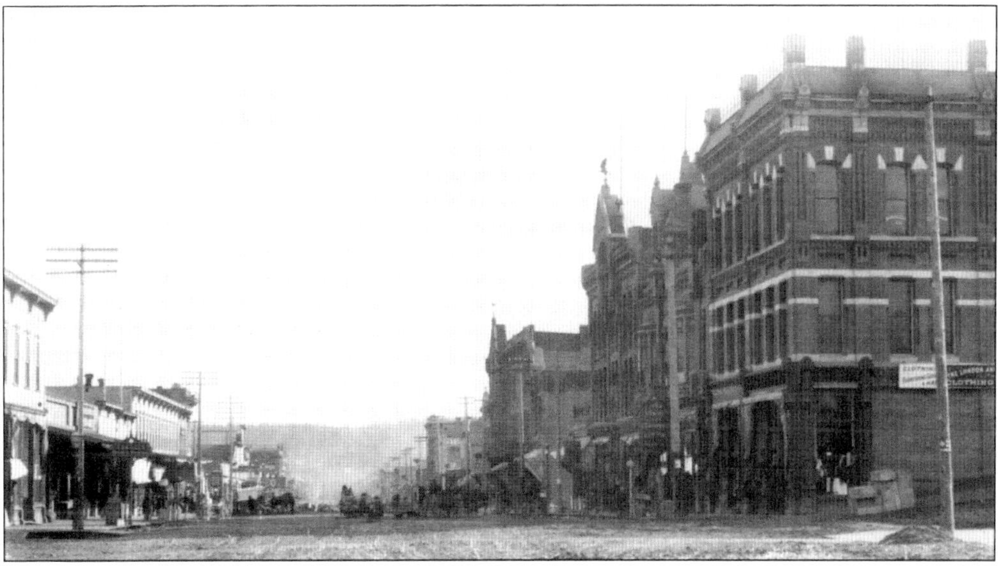

In the early 1890s, I.G. Davidson photographed Pacific Avenue south from South Ninth Street. On the right is the first brick building in downtown Tacoma, constructed around 1874 and owned by the town's benefactor, Charles B. Wright. The image also shows that not all businesses had changed their storefronts from wood to brick; the work was in progress.

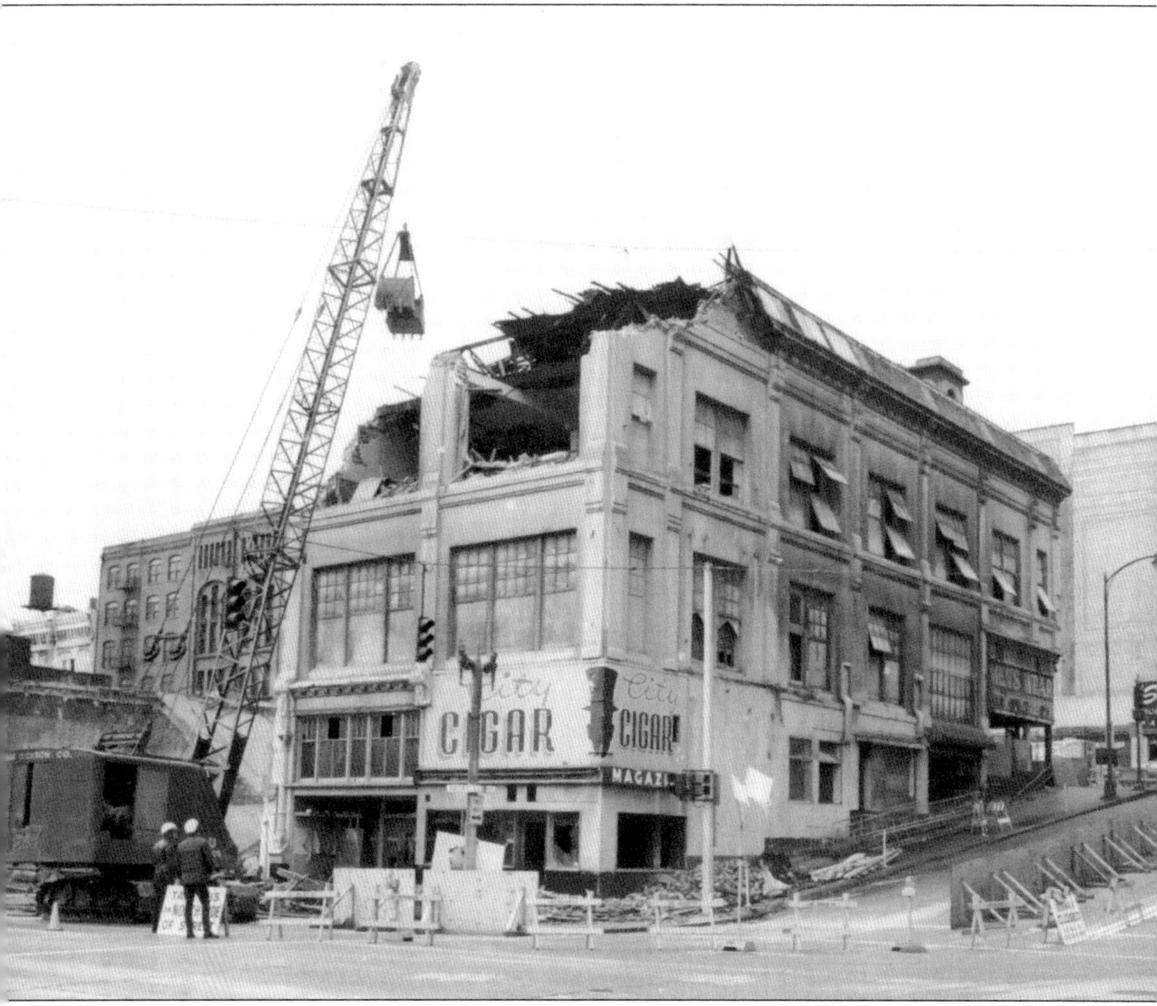

In 1969, the Wright Block was demolished, and clearly what is shown here is not the same building photographed in the 1890s. This is because in 1947, it was a candidate for what city officials called a "cleanup campaign" in the downtown area. Much of the original detailing was removed to completely change the architectural style. (Richards Studio, Tacoma Public Library.)

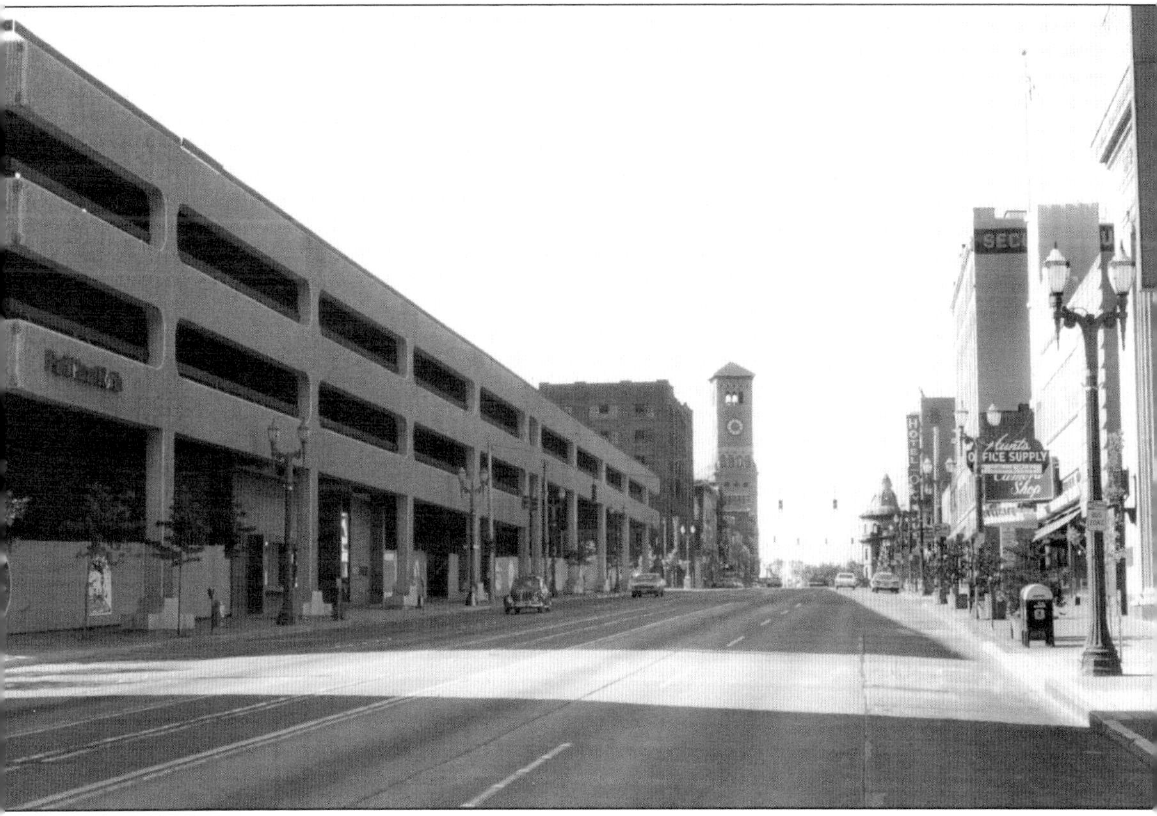

When the author worked for the City of Tacoma, she once overheard two employees discussing where they could go for lunch. One said to the other that he did not know because "we" have torn down all the good ones. If any images show the extent to which cities can do damage to the urban landscape, this view of the parking garage along Pacific Avenue looking north can serve the bill. On the previous page, buildings on the west side of Pacific Avenue are shown through two different stages of urban development. The third stage was the north and south parking garages where entire streets of buildings were demolished to once again cater to the automobile. The Wright Building would have been on the far left corner of the garage. The structure still stands, as does its sister to the south. In the latter instance, however, it had been redesigned in a new and different form of cleanup campaign.

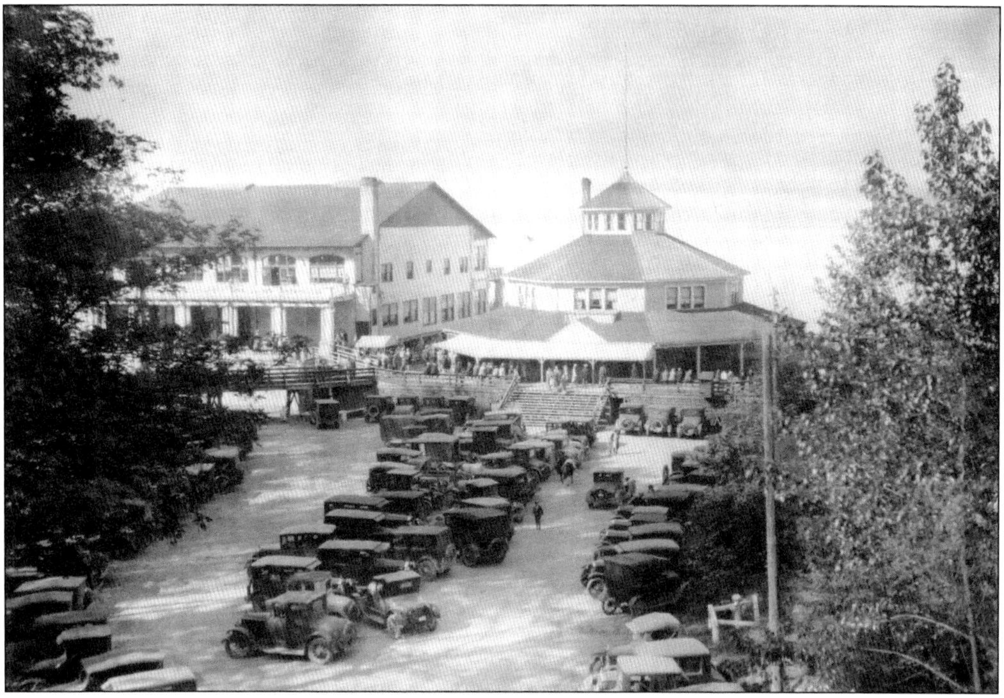

The history of Point Defiance Park has been told in many ways over the years, with each one agreeing with the landscape architects, Hare & Hare, in their 1911 report to the park district commissioners, that "no other city in the country has such a beautiful and natural park. . . . Every citizen of Tacoma should feel it a duty and a privilege to become one of the guardians." Even this park, however, has undergone generations of change as park district officers and employees decide how best to use the land in ways that both preserve it and provide amenities for all those wishing to enjoy it, especially along the shoreline. In 1903, Edwin Ferris (above) opened his restaurant and pavilion, situated adjacent to the boathouse shown below in 1929. Nereides Baths, located on a bluff above the boathouse, was opened in 1908. None of the buildings remain.

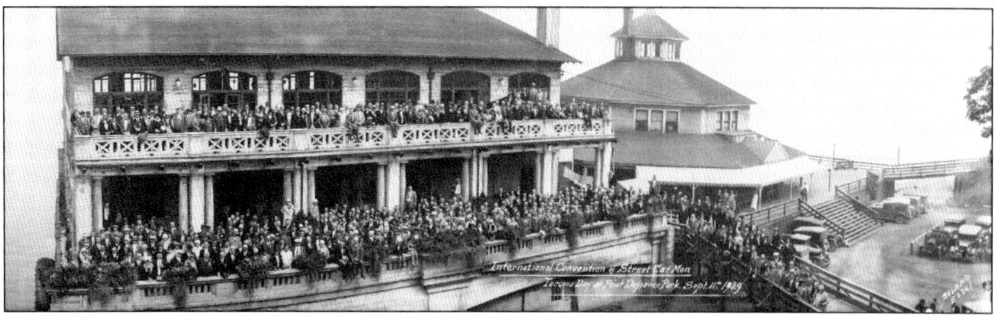

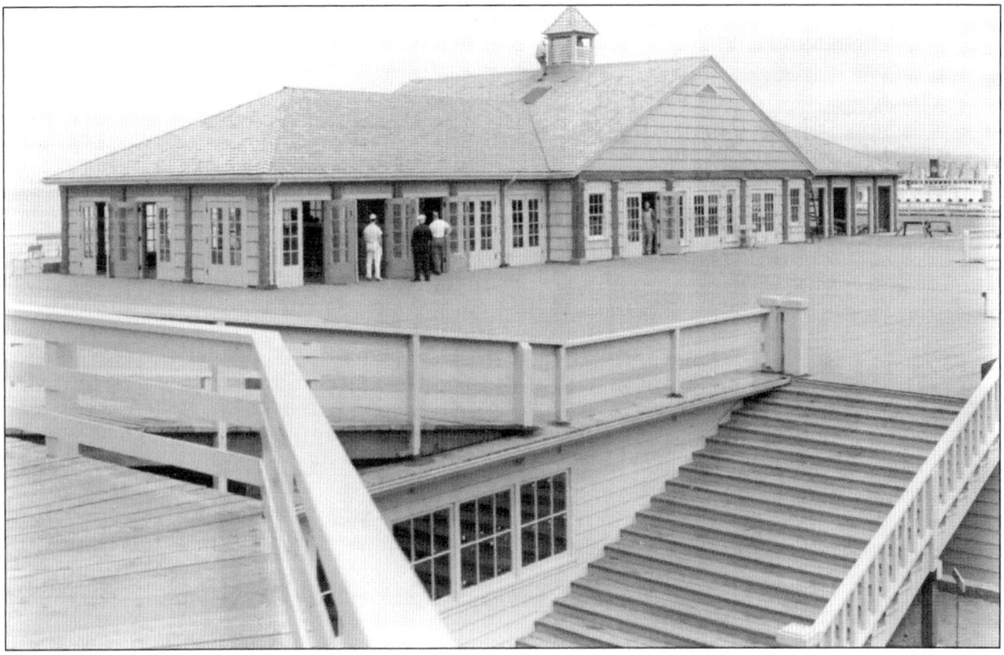

The facility was demolished a year after the preceding photograph was taken. In its stead, a new boathouse opened in 1940, and this image could have been taken at its dedication. At the restaurant, patrons could bring their own fish for the chefs to prepare. Fire destroyed the building in 1984. (Richards Studio, Tacoma Public Library.)

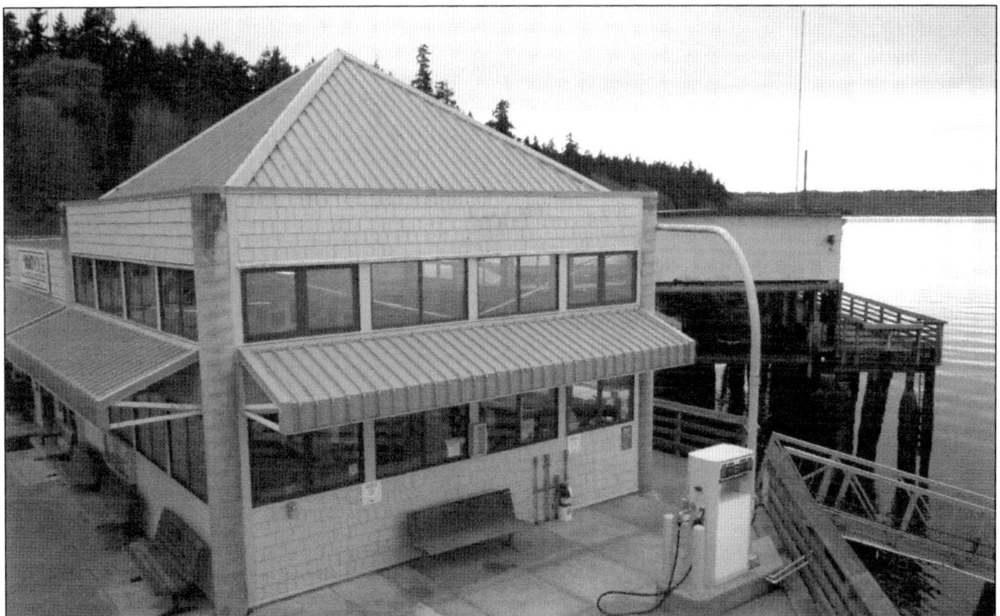

Following the fire, a new restaurant, originally known as the Boathouse Grill, opened for business in 1990. It is now part of Anthony's Home Port restaurant chain. A photograph display telling the history of Point Defiance and its various generations of change can be seen on the walls facing the promenade.

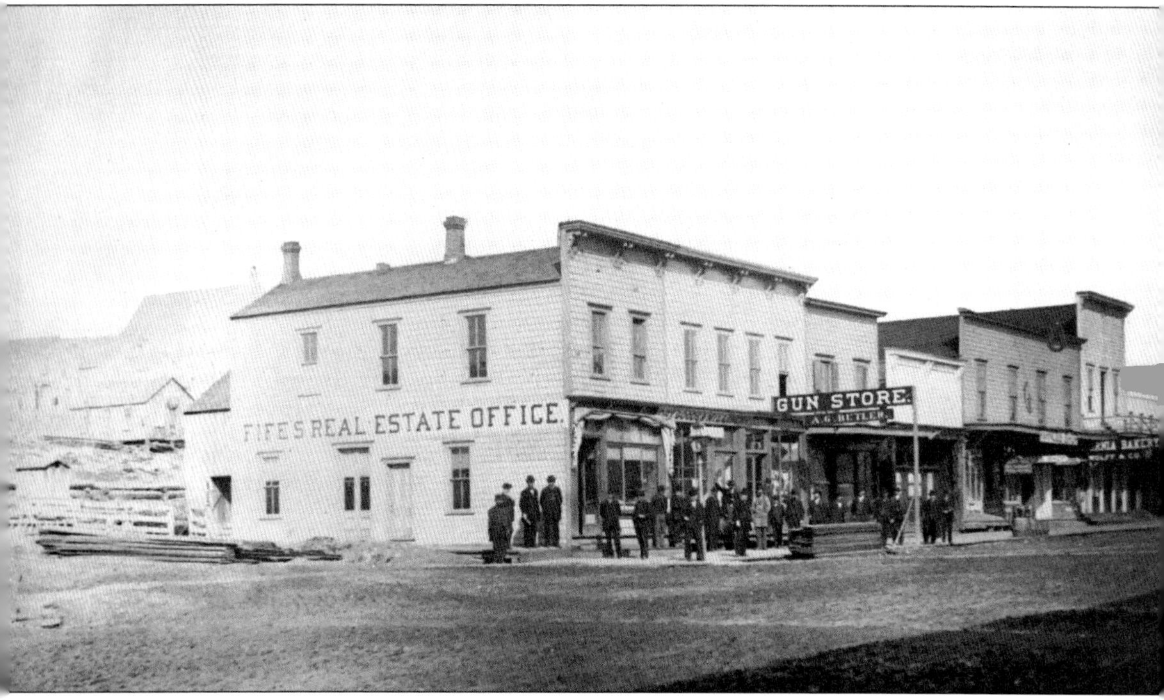

Two things determined the shape and subsequent development of a city in the latter years of the 19th century: One was the money to be had through the sale of real estate. The other was building, and later, zoning codes that determined where buildings were to be constructed as well as defining their appearances. Architects and builders worked—and still work—within these given parameters. The end result explains how Tacoma has witnessed such a variety of designs and uses over time. After 1873, when the Northern Pacific Railroad announced its wharf terminus location at Tacoma, the first businessmen to arrive were realtors, and early city directories list more people engaged in real estate sales and land development than any other occupation. One of the first was William H. Fife, who established his real estate company on the corner of South Ninth Street and Pacific Avenue in the late 1870s. After an 1885 fire destroyed this block of pioneer wood-framed businesses, Fife rebuilt using brick.

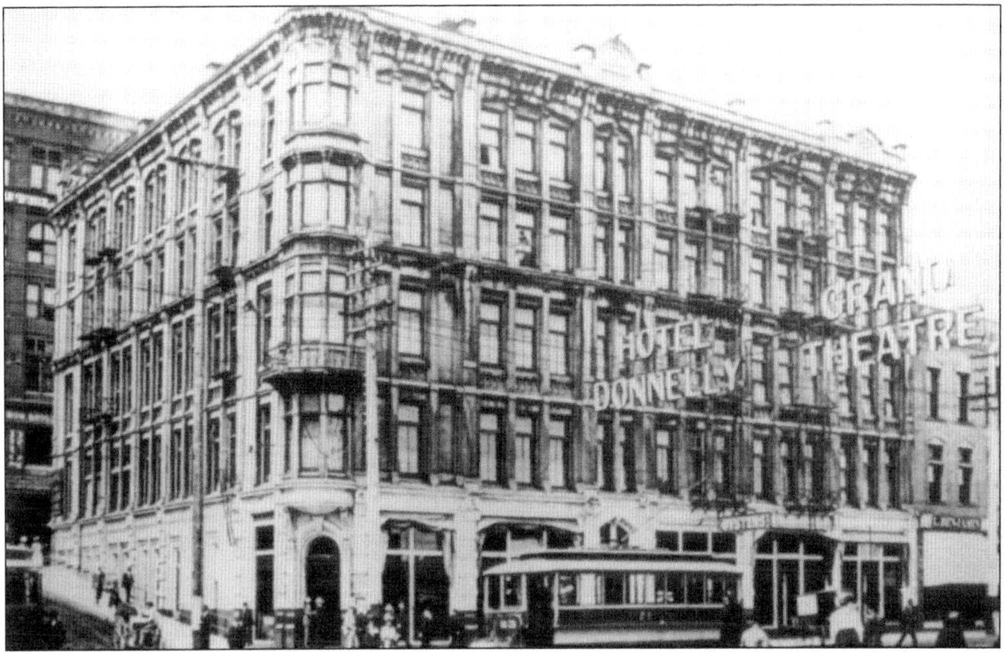

The Fife Hotel, designed by the Tacoma firm of Farrell and Darmer and constructed on the same corner as his real estate office at Ninth Street and Pacific Avenue, opened its doors in 1887. By 1897, the hotel had been leased to John Donnelly, and the name changed. It remained at this site until 1925, when it was demolished. (Historic Building Files, Tacoma Public Library.)

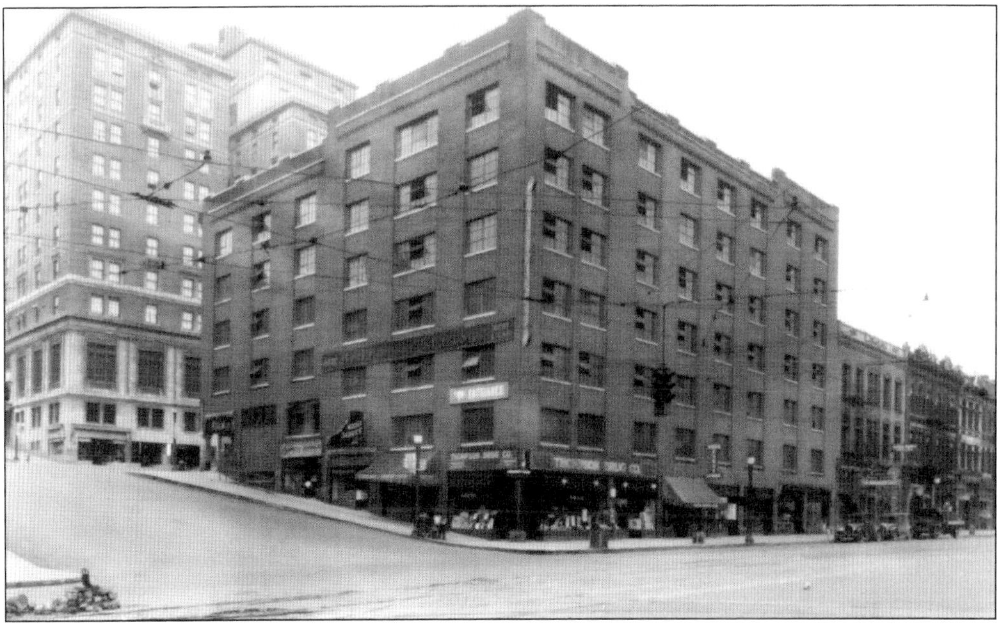

When the Donnelly Hotel was demolished, the *Tacoma Daily News* noted, "Another landmark passes into oblivion." A parking garage, designed by architect A.J. Russell, replaced it. The multistory building continues to accommodate cars, with businesses on the lower levels. With one exception immediately adjacent to the garage, the buildings shown here are now part of the Old City Hall Historic District. (Marvin D. Boland Collection, Tacoma Public Library.)

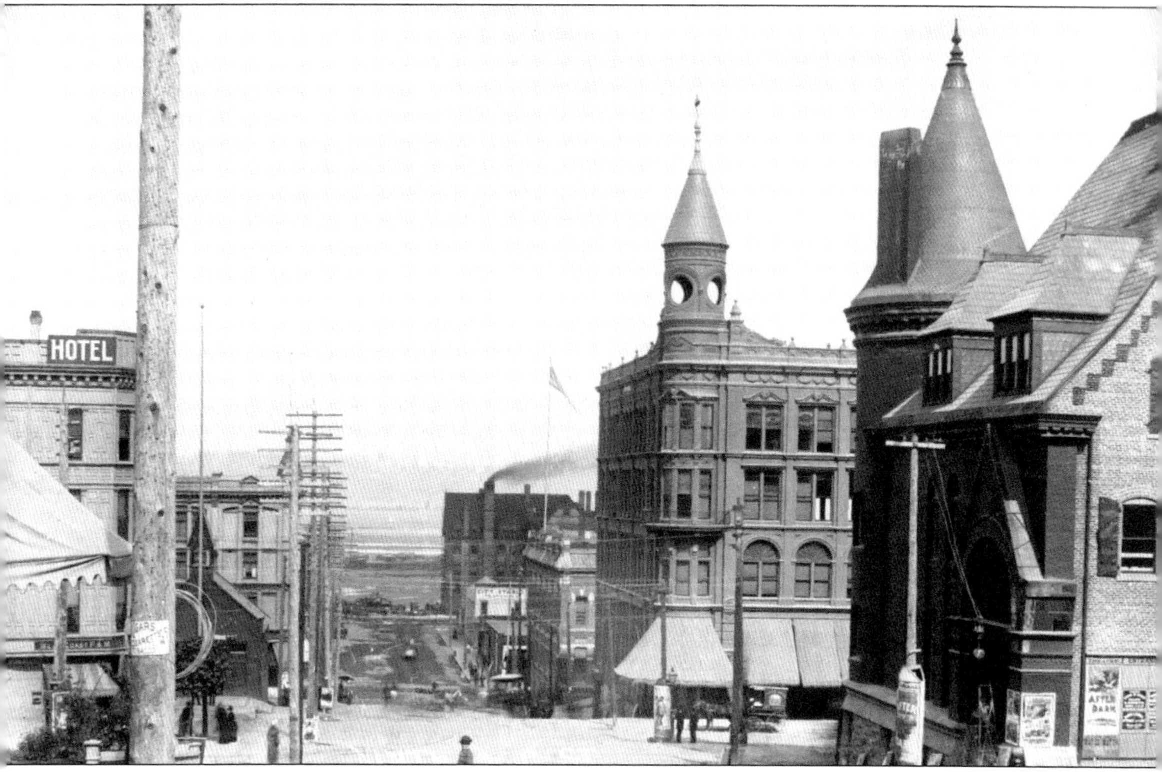

No street was immune from the tearing down and redesigning of downtown Tacoma. This 1890 view looking east along Ninth Street from Broadway Avenue shows the Gross Brothers Department Store constructed in 1889. Ten years later, it was called the Jones Block and housed a hotel along with street-level businesses. Prior to its demolition, there were theaters located in a part of the building as well as across the street, where Tacoma promoters built the Tacoma Opera House to provide a venue for opera and other forms of classical music. (Tacoma Public Library.)

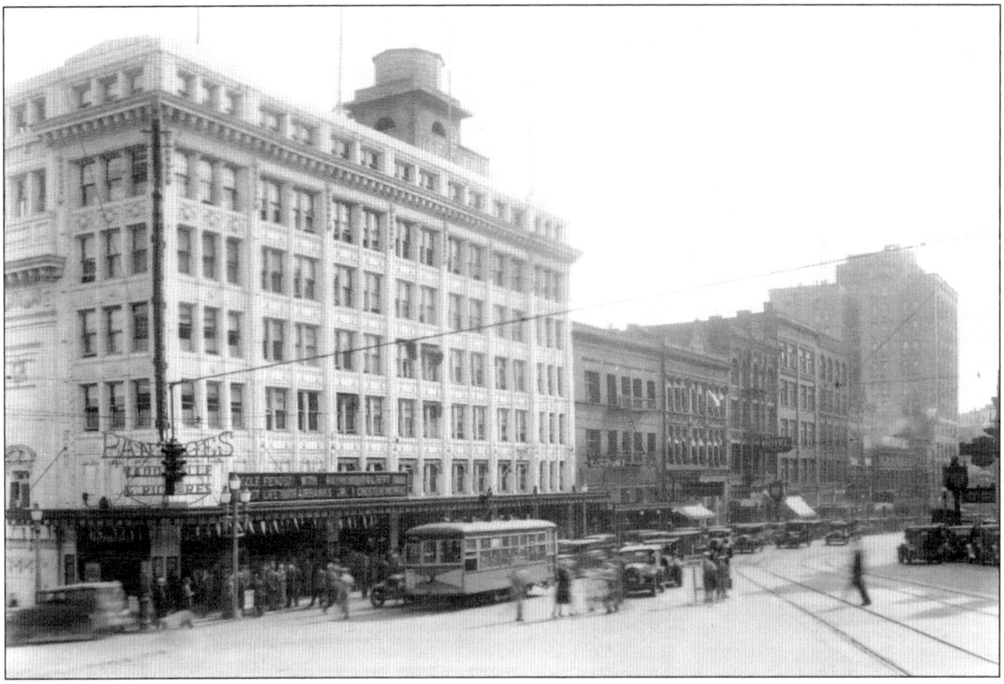

The Gross Brothers Building was destroyed in 1916 to make way for the B. Marcus Pritica–designed theater for Alexander Pantages's vaudeville enterprises. Spaces above were reserved for office space. The Pantages Theater building could have been demolished in the 1970s were it not for the City of Tacoma's commitment to preserve it, making it the core of the city's theater district today.

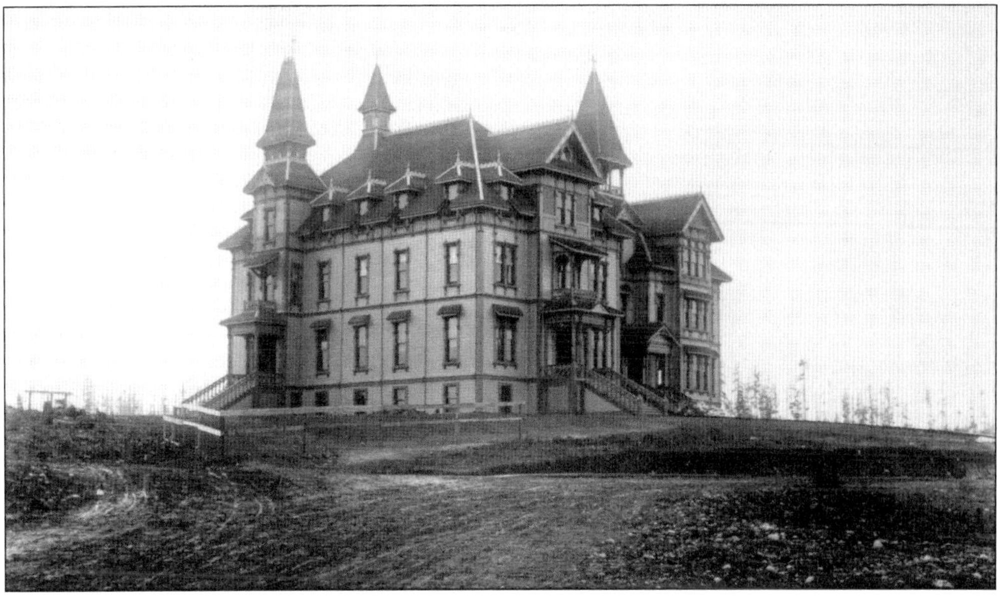

This history began (see page 9) with a photograph taken south along Tacoma Avenue North toward Division Avenue. Annie Wright Seminary, a private school for girls, was shown in the distance. A closer view, taken by U.P. Hadley around 1890, is shown here. The school remained here until 1925, when the present campus, located farther north along Tacoma Avenue North, opened for students. (Thomas R. Stenger collection.)

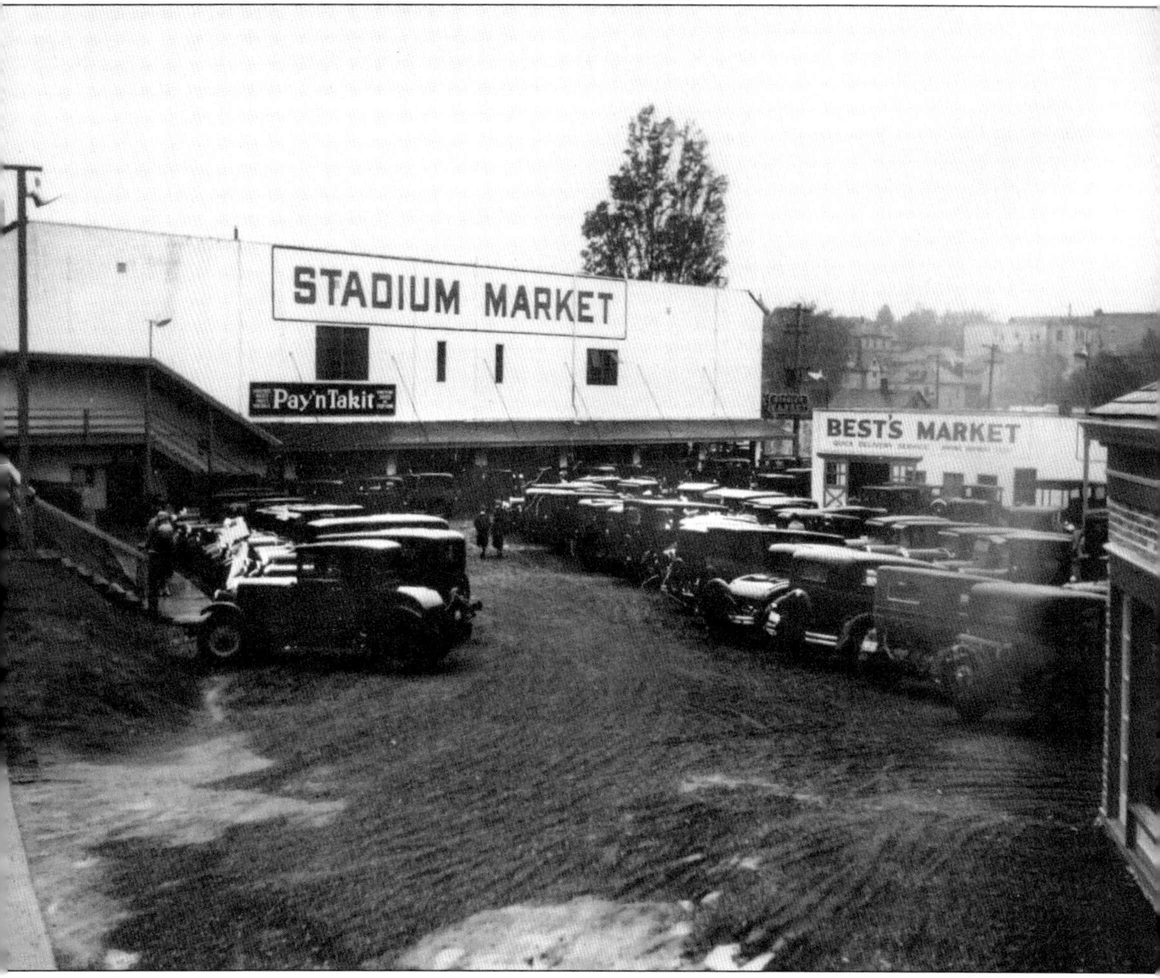

By the 1930s, the area surrounding Annie Wright was assuming its present character as a neighborhood business district, one formed first by the streetcar lines running through it as well as by the impacts of the automobile and city zoning codes. In 1929, Allen Motor Company constructed both a car dealership and garage. In 1931, the Lumberman's Improvement Company converted a part of the existing building into the Stadium Market, a business still in operation but now expanded into the area once home to automotive-related businesses.

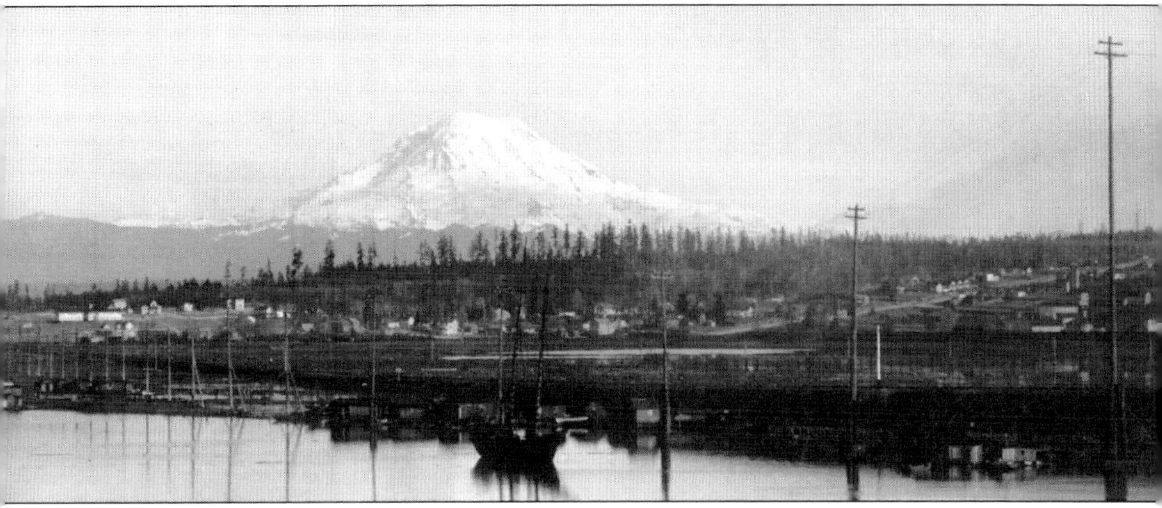

While it seems contrary to modern outlooks, Tacoma pioneers and past generations often thought within the context of "vanished peoples," pushing aside citizens of other cultural backgrounds. For Asian peoples, the exodus from downtown Tacoma was by force. In 1885, Chinese laborers were physically forced out of the city by vigilantes. In 1942, Japanese families were—by way of an executive order issued by Pres. Franklin D. Roosevelt—placed in concentration camps. The treatment of some so-called undesirables was subtler. Prostitutes were restrained along certain streets, for example. Once zoning became a fashionable tool, saloons and taverns were restricted to various sections of commercial business districts. Even given all of these examples, nationwide, only the Native American peoples were collectively referred to as "vanishing," seemingly compelled to live out their dying cultures on such places as the Puyallup Indian Reservation, shown here. However, for those pioneers wishing to lament or hoping for a rapid tribal passing, the exercise was wishful thinking. The Puyallup tribe was able to maintain its existence and provide for its members regardless of what many Tacomans thought. (Thomas R. Stenger collection.)

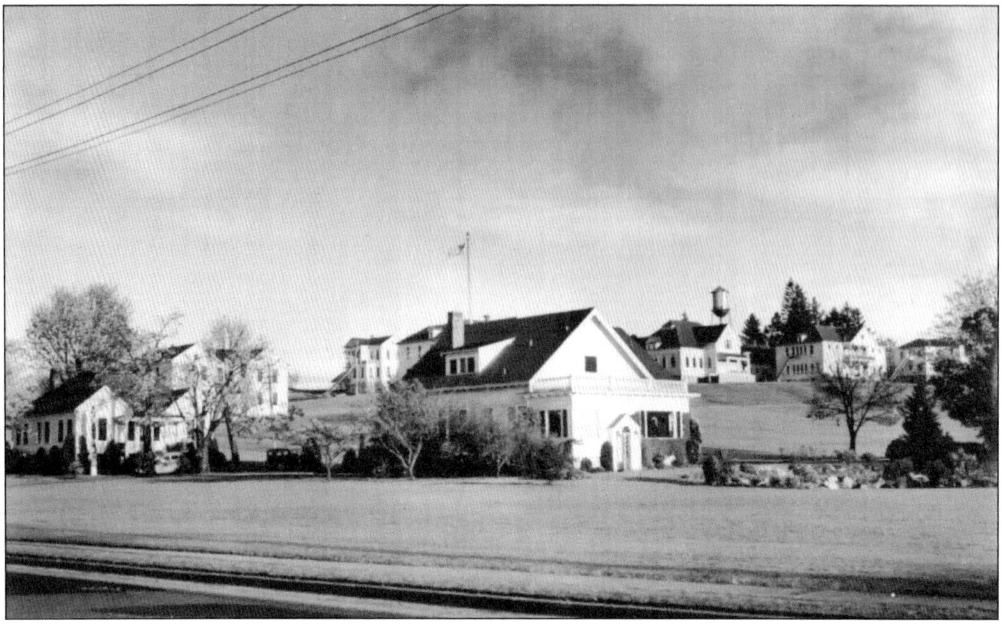

Education and health care were two areas of specific concern as the Puyallup leadership became stronger over time. Education was funded through congressional legislation requiring that a part of the reservation lands be platted and sold. This endeavor began the creation of Tacoma's East Tacoma neighborhood. This 1940 photograph shows the Cushman Indian Hospital that at this time was devoted to Indian tuberculosis patients. (Richards Studio, Tacoma Public Library.)

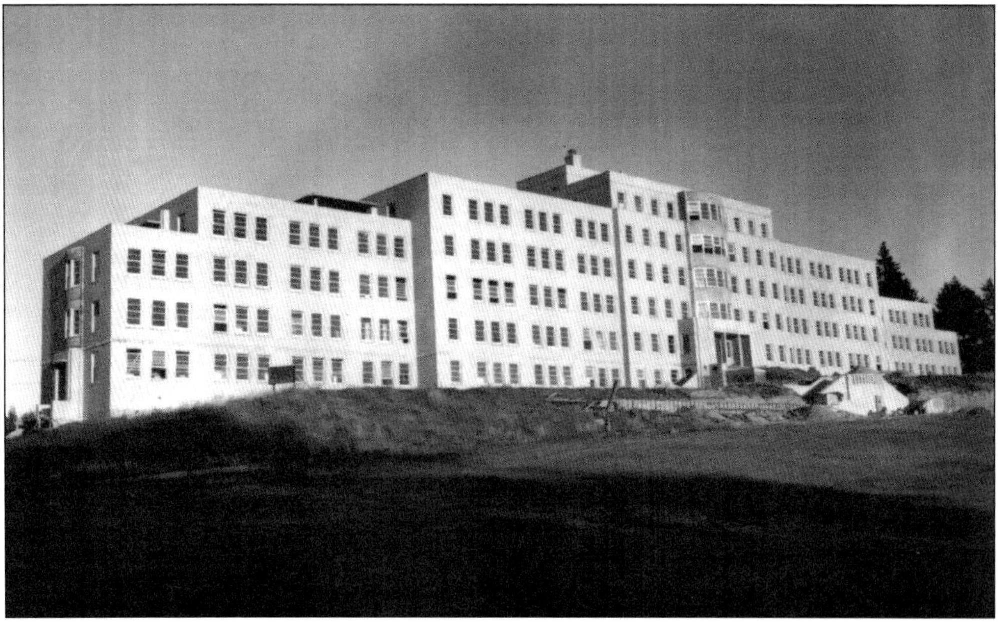

Prior to the outbreak of World War II, Congress approved the construction of a new Cushman Hospital, shown here nearing completion in 1943. By the 1960s and 1970s, the building became the symbol of Puyallup Indian rights over their own lands and lives. Through intricate negotiations, the tribal council proved its point. The land was theirs, and the hospital was subsequently demolished and replaced by a casino. (Richards Studio, Tacoma Public Library.)

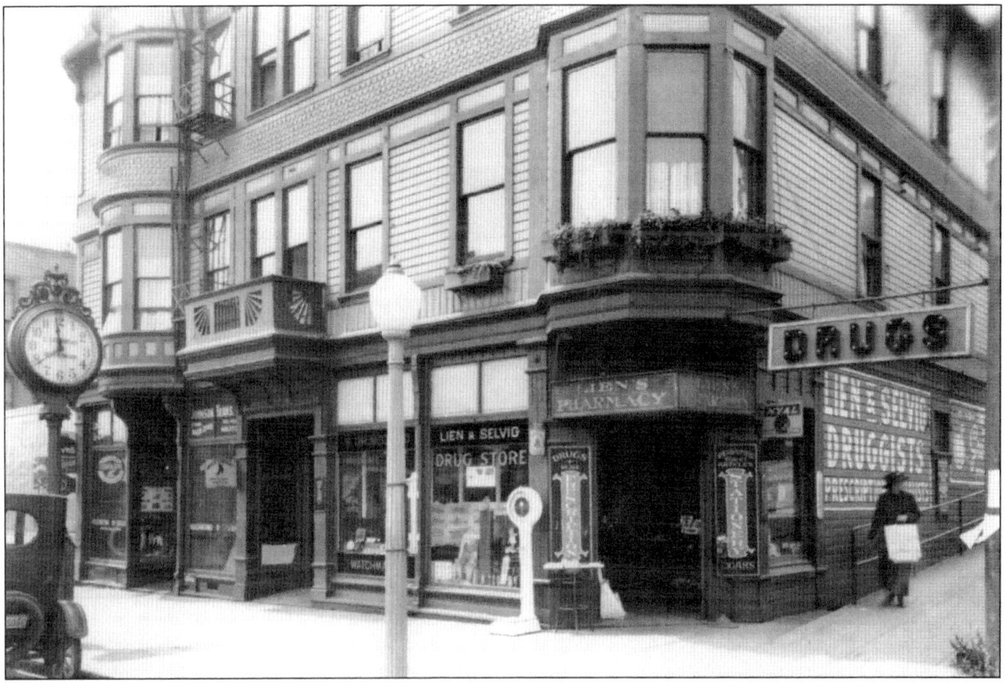

In 1888, the Tacoma architectural firm of Farrell and Darmer designed the George H. Greer Building, located at 1102 Tacoma Avenue South. In 1923, when Marvin Boland took this photograph, the city's Carnegie library had been opened for 20 years. In March 1951, the *Tacoma News Tribune* reported that a new library building "forces out landmark" occupants, including those living in the Wheeler Apartments. (Marvin D. Boland Collection, Tacoma Public Library.)

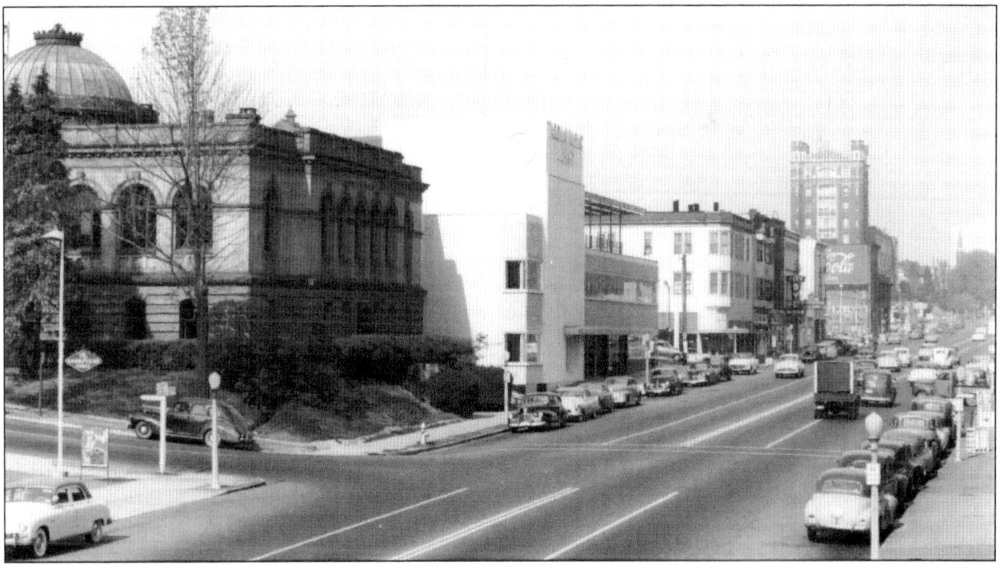

The main branch of the Tacoma Public Library, shown here in 1952, was designed by local architect Silas E. Nelson and was dedicated in November 1952. In this northward view, other primarily wood-framed buildings are seen facing Tacoma Avenue South. Within a couple of years, these building would be demolished to make way for the County-City Building. (Richards Studio, Tacoma Public Library.)

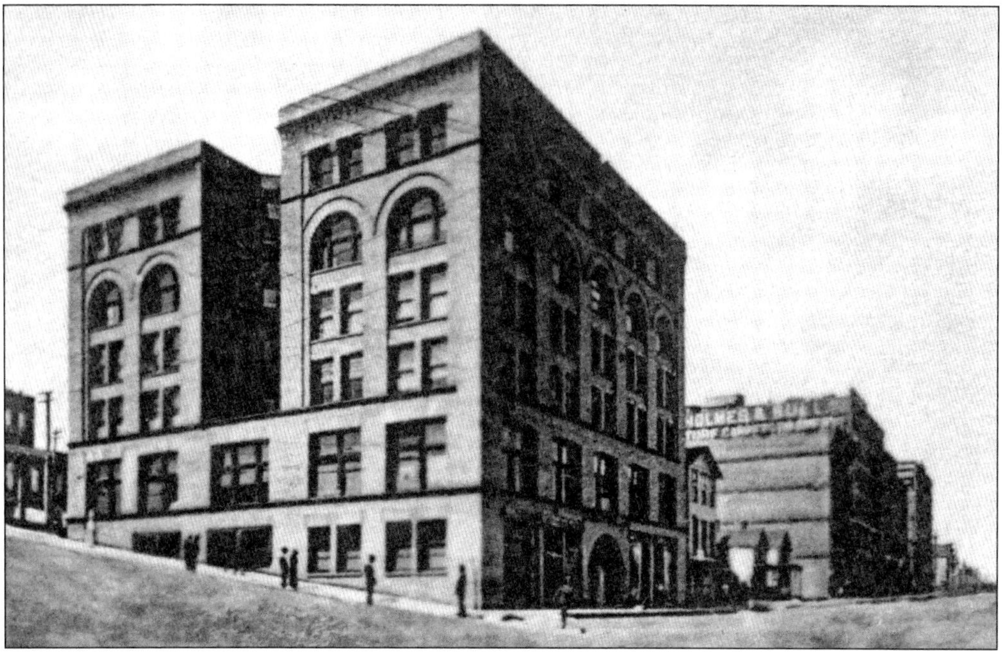

The Chicago architectural firm of Burnham and Root designed the Fidelity Building, shown here in 1890 near its time of completion. It was one of two designed in Tacoma by the nationally known firm and one of a few built in the Pacific states. In 1909, an additional six stories were added. The building stood until 1949.

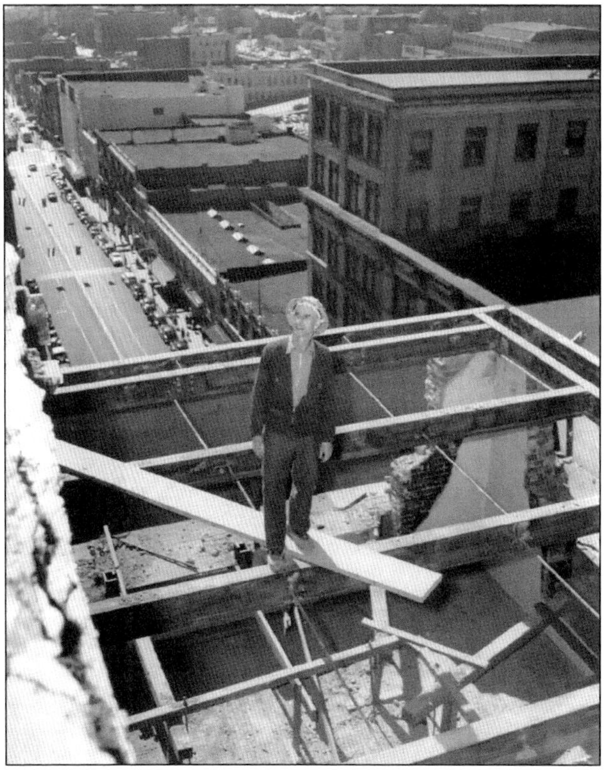

Available information does not make it clear if the 1949 earthquake that damaged many downtown buildings caused the demolition of the Fidelity Building or if another development was planned for the site prior to the disaster. Whatever the reason, by September 1949, demolition had begun, as shown here in a view taken at the time. (Richards Studio, Tacoma Public Library.)

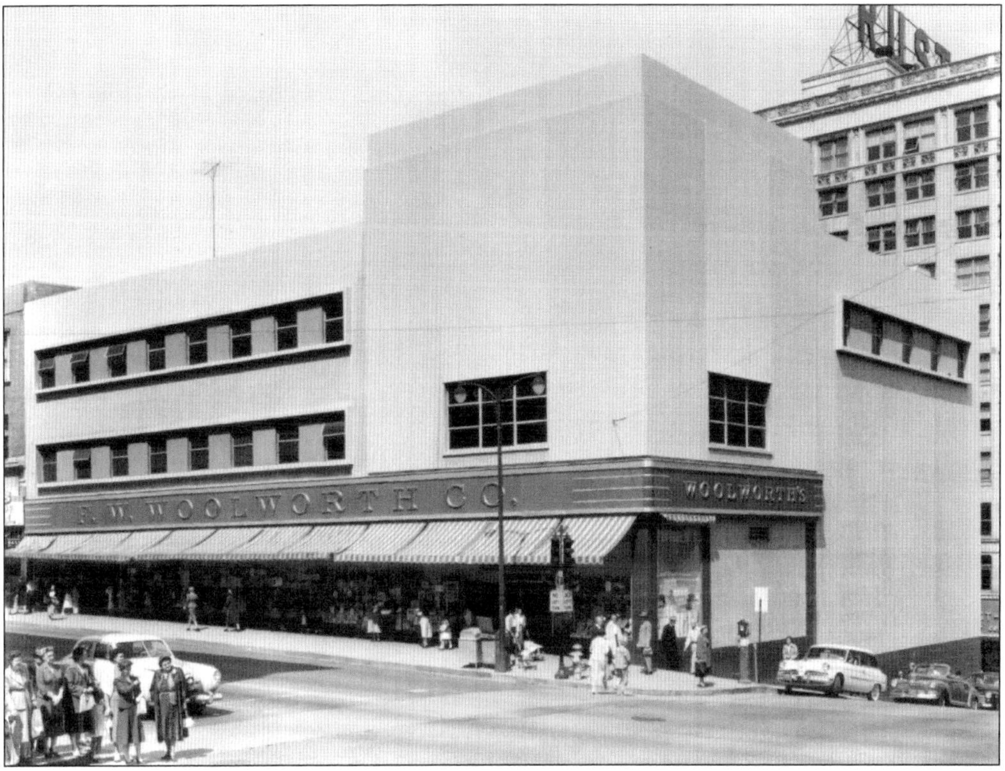

The month before the earthquake occurred, the *Tacoma News Tribune* reported that plans had been drawn for a replacement for the Fidelity Building. By January of the next year, the newspaper reported, "Landmark gone, new one rising." This was the Woolworth department store shown here in 1954. While the store closed its doors in 1993, the building still remains. (Richards Studio, Tacoma Public Library.)

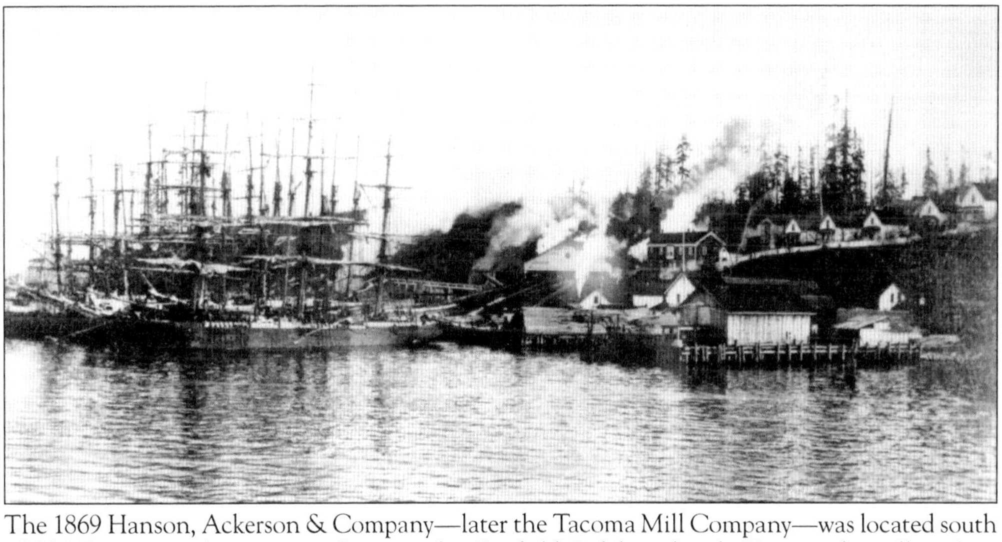

The 1869 Hanson, Ackerson & Company—later the Tacoma Mill Company—was located south of Old Tacoma in the vicinity of present-day Garfield Gulch and park. Housing for mill workers was constructed west of the facility, and a company store was a fixture on the mill dock. It was, in some ways, a town within a town.

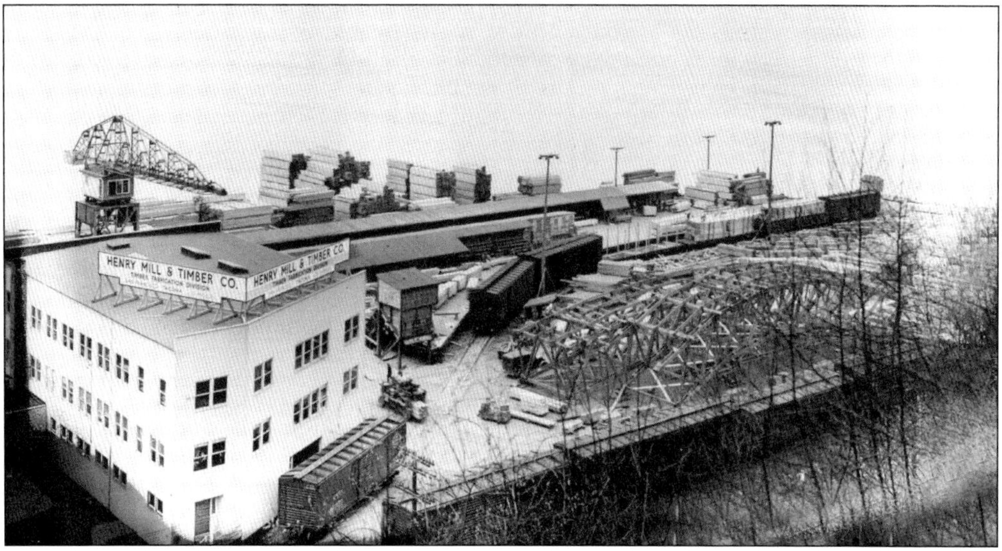

In 1925, after the Tacoma Mill closed, the Henry Mill and Timber Company rebuilt on the site, specializing in prefabricated wood products for the Army and Navy. The company experienced two fires—one in 1942, and another in 1950 that completely destroyed the facility. The site remained undeveloped for another generation. (Richards Studio, Tacoma Public Library.)

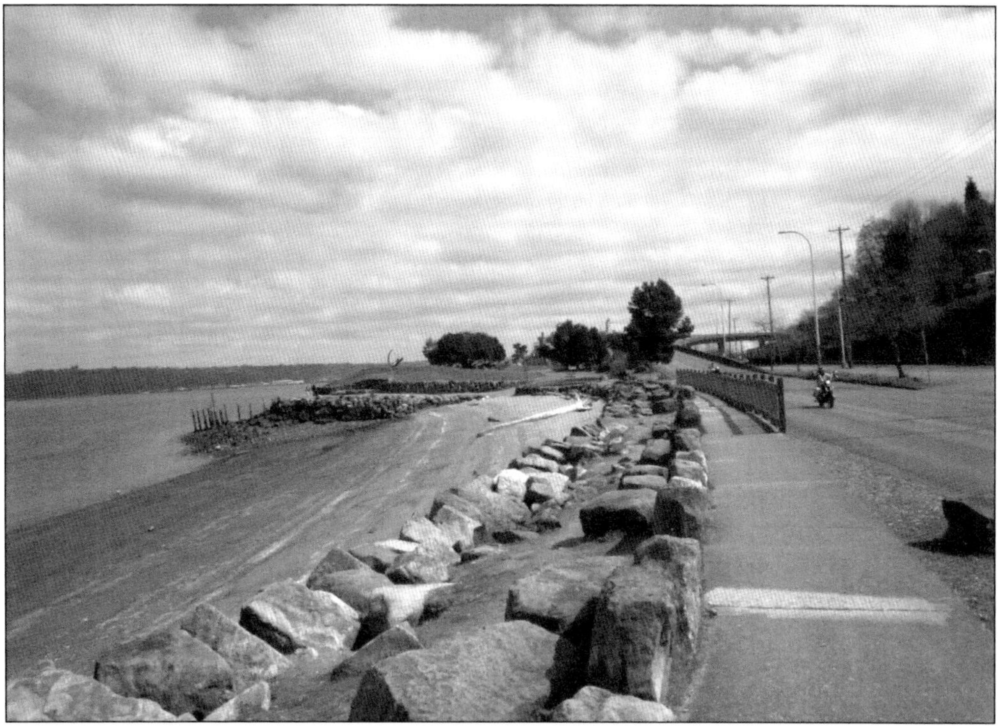
In the early 1970s, the Metropolitan Park District, the City of Tacoma, and other agencies began designing a park at the Henry Mill location, which was originally called Commencement Park. Following the death of Mayor Jack Hyde in 1994, the city council changed the name. The city's Reconciliation Park, dedicated to Tacoma's Chinese immigrants and citizens, is located south of Hyde Park.

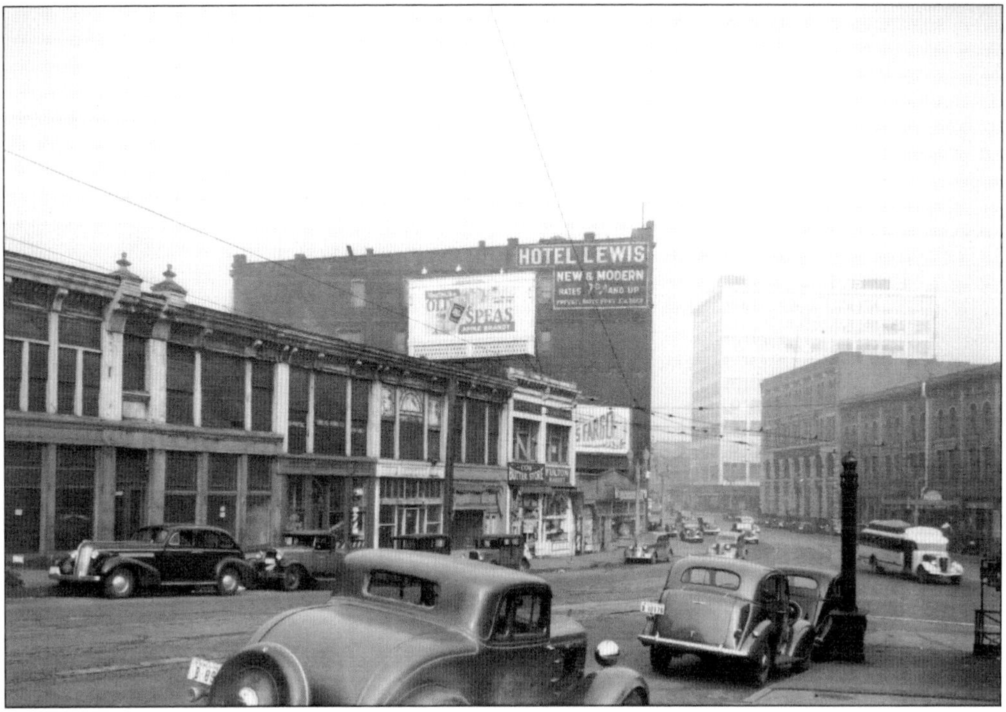

Originally, the intersection of South Seventeenth Street and Pacific Avenue, shown in the 1933 photograph below, was a dividing line between commercial and industrial areas in downtown Tacoma. The Northern Pacific rail line crossing Pacific Avenue defined the division. The tracks were a constant bone of contention between the city and the railroad for decades, and it has only been recently that they were removed. In the below photograph by Chapin Bowen, the view is looking north along Pacific Avenue and Commerce Street. The above image was taken the same year and is a closer view of the same intersection. Of all of the buildings shown in the below image, only a portion of the 1889 Sprague Building at 1509 Pacific Avenue and the high-rise Schoenfeld Building have survived. The 1890 Waddell Building on Pacific Avenue across from the Sprague Building is the only other major survivor. (Both, Chapin Bowen, Associated Photographic Services.)

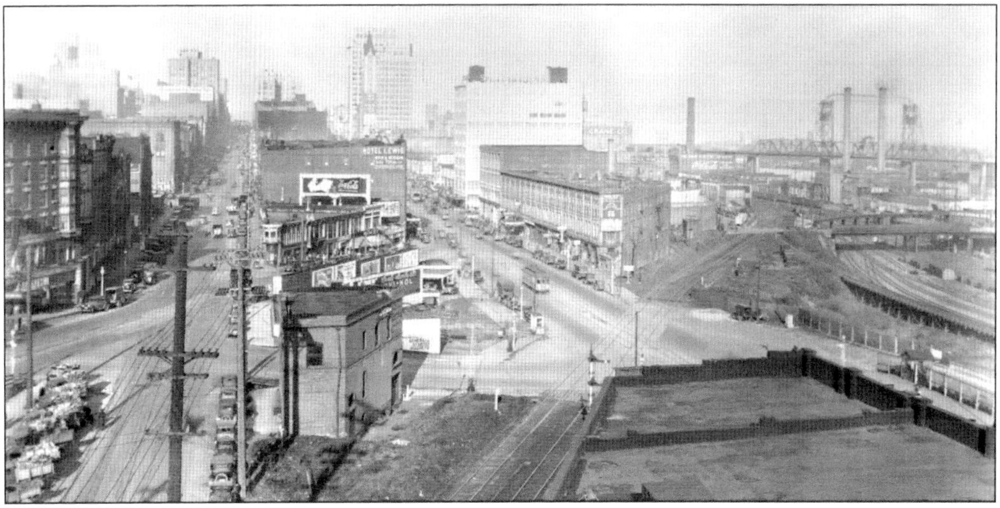

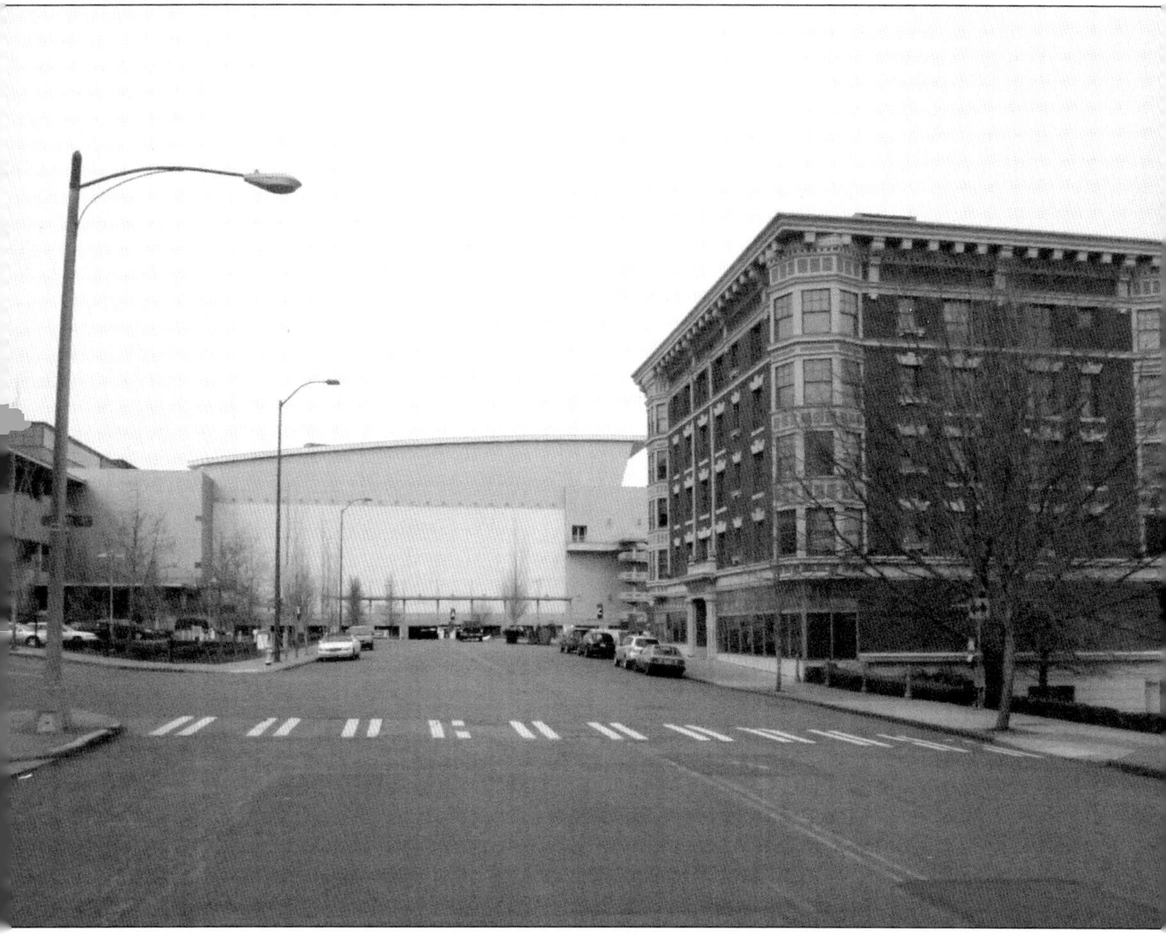

Since the beginning of cities, urban dwellers have sought to improve urban landscapes. Many reasons, like "city beautification" or "urban renewal," which are catchphrases here in the United States, have been given for this continual need to change a city's appearance. Economic development and improving urban transportation are actually the two major reasons why beautification is deemed necessary. In all instances, plans include the demolition of buildings. One of Tacoma's earliest efforts was a "things that mar" the city section in the newspaper, where photographs of unkempt buildings and yards were printed so as to embarrass the owners. Economic development motives are best seen in the Greater Tacoma Convention and Trade Center, designed by the architectural firm of Merritt and Pardini and completed in 2004. This photograph was taken looking north from the corner of South Seventeenth Street along Broadway Avenue. The 1909 Carlton Hotel on the right was rehabilitated by private developers and then sold to the city.

Six

DEMOLITIONS

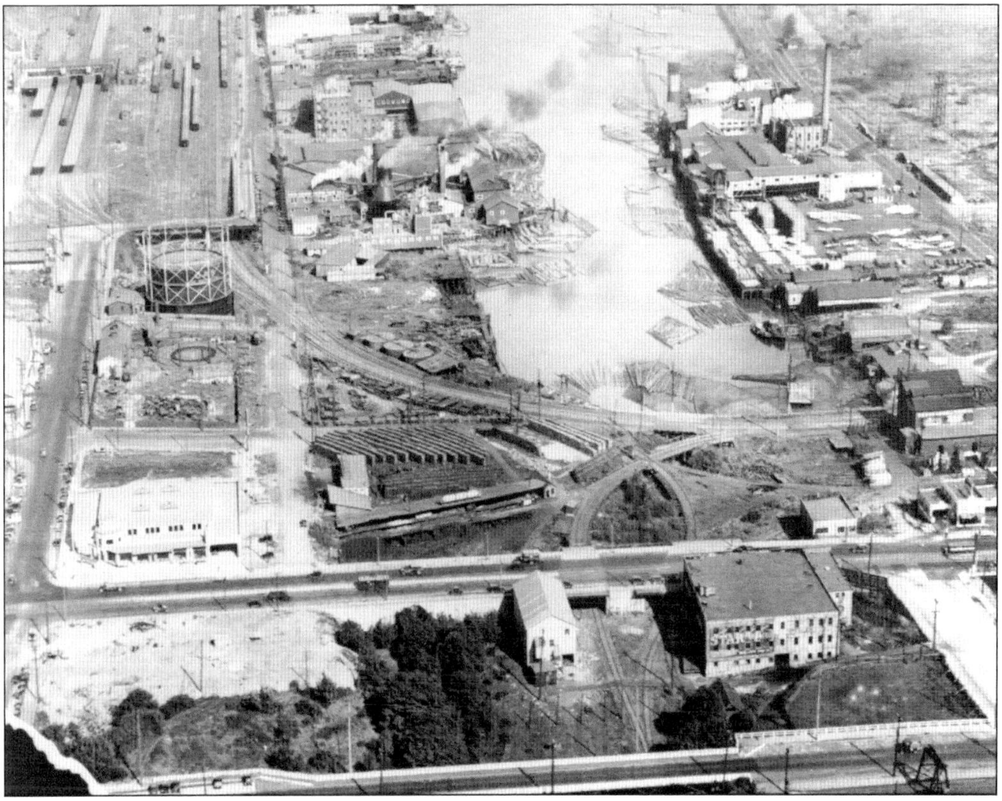

Throughout urban history and in all American cities, beautification or economic development plans have included the demolition of buildings and other changes to the landscape. Even though there are additional reasons discussed in this history, demolition has been a conscious tool used to make cities pleasant for work and play. Public opinion and government decision-making regarding these goals and how they can be carried out are constantly changing over time. This undated aerial photograph shows the head of the Thea Foss Waterway at it appeared before urban renewal began to change the area following World War II. Industrial uses prevailed on the west side of the waterway. A current view of this area would include the I-705 freeway, the Museum of Glass, and condominiums. While industrial uses have been retained on the east side of the waterway, marinas have replaced log booms in the water. (Thomas R. Stenger collection.)

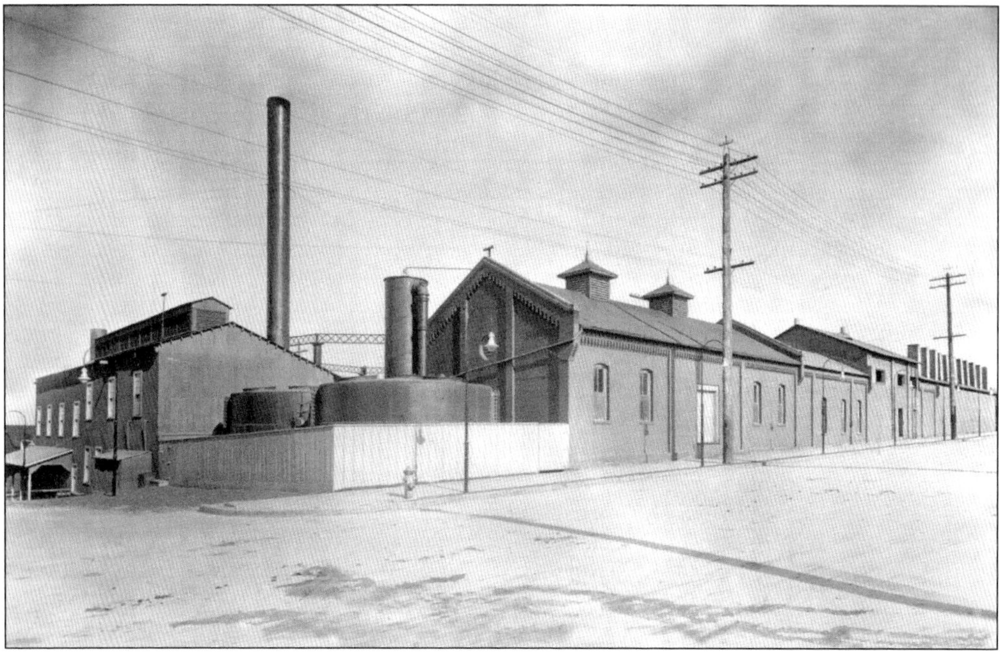

One of the buildings destroyed in 1975 for a freeway to downtown was part of the Tacoma Light and Water Company, the Tacoma Gasworks Building complex, constructed in 1884 by Charles B. Wright, then president of the Northern Pacific Railroad Company. When Wright sold his franchise to the city, those parts related to gas production were retained as a private concern.

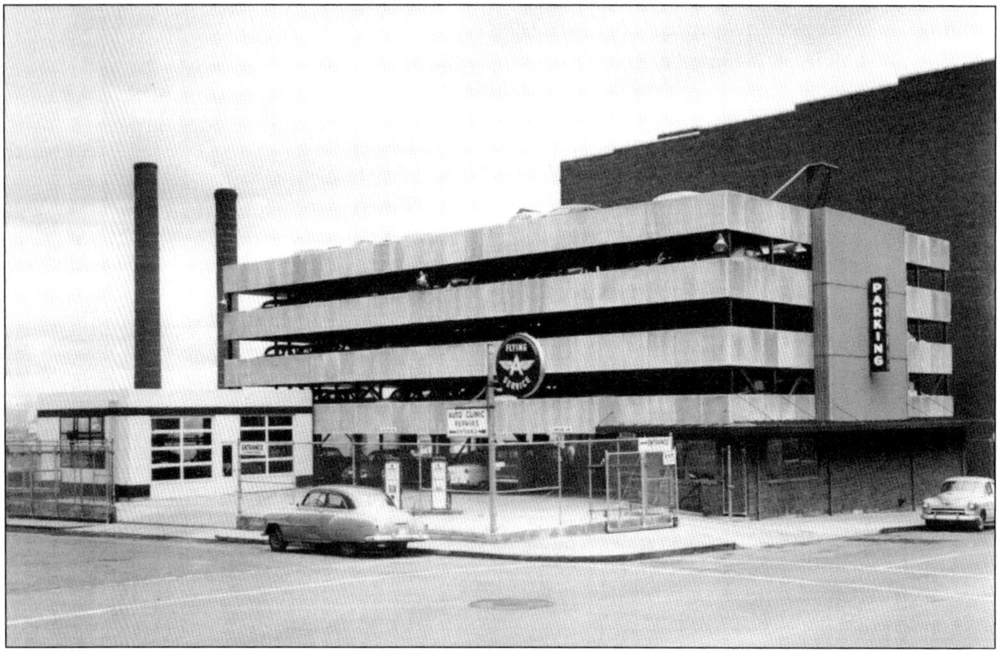

In December 1953, owners John T. Long and Lily Schweizer introduced "pigeon-hole" parking to Tacomans. Under this system, hydraulic hoists could move cars from level to level without the need for ramps. It is unknown when the structure was demolished, but the site is now a surface parking lot on the corner of South Twelfth and A Streets. (Richards Studio, Tacoma Public Library.)

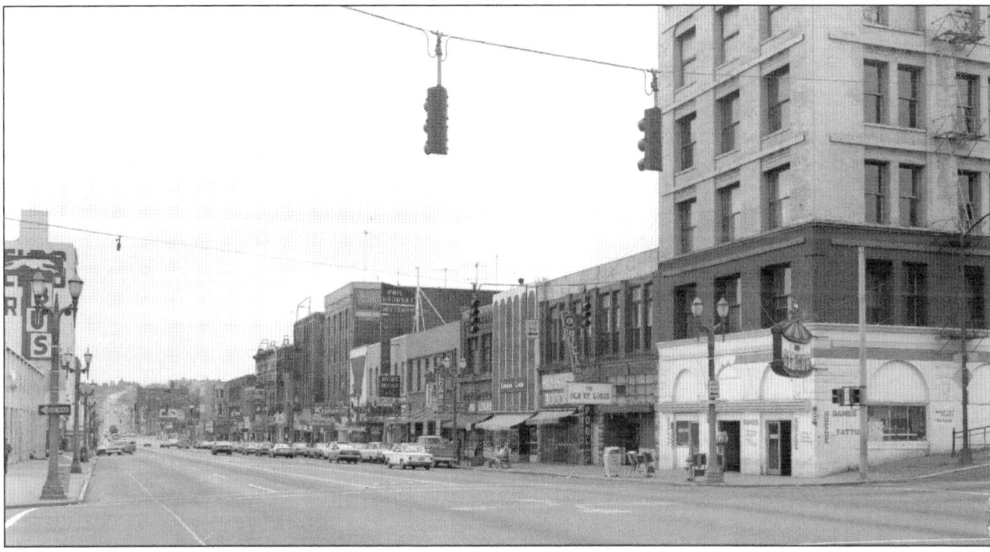

The Motor Ramp Garage at Ninth Street and Pacific Avenue and the Long-Schweizer garage at Twelfth and A Streets were the earliest multistory parking structures in downtown Tacoma. In both instances, the facility only took up a lot or two. By the late 1960, city officials, through the process of urban renewal, were planning for the total destruction of city blocks throughout Tacoma's central business district. The photograph below shows the Park Plaza South under construction in 1969. The Luzon Building, designed by the Chicago firm of Burnham and Root in 1890, is seen on the far left. The 1975 photograph shown above, of Pacific Avenue viewed southward from South Thirteenth Street, shows how all of Pacific Avenue looked before urban renewal. Within a generation, however, this block too would see the wrecking ball, again for more parking. (Below, Richards Studio, Tacoma Public Library.)

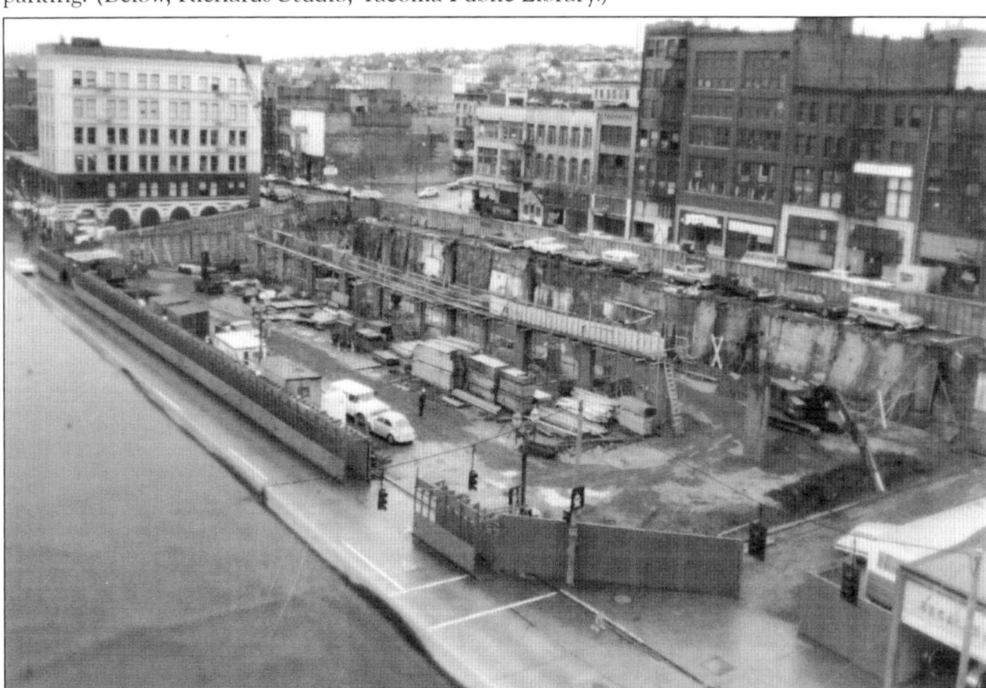

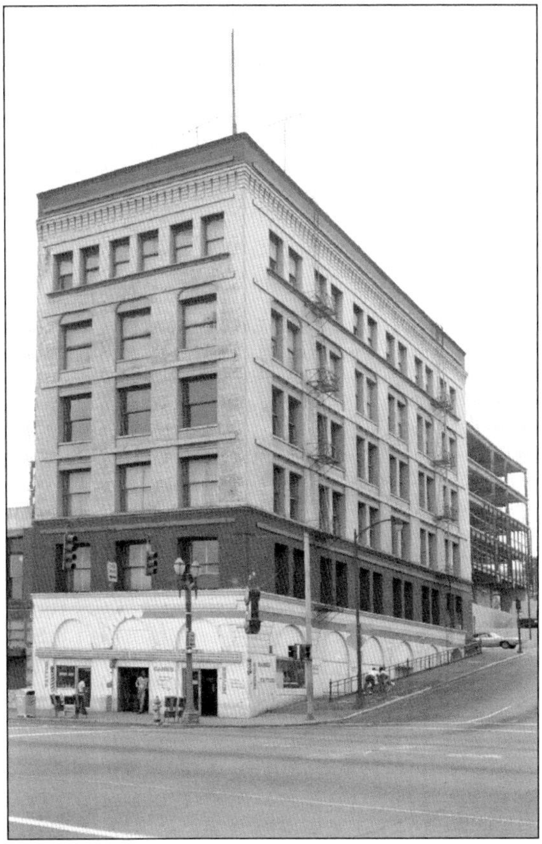

In the November 15, 2012, *News Tribune* columnist Peter Callaghan introduced to Tacomans a new malady, the "Luzon Hangover." The verb, introduced later by a Tacoma Landmarks Commission member, was "Luzoned." Callaghan's comments pertained to what historic preservationists call "preservation by neglect." In the instance of the Luzon, the demolition of the building in 2009, shown below, is all the more tragic because, at the time, it was publicly owned. The tragedy was even greater because there were private developers wanting to preserve the building, but the ever-prevalent problems imposed by banking institutions and city codes were sufficient barriers to prevent the restoration of this designated landmark. The building itself (left) is not pretentious, but in terms of architectural and engineering history, it was significant. It was in Tacoma that the Chicago firm of Burnham and Root pioneered the use of metal framing in a building's construction. This, in turn, ultimately led to the skyscrapers that revolutionized city development.

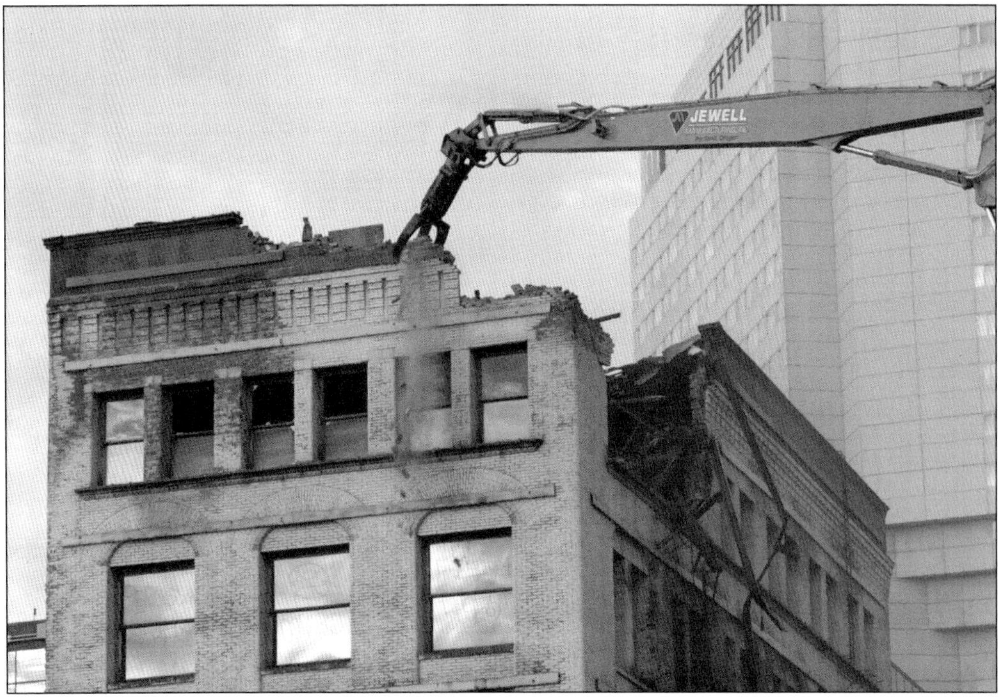

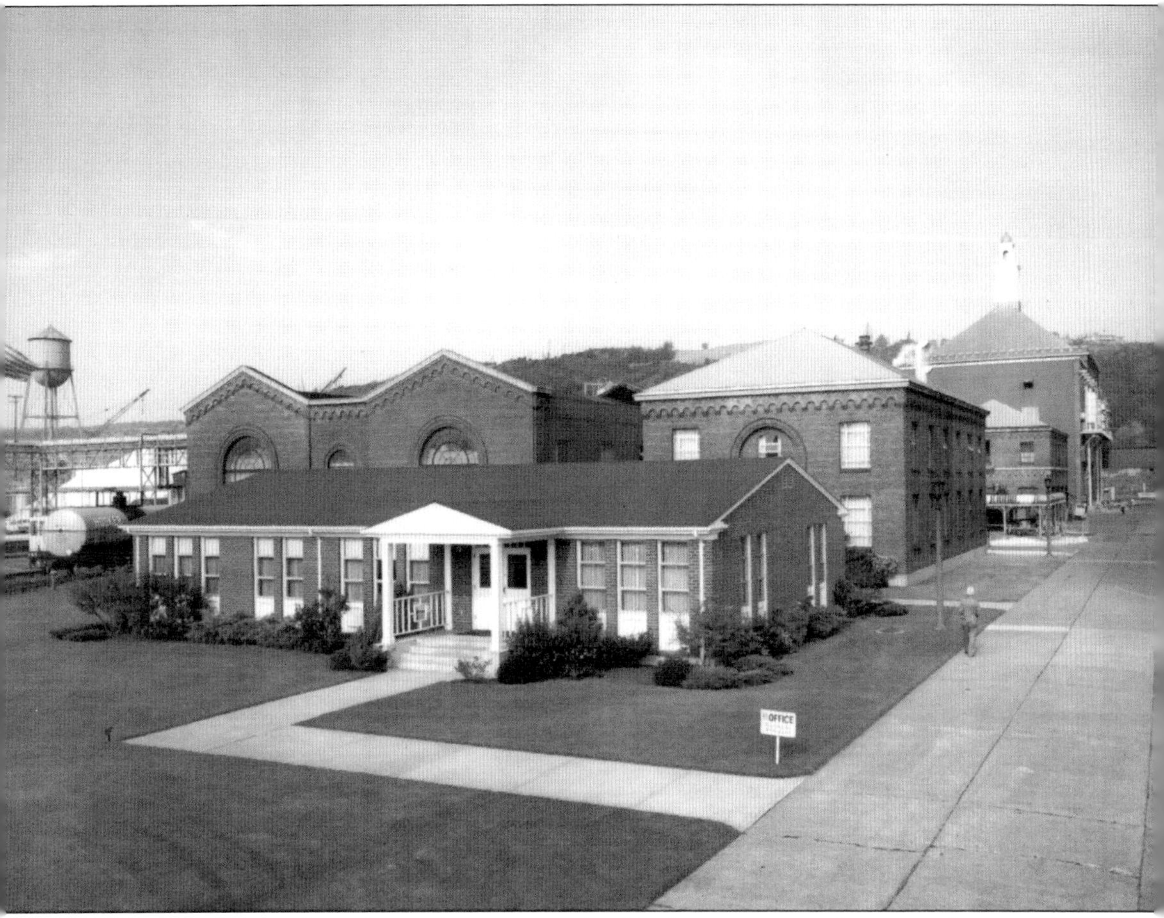

Tacoma's port-industrial area has undergone considerable changes, most unknown to the general public. The land continues to undergo alterations related to port and industrial uses reflecting new technologies. The most obvious transformation of the area is the filling in of the elongated slips to expand the land for container cargo shipments. Buildings have been lost through fires and demolitions, as they lost their usefulness. Chemistry-related industries found the port area particularly desirable because of the availability of water, especially salt water, and inexpensive power. Hooker Chemical Company, shown here in 1964, was one of first to establish a plant of this nature. Its prim and pristine industrial yard and landscaping made it unique in 1929, when the facility was built. The plant operated until 2002 and is now a Superfund site. (Richards Studio, Tacoma Public Library.)

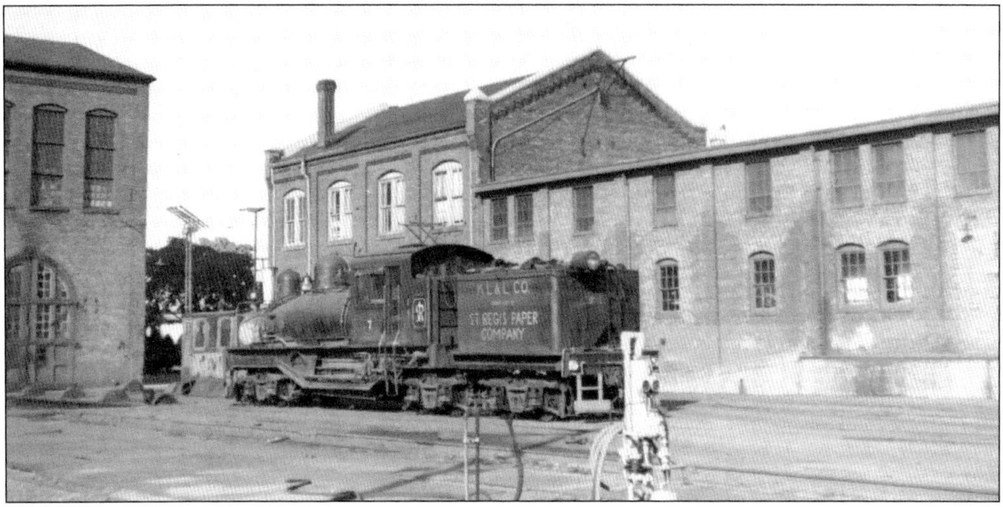

The history of the Northern Pacific Shops in South Tacoma has been told many times. Originally, the complex was located on the Columbia River near Kalama, Washington, where trains would be ferried from the Oregon side of the river. The next location was in downtown Tacoma, approximately in the vicinity of today's Union Station near the Lister Foundry at South Fifteenth Street and Pacific Avenue. Nothing is left in the way of shop activity at either of these two locations; however, there are few buildings that remain. The same can be said of the South Tacoma shops, which were first established there in 1891 and closed in the mid-1970s. While Burlington Northern Santa Fe Railway did plan for an industrial park at the site, environmental concerns have impeded any development. (Above, Thomas R. Stenger collection.)

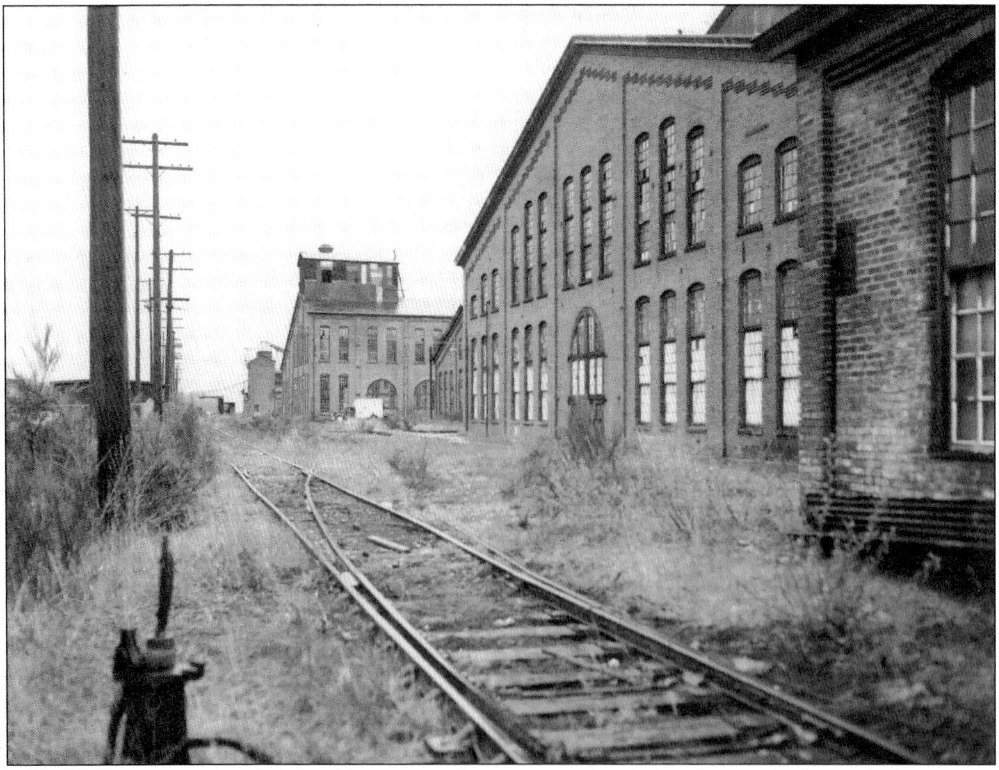

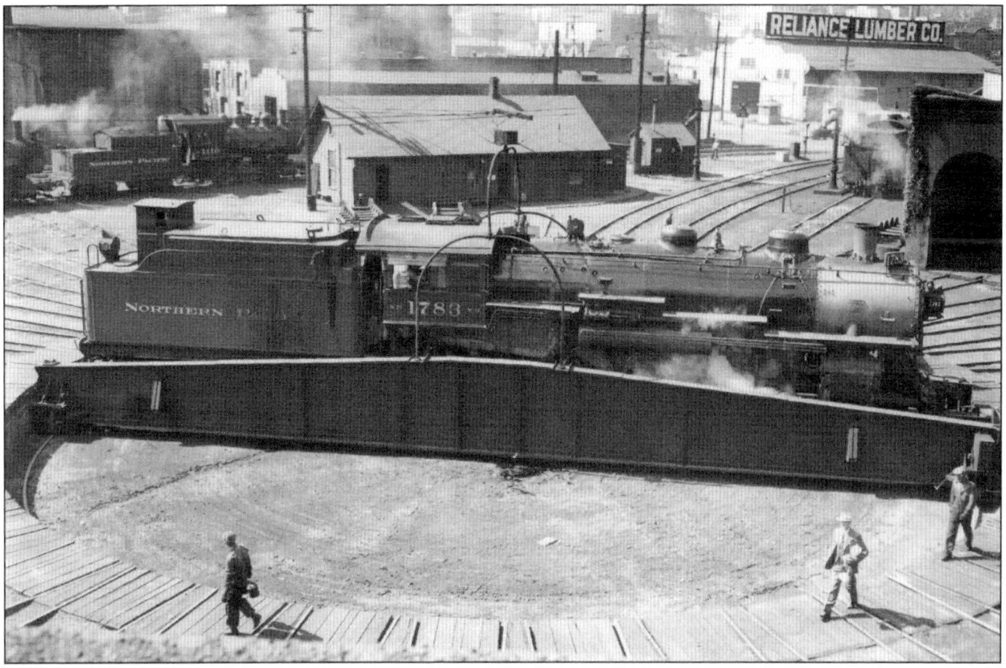

The Northern Pacific Railroad roundhouse has also been demolished, although the turntable remains at its location a 2211 East D Street. Constructed in the late 1890s to service steam engines, it was closed by 1971, when this photograph was taken, primarily because diesel-electric engines required a more modern form of maintenance. (Richards Studio, Tacoma Public Library.)

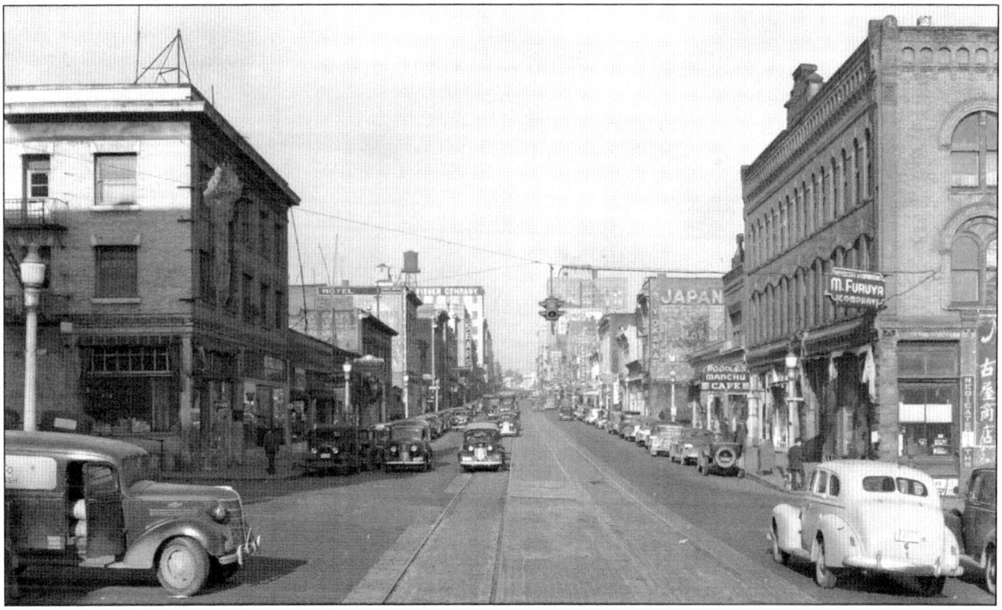

Prior to World War II, a neighborhood of Japanese businesses centered around South Thirteenth and Fifteenth Streets between Broadway Avenue and Market Street. All of this was lost when the city's Japanese community was put into concentration camps. Most of the buildings and all of the businesses shown in this undated Chapin Bowen photograph are no longer there, as each fell victim to urban renewal.

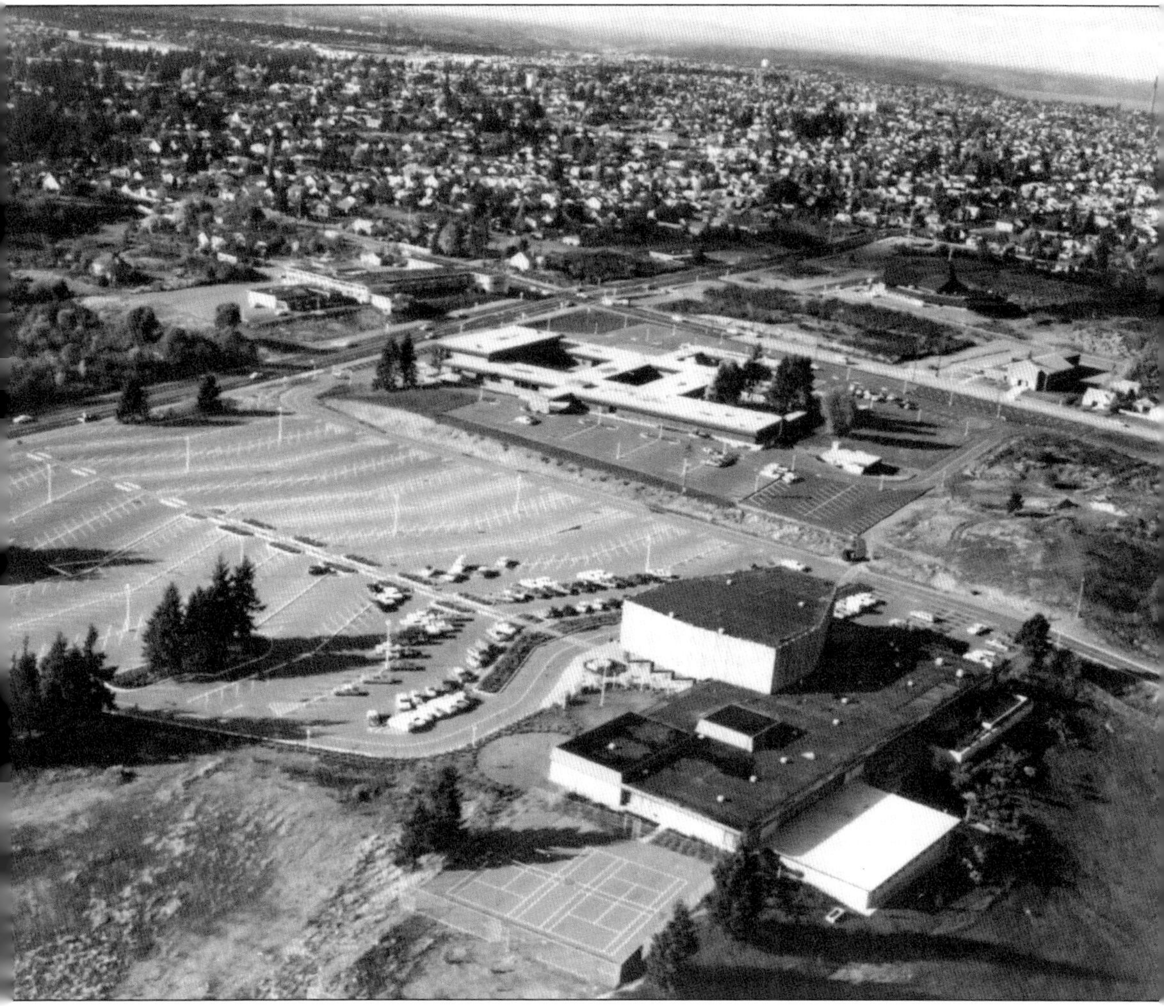

"Walls tumble down at Tacoma Elks Lodge to make way for first Wal-Mart inside city limits," reads a headline in the *News Tribune* on September 5, 2012. Tacomans were less concerned about the destruction of the Elks Building (shown here in 1967) and more about a Walmart on South Union Avenue in the Allenmore neighborhood. For unknown reasons, the historical significance of the Elks Building was not taken seriously at the time of its demolition. Edgar L. Mills (1921–1967) was the architect; prior to his untimely death at age 46, he also designed Ben Cheney's baseball stadium. Mills was associated with two Tacoma architectural firms—Heath, Gove, & Bell and Lea, Pearson & Richards. Perhaps people in 2012 thought that a building constructed in 1967 was too new to be considered historic. There is a lesson in the loss of a building whose significance was not seriously considered prior to its demolition, however: It is time to start considering that what many think are newer buildings might really be historic. (Richards Studio, Tacoma Public Library.)

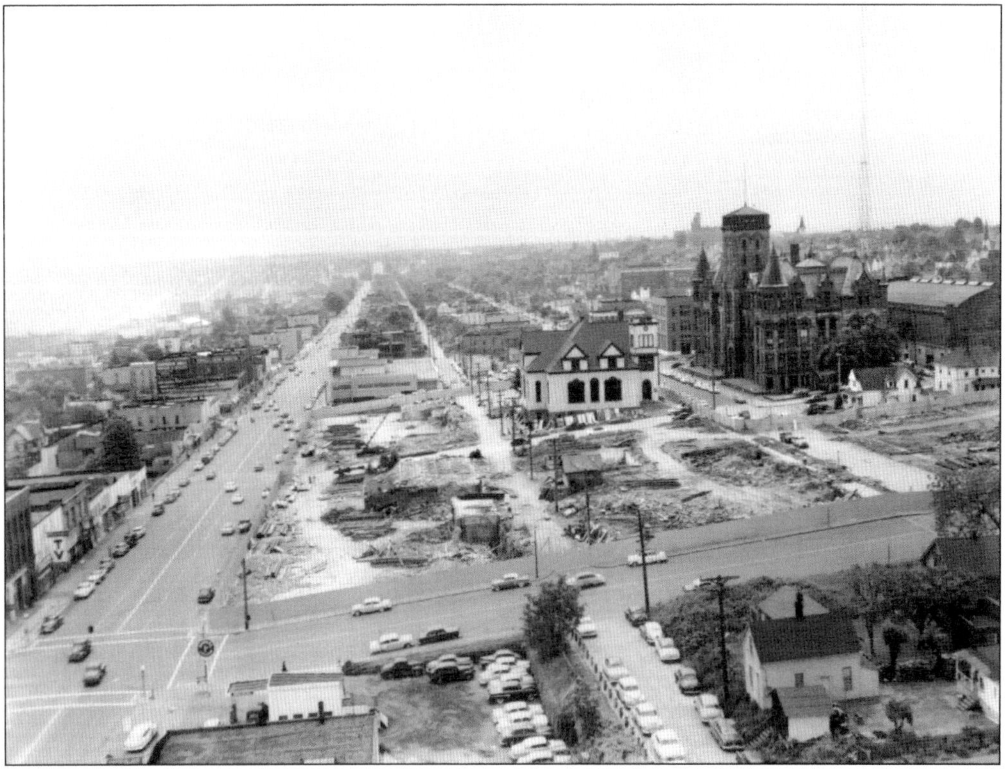

Demolition needed for the construction of today's County-City Building was almost complete in 1955 when this photograph was taken. All that is needed to finish this phase of the project is the demolition of the Central Lutheran Church near the Pierce County Courthouse seen in the upper right of the image. (Tacoma Public Library.)

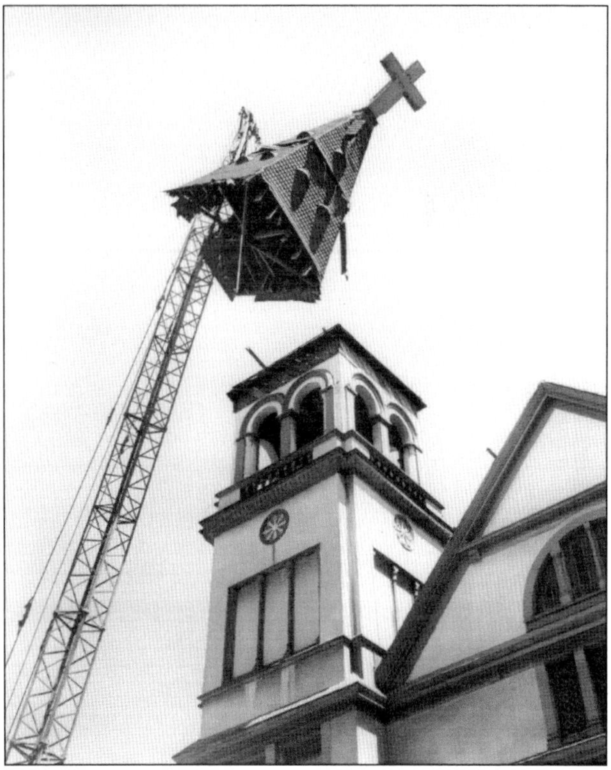

Central Lutheran (originally the First Presbyterian Church) was constructed in 1889. In 1949, following the earthquake of that year, city officials condemned and ordered the removal of the steeple from the bell tower. The complete demolition in around 1955 meant that the congregation needed to seek a new church location for worship and the church school. (Richards Studio, Tacoma Public Library.)

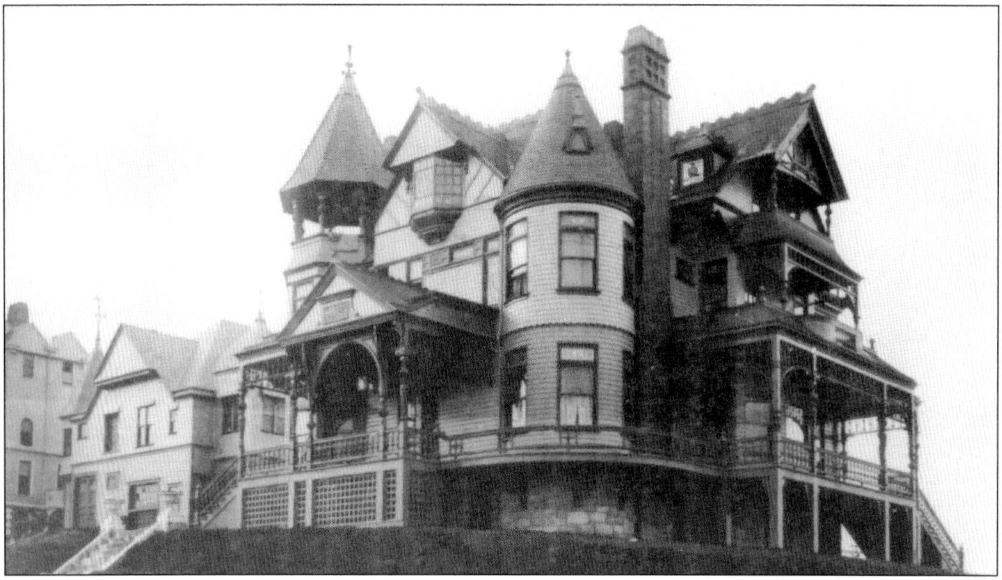

The Lutheran congregation acquired property at the corner of Fourth Street and Tacoma Avenue North for its new church. In 1956, prior to beginning construction, the Henry Hewitt Jr. house sitting on the property was demolished. Hewitt was one of the founders of the St. Paul and Tacoma Lumber Company in 1889, the same year that the house was built. (Richards Studio, Tacoma Public Library.)

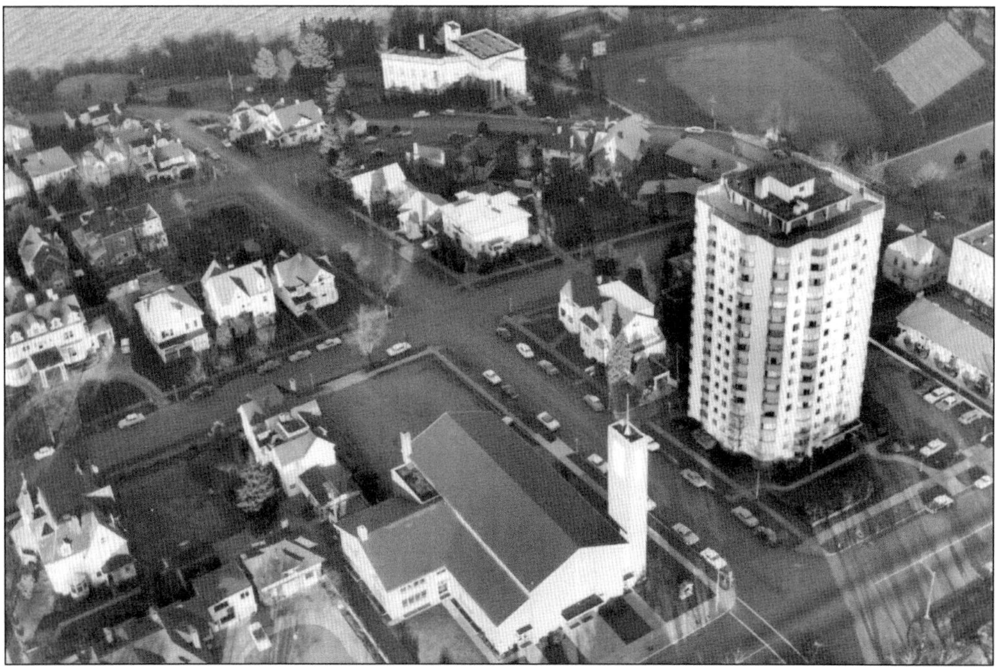

A 1960s aerial shows the new Central Lutheran Church and School. The building still stands and is designated as a Tacoma Landmark. Other buildings seen in the photograph include the then Washington State Historical Society Museum, Stadium Bowl, and Vista Manor. All of what is seen in this image is part of the Stadium-Seminary Historic District. (Richards Studio, Tacoma Public Library.)

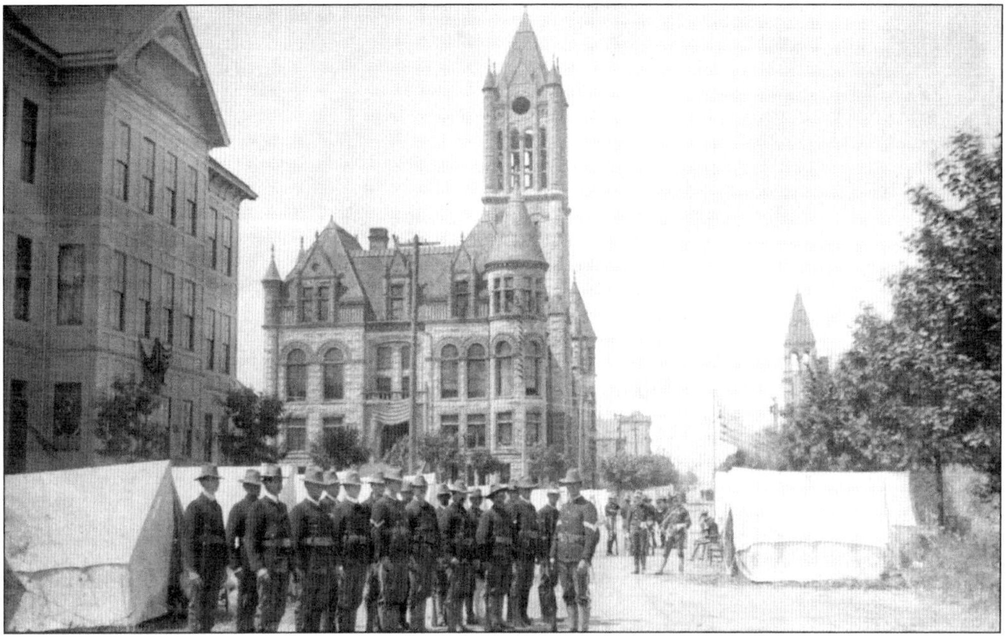

The Pierce County Courthouse serves as a backdrop for a National Guard muster (above) and an impromptu baseball game (below). While the dates of the two photographs are unknown, they were taken before and after 1905. The architectural firm of Proctor and Dennis modeled the building after a similar Richardsonian Romanesque courthouse in Pittsburgh, Pennsylvania. From the time of its completion in 1892, the Pierce County Courthouse was the city's jewel. Positioned on the top of a ridge, the building was easily seen, making its urban impact all the more wondrous. After the 1949 earthquake, city officials mandated the removal of the bell tower just as they had for the Central Lutheran Church down the street (above). The present-day Tacoma Armory, a designated landmark, is seen in the below image. (Both, Tacoma Public Library.)

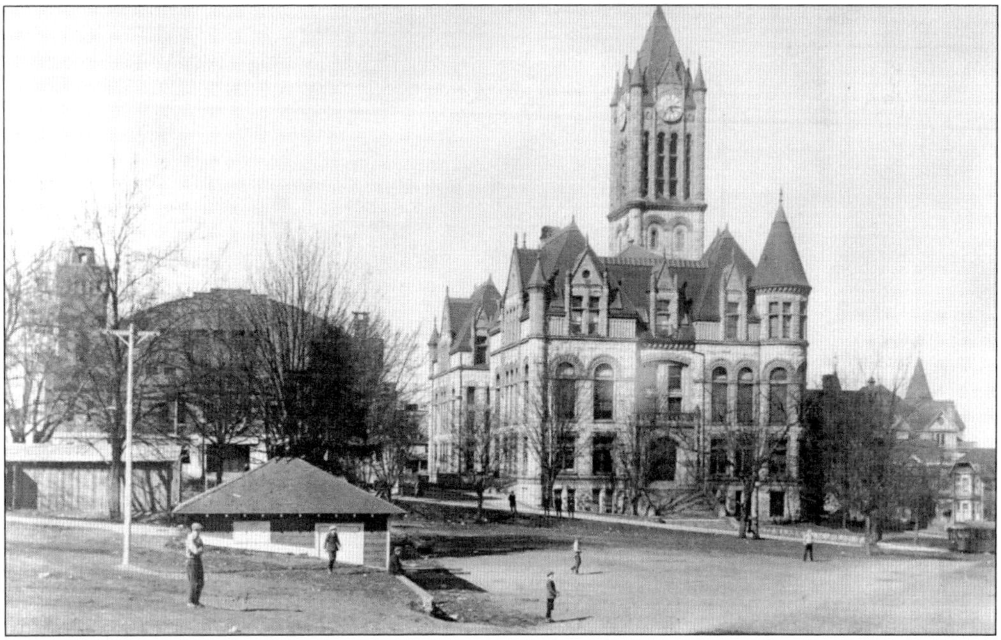

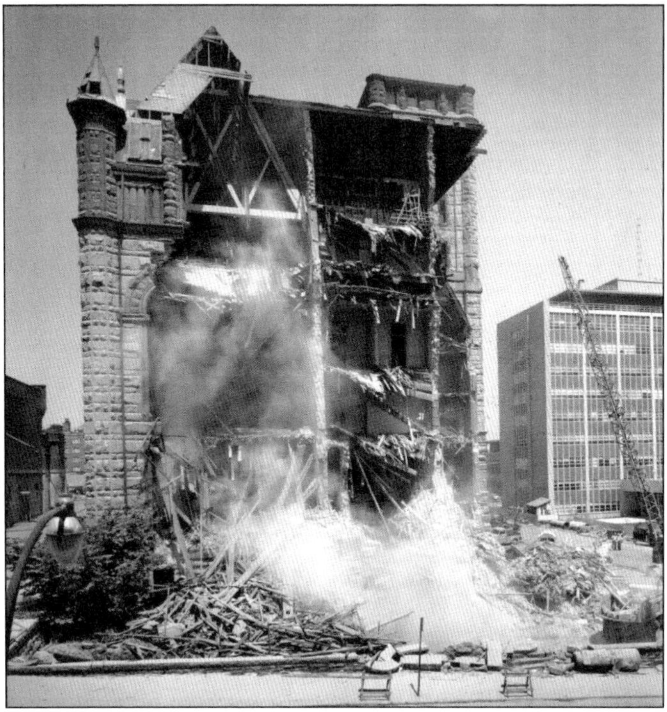

Courthouse demolition occurred in 1959 following the completion of the new County-City Building. Newspaper accounts in 1955 report that a survey was to be undertaken to determine alternative uses for the building, but none were evidently found. There is more than one example of public officials claiming that a building was unsafe or that alternative uses were sought to save a building. In the case of the Pierce County Courthouse, the building was demolished to provide more space for parking, a use still currently in mode when older buildings become problematic. (Richards Studio, Tacoma Public Library.)

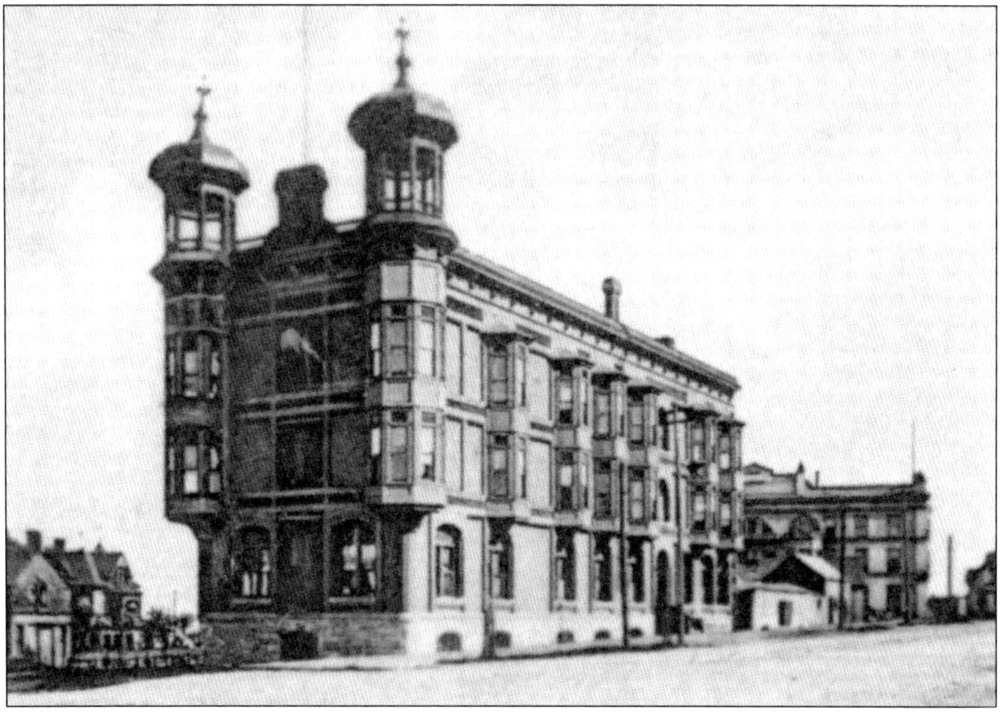

Charles N. Daniels designed the Hotel Rochester, located at 109 Tacoma Avenue South, in 1888. The residential hotel experienced rounds of rehabilitation and fires prior to its demolition in 1966. The site is now a parking lot midway between the First Presbyterian Church and the Masonic temple on the edge of Stadium's commercial district. (Thomas R. Stenger collection.)

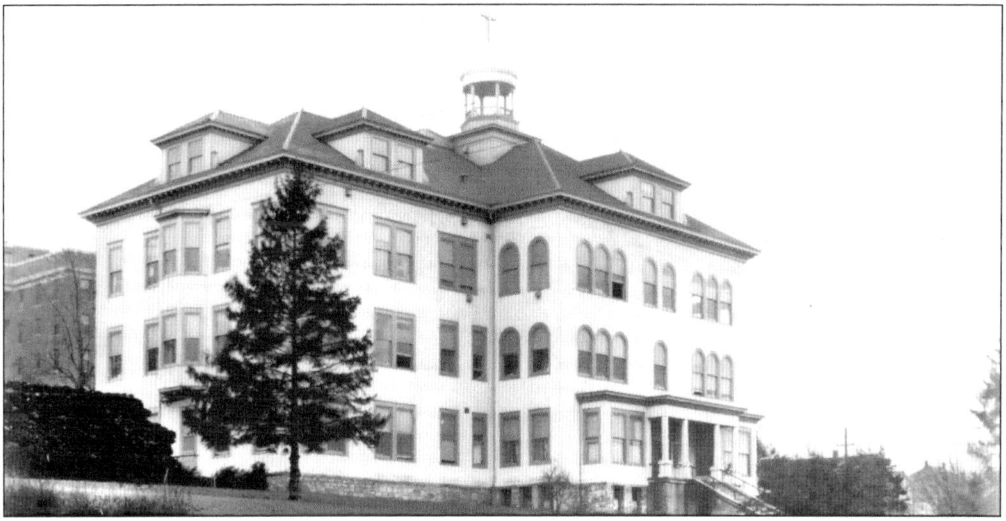

The Roman Catholic Church constructed Visitation Academy on Yakima Avenue South east of St. Joseph Hospital. By 1926, the academy had moved to new facilities in South Tacoma, and the building, shown here in 1930, became the Ozanam Home for the Aged. It closed in 1966, and the land became a parking lot for the hospital. (Marvin D. Boland Collection, Tacoma Public Library.)

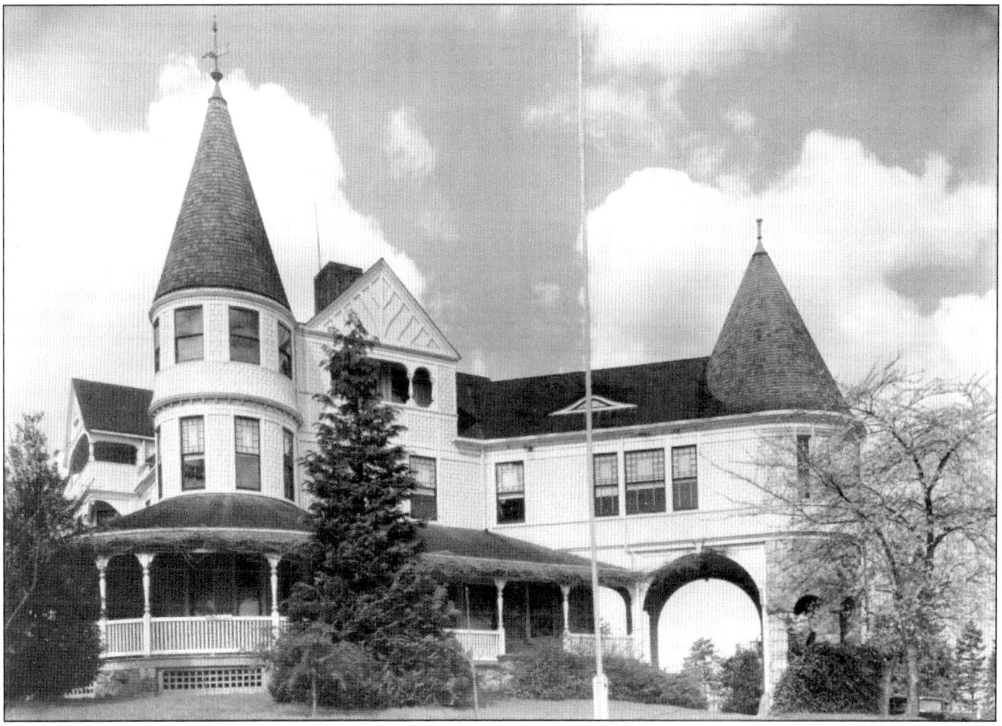

The Saint Ann's Home and orphanage overlooked Wapato Lake, located south of Tacoma's business district. Alan C. Mason built the house in the early 1880 before moving his family to another mansion in Tacoma's North End. After that time, there were various owners until 1938, when the Catholic Sisters purchased it for an orphanage. The mansion was demolished in 1971. (Richards Studio, Tacoma Public Library.)

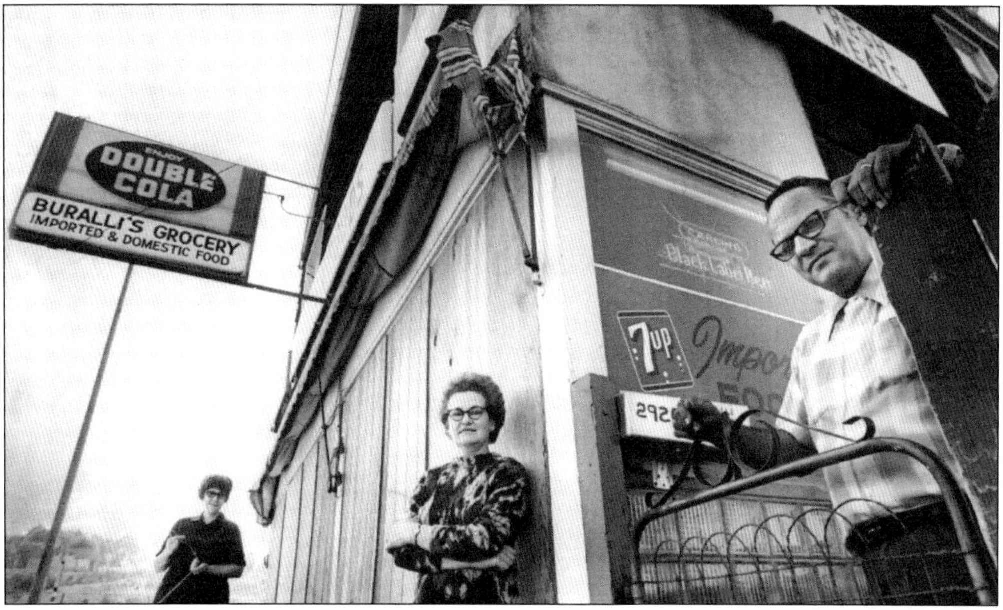

Attilio Buralli's Grocery was a victim of Interstate 5 freeway construction. The building, located at the northern foot of McKinley Hill on East D Street, was constructed in 1905. While freeway construction did not cause the loss of the building, Buralli was forced to close the business because of the demolition of properties surrounding it. This photograph was taken in 1972. (Tacoma Public Library.)

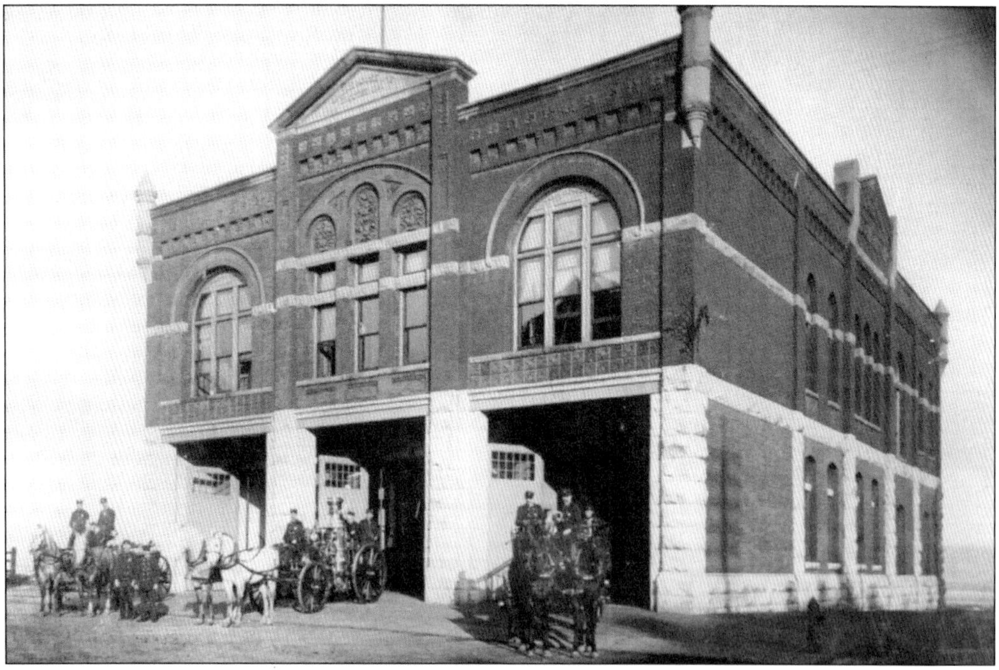

The March 23, 1974, *Tacoma News Tribune* reports that the "Old Station 6 goes way of the fire Horse." There were architects, developers, and historic preservationists wanting to save the building, located at the foot of South Ninth and A Streets. However, demolition was necessary to construct the Interstate 705 freeway.

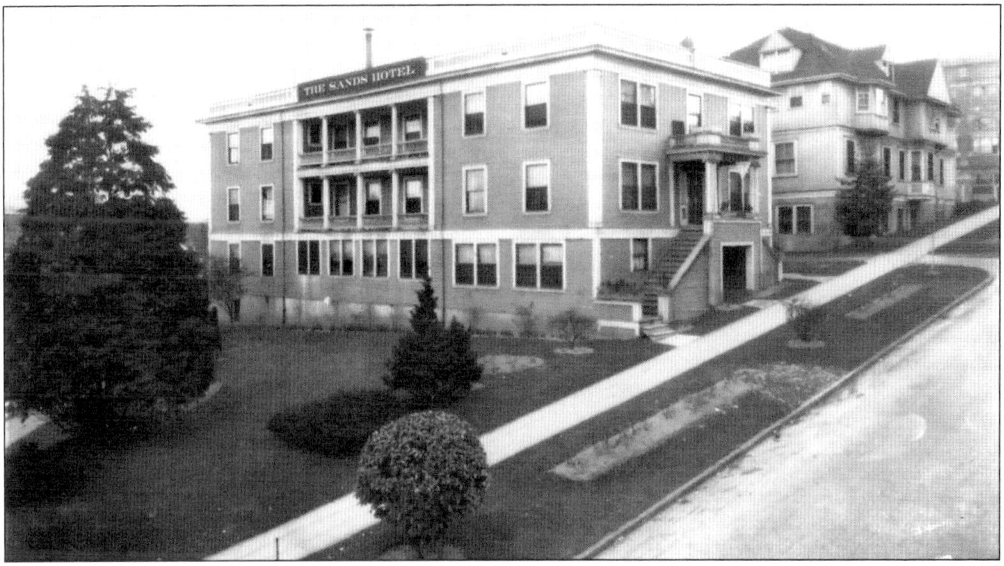

Tacoma's architectural firm of Russell and Babcock designed this residential hotel, pictured in 1927, for Alva C. Sands in 1905. The hotel was located at 410 Sixth Avenue. Sands became district manager for the Sunset Telephone Company in 1883 and remained in that position until his death in 1911. Located north of downtown Tacoma, this area became the focal point for apartment houses. The Sands Hotel was demolished in the 1970s and was replaced by modern condominiums. (Marvin D. Boland Collection, Tacoma Public Library.)

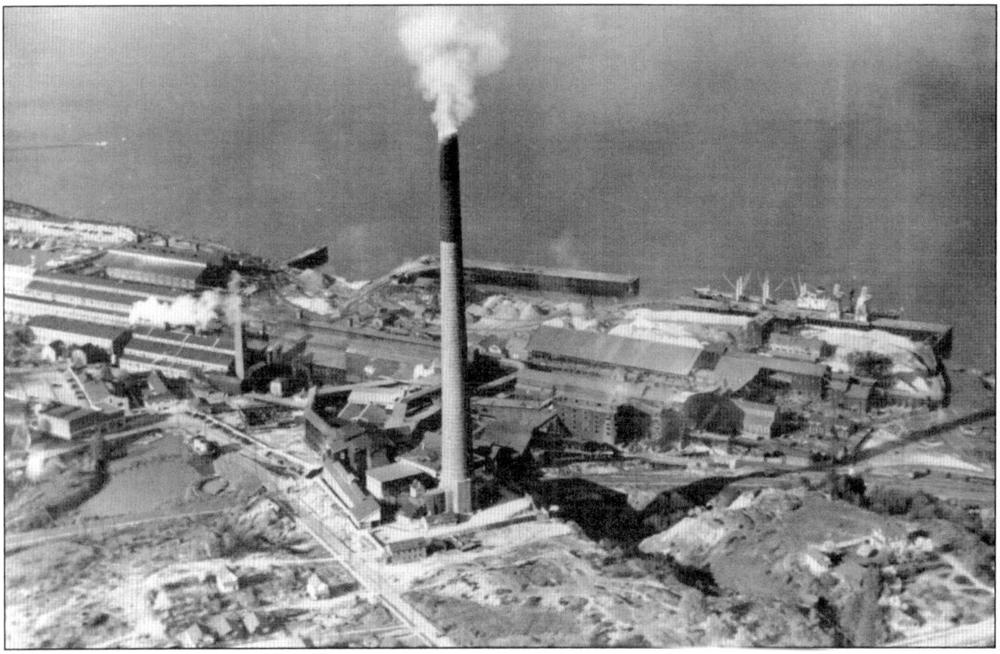

The story of Tacoma's American Smelting and Refining Company (ASARCO) smelter is well known to those who live around Puget Sound. The facility began in 1887 and grew over the years to encompass acres of land southeast of Point Defiance Park. Environmental concerns caused ASARCO to close its doors in 1985, beginning years of demolition and cleanup prior to its development as a residential community. Few mourned the industry's demise.

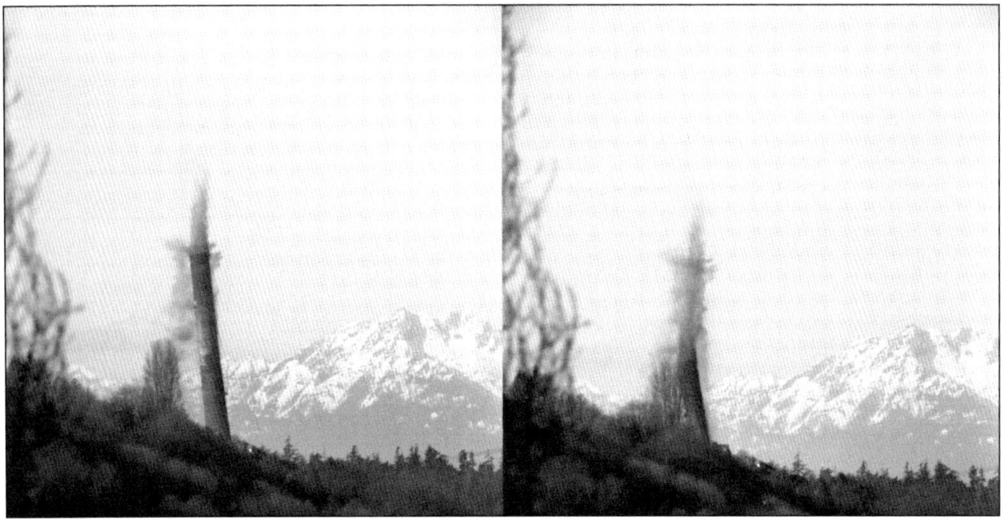

The demolition of the ASARCO stack was a social and media event when it occurred in 1993. Unlike the gradual demolition of the plant itself, the stack was to be imploded, but there were those who thought that the stack should remain either as a landmark or a navigational beacon. The environmental effects of the stack's existence, however, overrode those with historic preservation in mind. (Photograph by the author.)

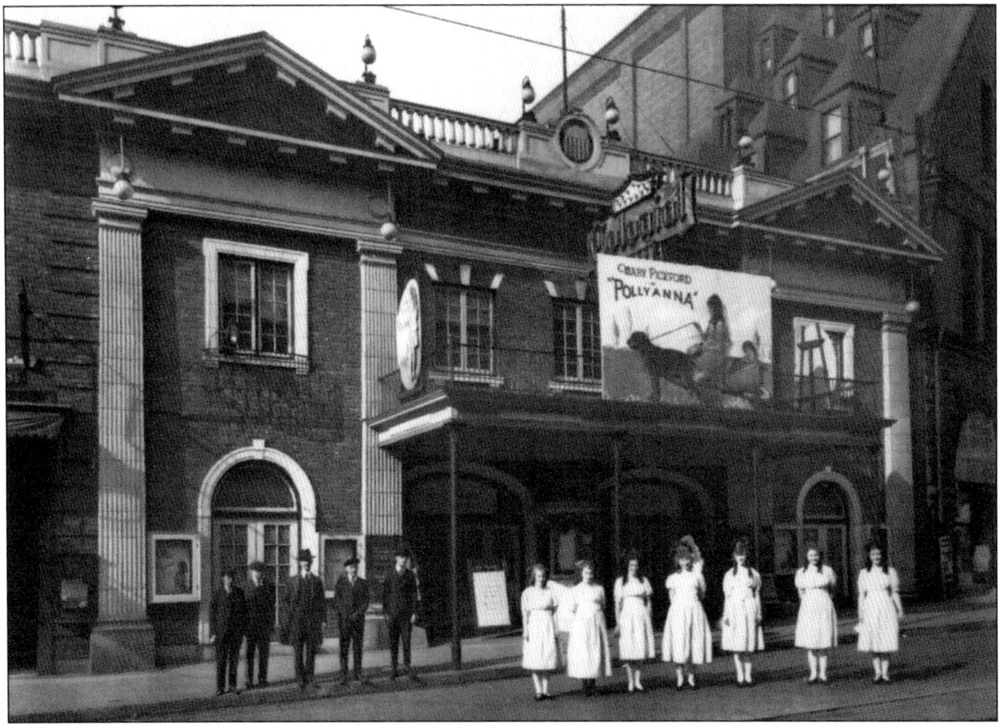

The Colonial Theater was constructed in 1914 at 916 Broadway Avenue. Designed by Roland E. Borhek, it was one of the earliest devoted to motion pictures. Marvin Boland photographed the ushers in front of the theater in 1920. It underwent numerous remodels under various owners, but the theater was in operation until its demolition in 1988. The site is now a parking lot. (Marvin D. Boland Collection, Tacoma Public Library.)

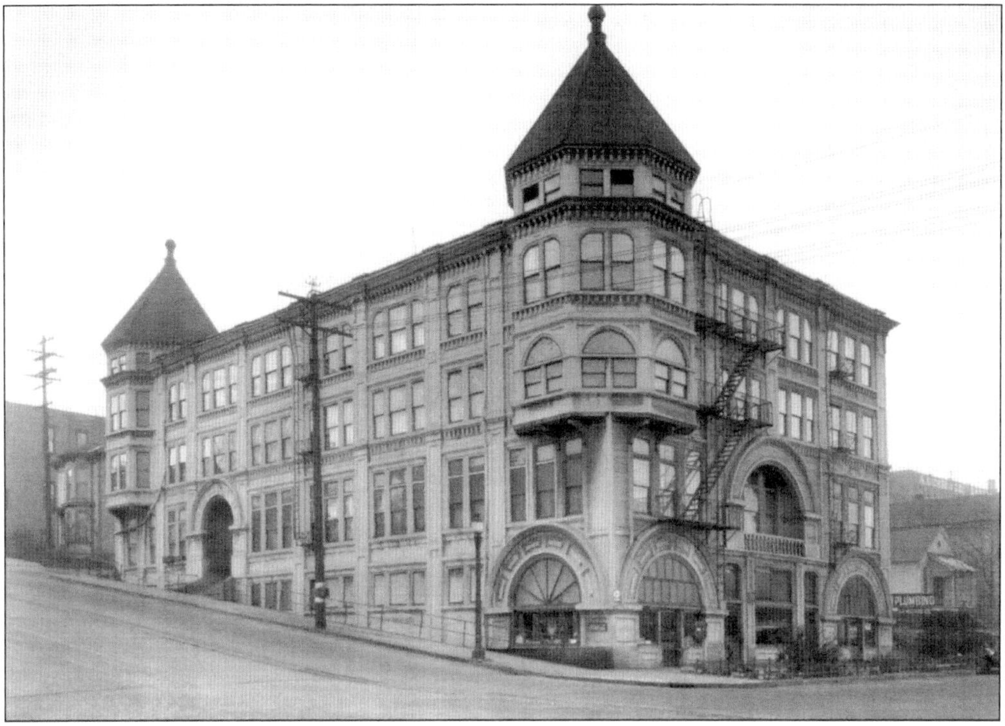

The Astor House, designed by architect F.A. Sexton, was renamed the Samson in 1902 and was subsequently converted into an apartment house in the 1920s. Even though the building was designated both a local and national landmark, fire forced its demolition in 1989. After the location was a vacant lot, a parking garage for an adjacent building was constructed sometime after 2007.

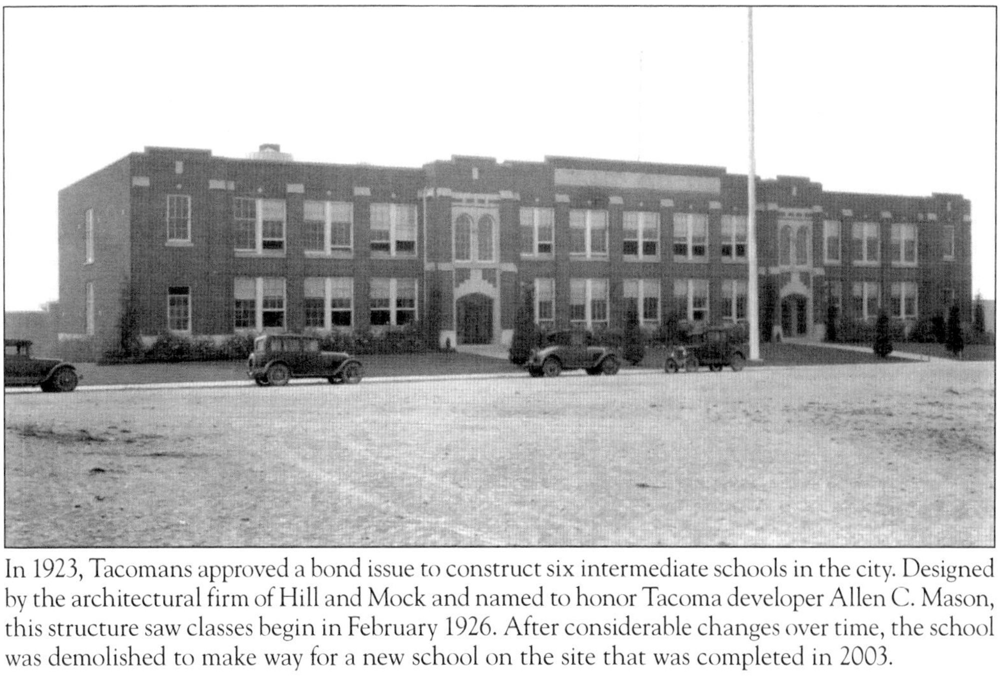

In 1923, Tacomans approved a bond issue to construct six intermediate schools in the city. Designed by the architectural firm of Hill and Mock and named to honor Tacoma developer Allen C. Mason, this structure saw classes begin in February 1926. After considerable changes over time, the school was demolished to make way for a new school on the site that was completed in 2003.

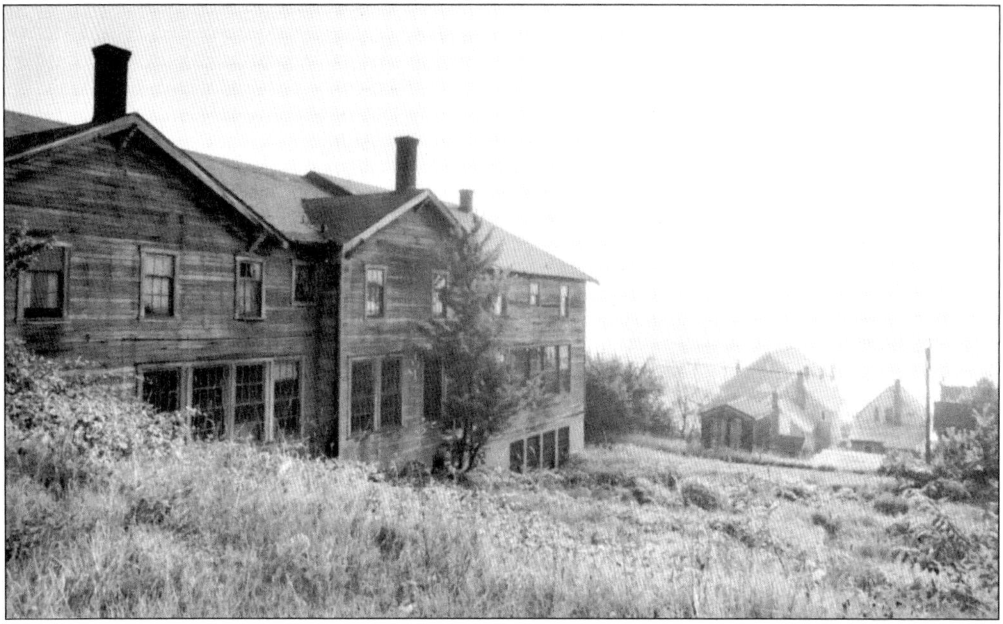

Heath and Gove designed the Nihon Go Gakko, or Japanese Language School, in 1922, and it was closed in 1942 after the building was used to register local Japanese citizens prior to their incarceration during World War II. As the University of Washington planned its Tacoma campus, it acquired the Japanese School property for future development and demolished the historic building around 2003. Today, the land is a vacant lot. (Cysewski Collection, Tacoma Public Library.)

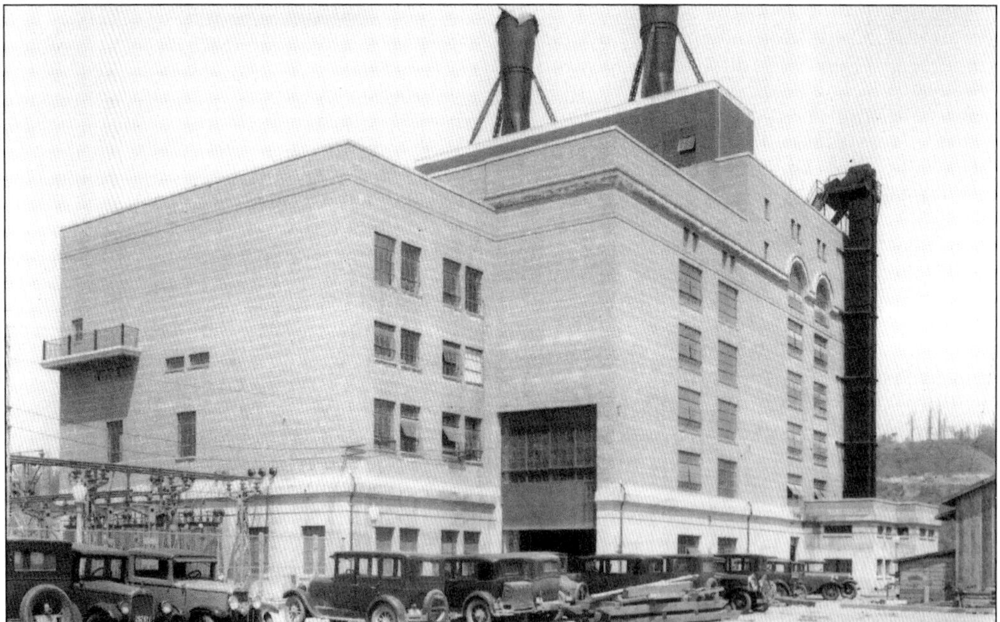

This photograph of the Tideflats Steam Plant, located at 1171 Taylor Way, was taken in 1931 shortly after it began operations. Over the years and following various refittings, different fuels, from coal to garbage, were unsuccessfully tried as energy alternatives. The city demolished the plant in 2007, and the land remains vacant. (Tacoma Public Library.)

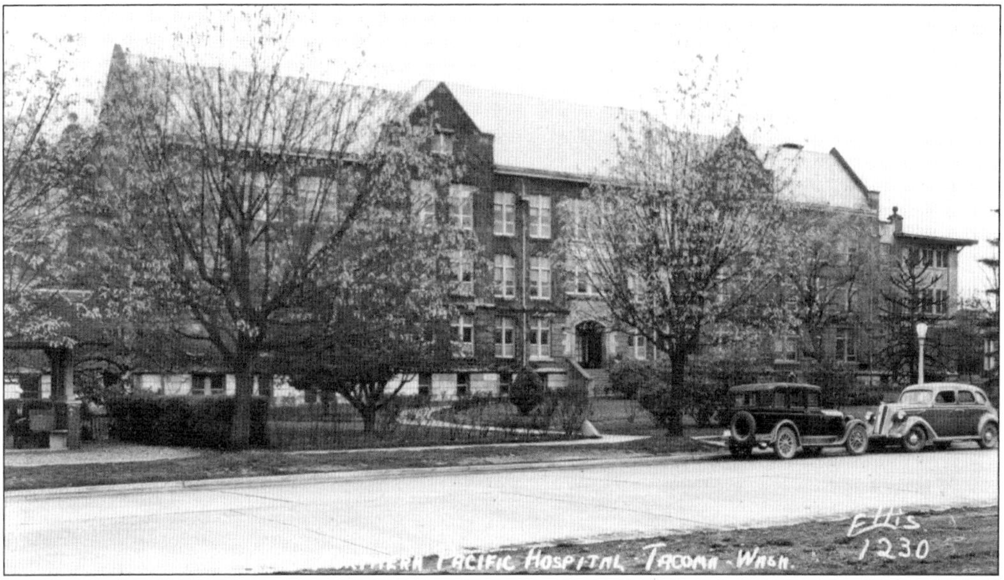

In 1904, the Northern Pacific Beneficial Association retained the architectural firm of Reed and Stem to design a hospital on McKinley Hill at 801 East Wright Avenue for railroad employees. It remained in operation until 1968 and was demolished in 1973. On the site today is a federally funded senior housing complex. (Thomas R. Stenger collection.)

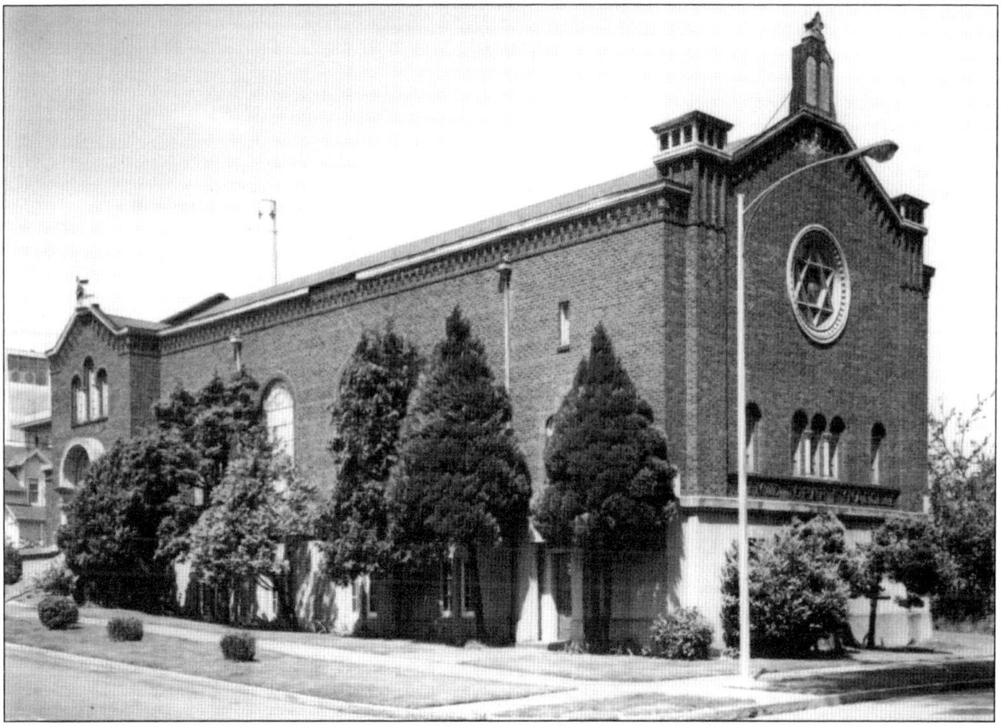

The Talmud Torah Synagogue and Sinai Temple, located at 901 South Fourth Street, was designed by the architectural firm of Hill and Mock in 1925. After the merger of the two Tacoma Jewish congregations in 1960, this synagogue was sold to the Tacoma Blood Bank adjacent to Tacoma General Hospital. The site became a parking lot. (Richards Studio, Tacoma Public Library.)

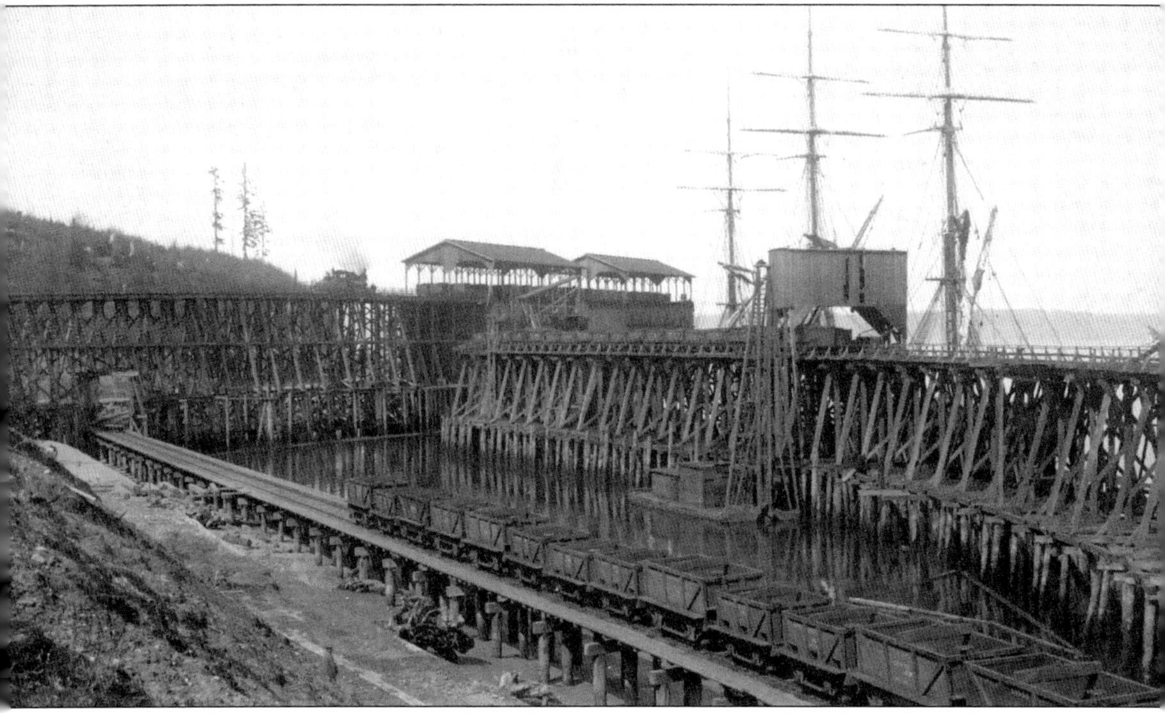

In 1882, the Northern Pacific Railroad began constructing coal bunkers along the shoreline below the present-day location of Stadium High School. This photograph was probably taken after the company expanded the facility in 1887. By 1914, the *Tacoma Daily Ledger* was reporting the construction of the current waterfront rail line and the need to demolish the bunkers. When driving Schuster Parkway today, riders can still see the coal bunker piers that have survived. (Thomas R. Stenger collection.)

Seven

Landmarks

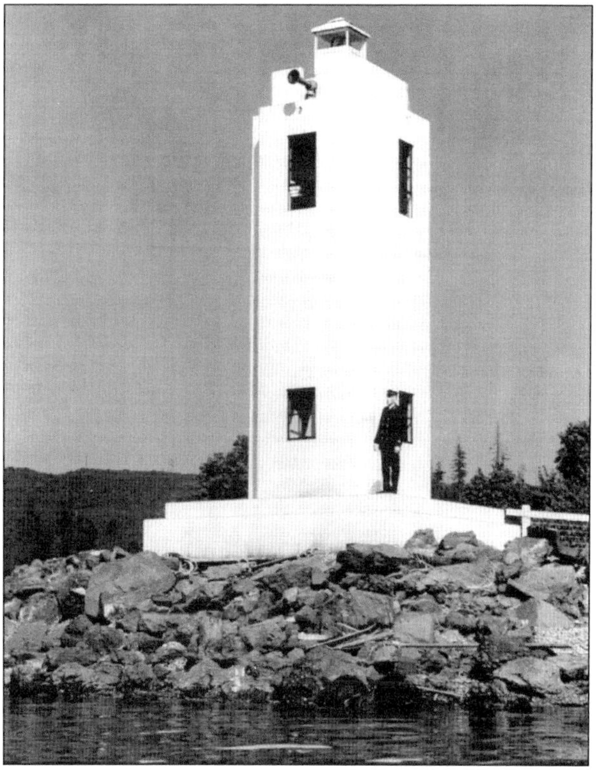

By 1903, a wood-framed light station and caretaker's cabin overlooked the entrance to Commencement Bay, guiding ships into Tacoma's harbor. The US Coast Guard constructed a second Art Deco–influenced Browns Point Lighthouse in 1934. Oscar V. Brown, who retired in 1939, was caretaker for most of his life. While now electronically operated, the lighthouse continues to do its duty. (Richards Studio, Tacoma Public Library.)

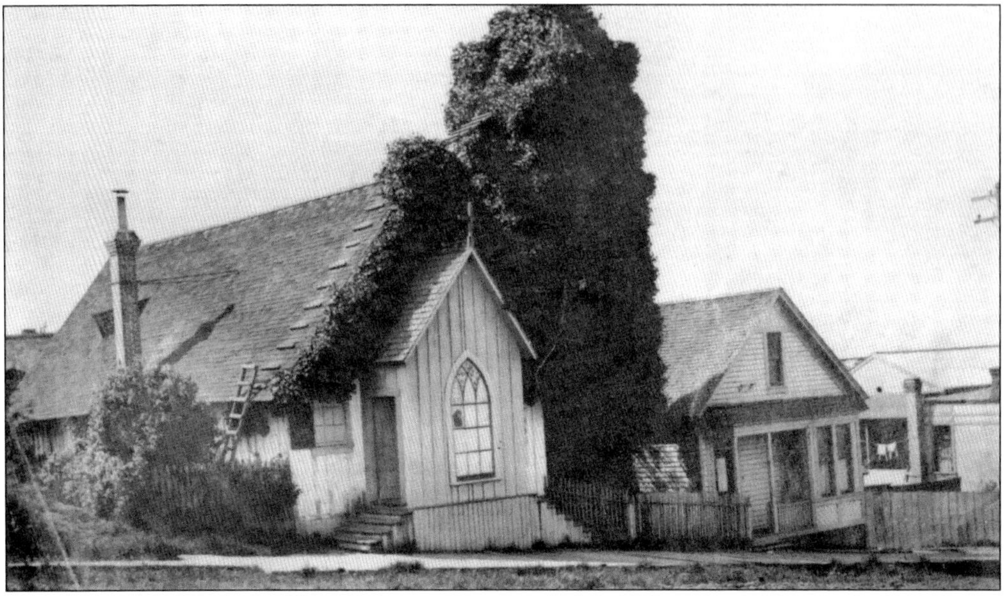

The first service held in Old Tacoma's St. Peter's Episcopal Church at 2910 North Starr Street occurred in 1873 shortly after local settlers built it. Sunday school students from Philadelphia donated the bell, which was placed on a cedar tree, thus allowing (because of the tree's age) Tacoma to claim "the oldest bell tower in the world" at the time. Services are still held in this simple wood structure.

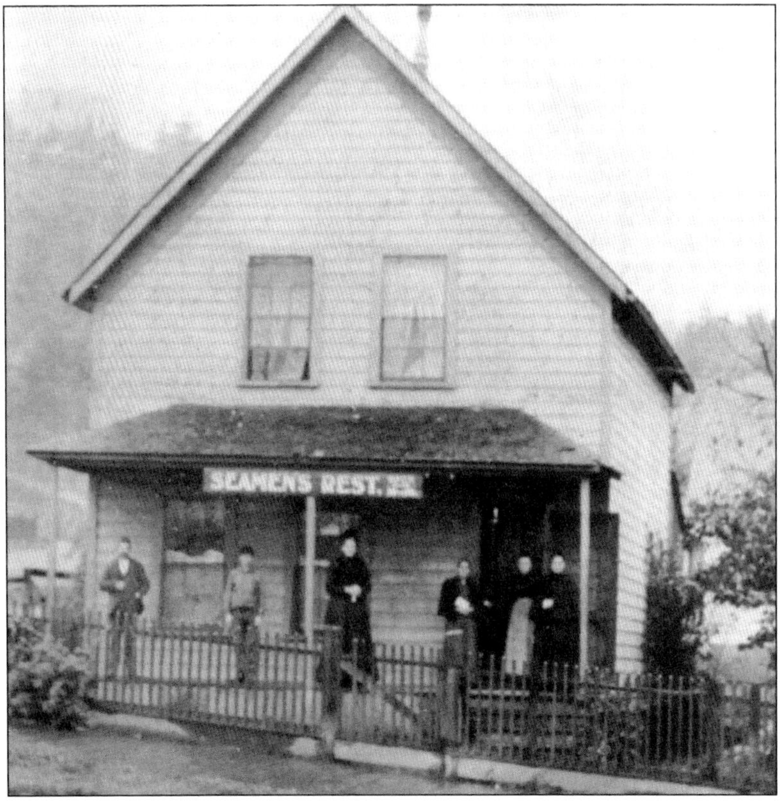

In 1897, Birgitte Funnemark and her daughter Christine opened one of the first rescue missions, called the Seaman's Rest, in the city at 2802 North Carr Street in Old Tacoma. Sailors not wanting to frequent one of the many bars along the shoreline had a place to go. Built in 1883, the house has undergone changes over the years and has had many owners but remains a private residence.

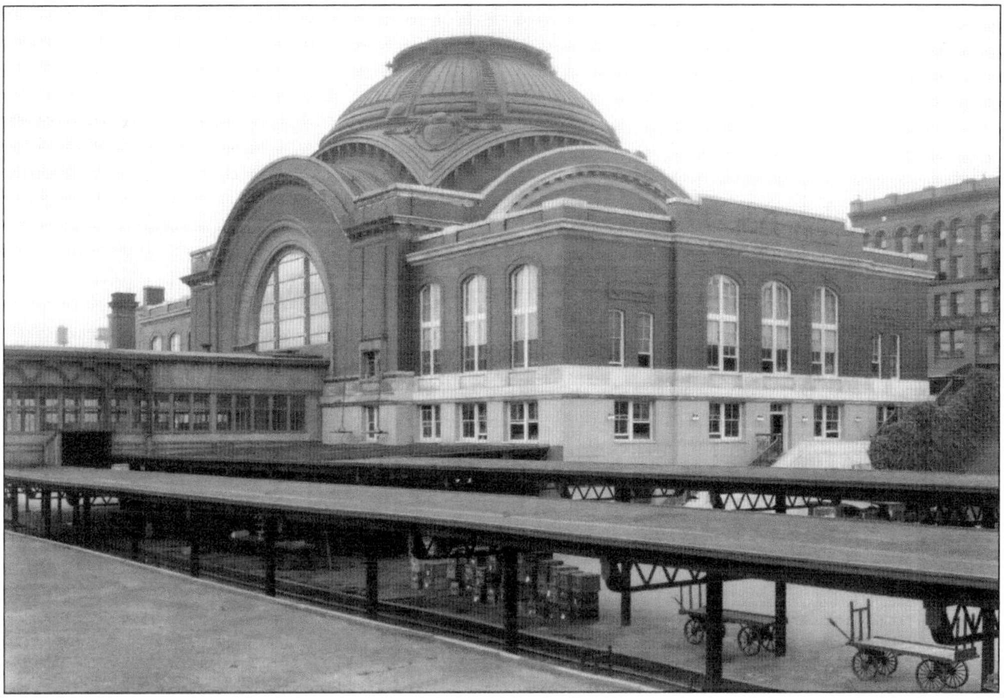

Considered by some historians as the southern anchor of Tacoma's original central business district, the Union Station—so called because the facilities were to be shared by both the Northern and Union Pacific Railroads—was designed by Reed and Stem, New York architects, and opened in 1911. It served as a station until 1984 and was then converted into a federal courthouse.

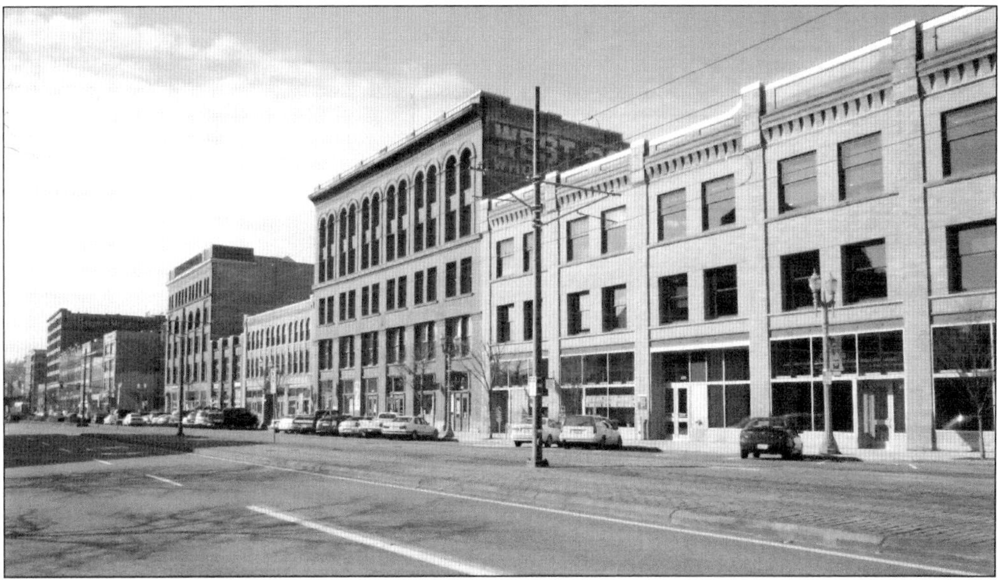

The Union Station Historic District across Pacific Avenue from the Union Station began as a neighborhood prior to 1911. Here, warehouse owners received and resold dry goods and groceries sent by ship or rail. Manufacturing companies mixed with the jobbers, making this area the hub of Tacoma's commercial economy. Most of the warehouse district is now part of the University of Washington's Tacoma campus.

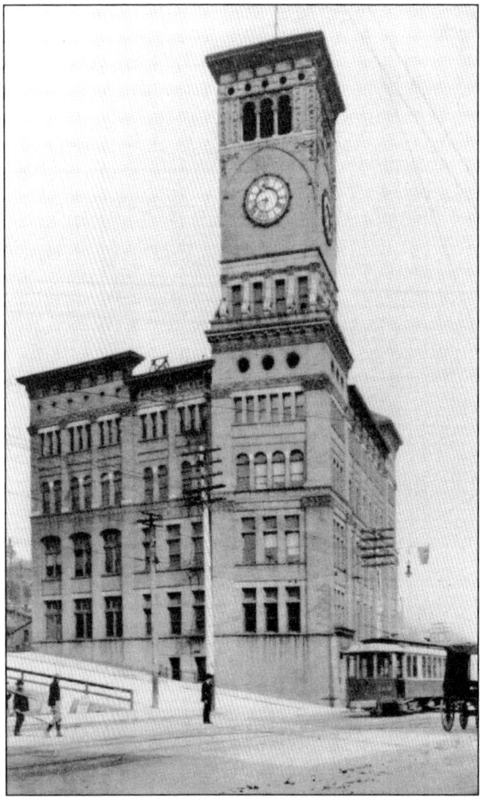

Tacoma's first city hall was designed by E.A. Hatherton and completed in 1893. The city hall and the Northern Pacific Headquarters Building, constructed in 1887 and located across Pacific Avenue from the city hall, formed the northern anchor of the city's original central business district. The potential loss of these two buildings led to the City of Tacoma's historic preservation program.

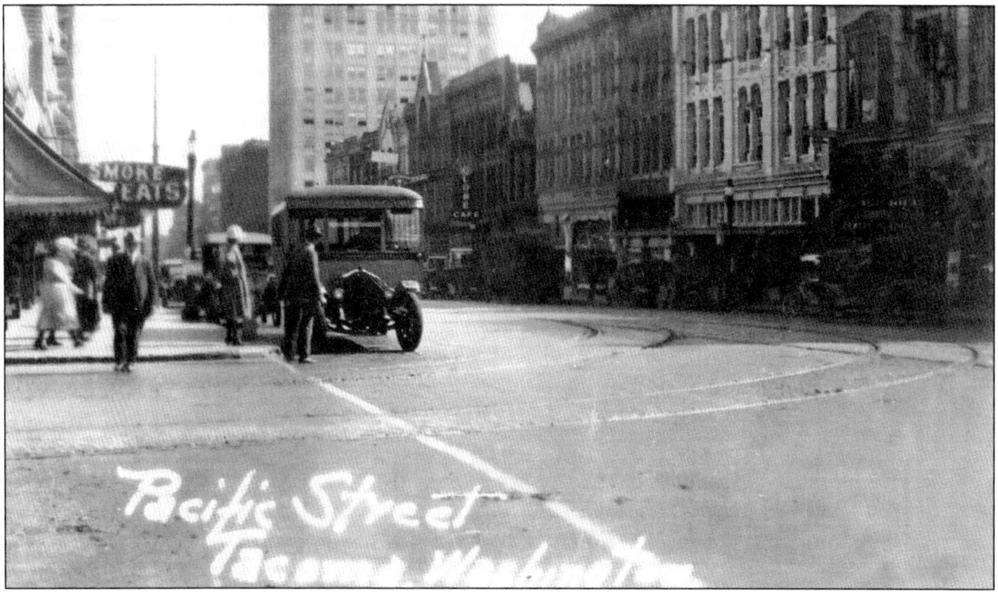

While commercial and industrial buildings accumulated around Union Station, retail shops, businessmen, and bankers encircled the city hall and railroad headquarters building and gradually moved south along Pacific Avenue. The initiative to establish the Old City Hall Historic District—the first one in Tacoma—came from the business owners in the area. (Thomas R. Stenger collection.)

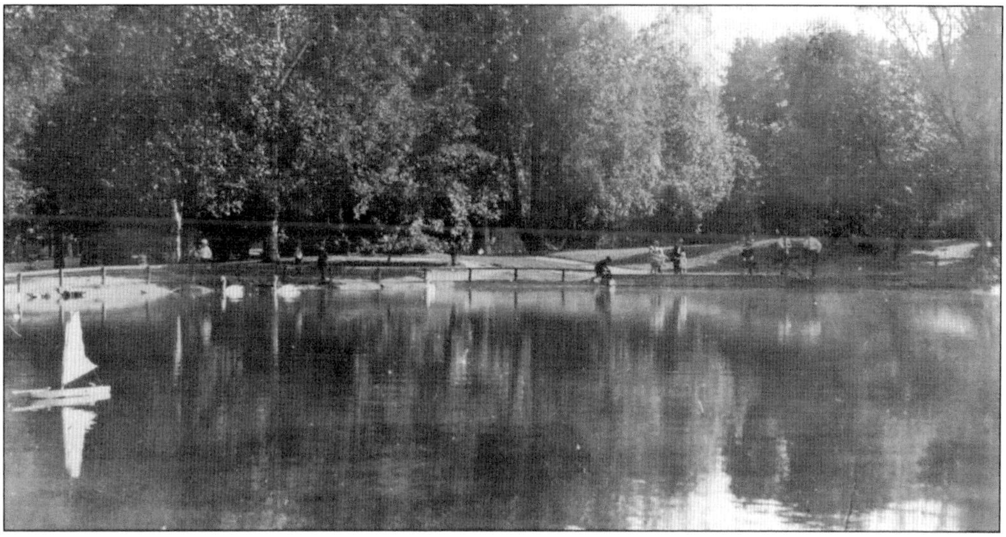

In 1886, the Tacoma Land Company donated a parcel of land to Tacoma with the understanding that the city would develop it as a park. Located in the present-day Stadium District and named Wright Park to honor Tacoma's benefactor, the open space competes with Point Defiance Park as one of the oldest and most popular in the city. (Thomas R. Stenger collection.)

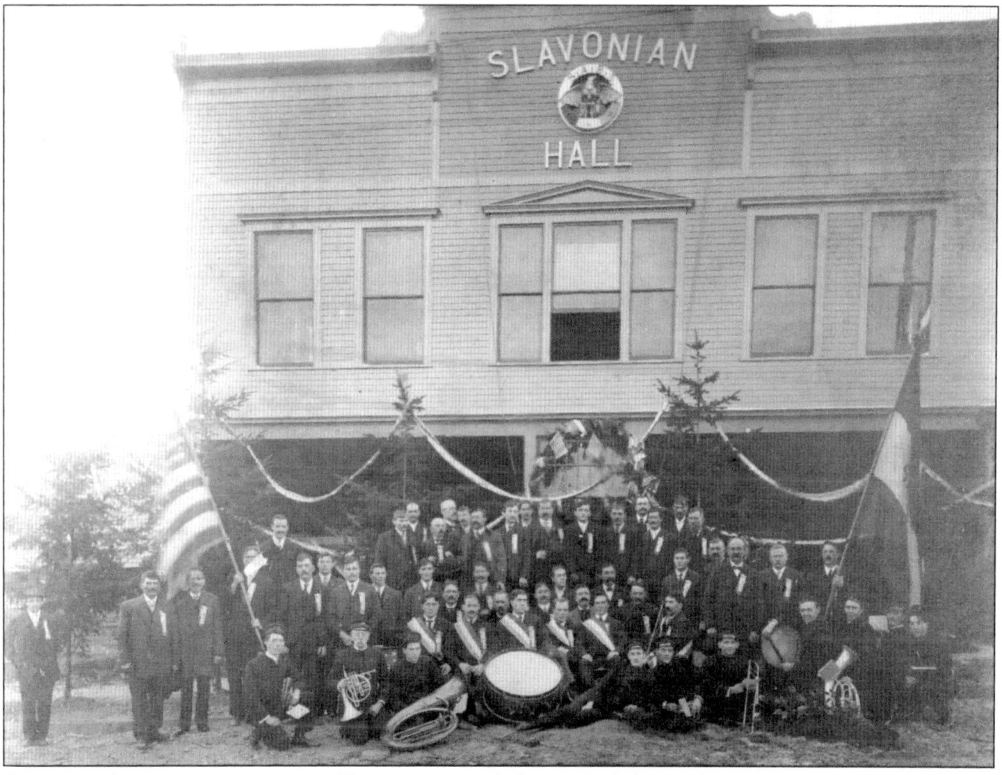

Croatians begin immigrating to Tacoma toward the end of the 19th century and settled in Old Tacoma, where they would be close to the water and fishing. As with all ethnic populations that came to the United States, the group established a fraternal hall to provide for the welfare of its families. The Slavonian Hall was dedicated in 1906 and is located at 2306 North Thirtieth Street.

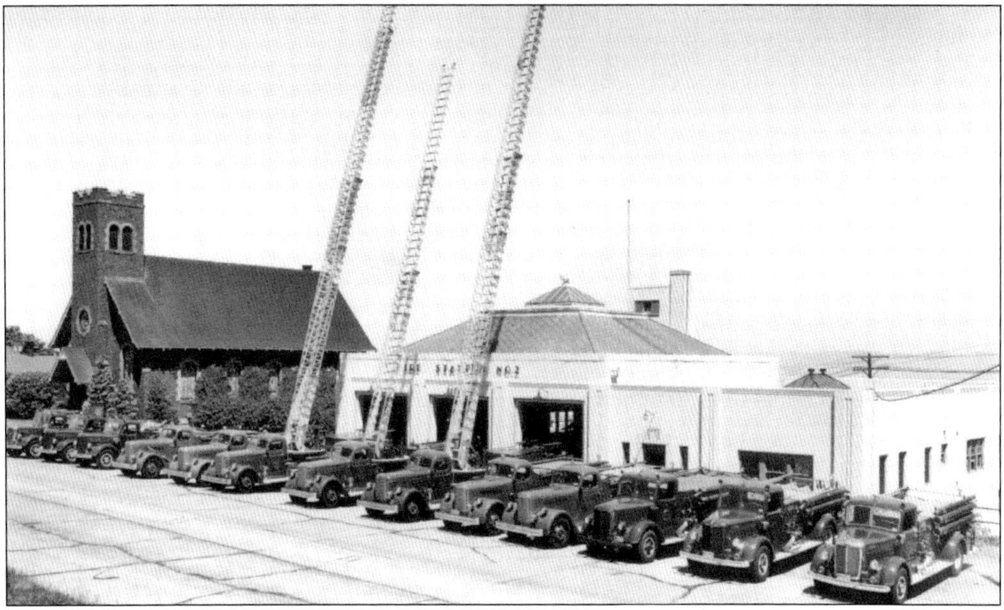

In recognition of the role that firefighters play in safeguarding local citizens, Tacoma has provided landmark status to several of the stations and engine companies. Engine House No. 2, constructed in 1907 and located at 2701 Tacoma Avenue South, is shown here in 1948, along with the entire fire department's fleet of trucks. (Richards Studio, Tacoma Public Library.)

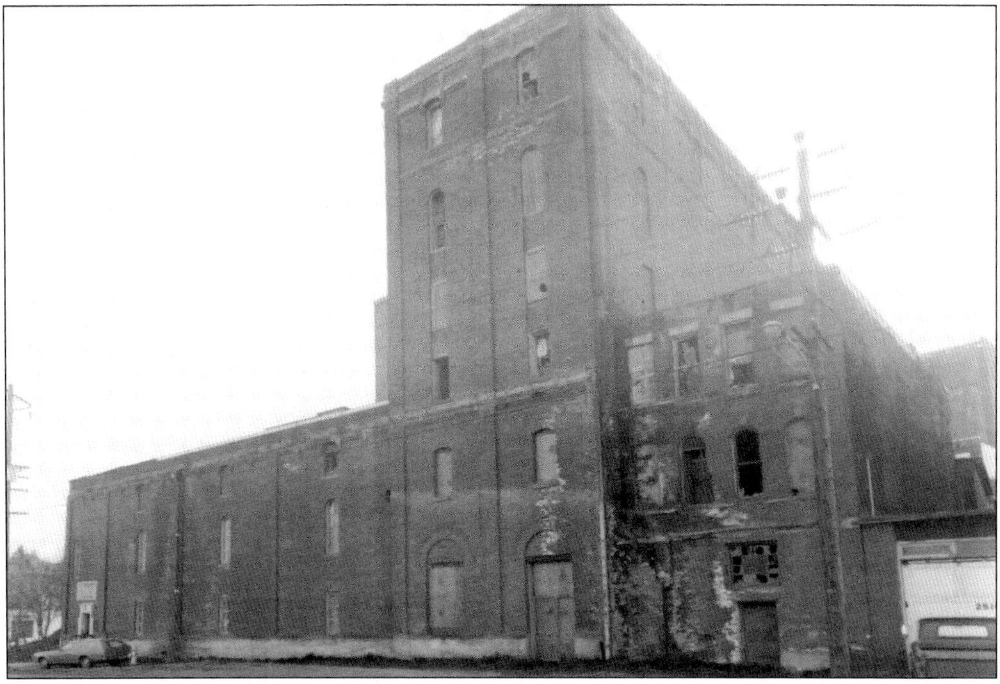

Prior to 1915, when prohibition was introduced in Washington State, breweries were one of the manufacturing concerns established in the southern part of Tacoma's downtown. Anton Huth founded one the first—the Puget Sound Brewing Company—in 1888 on South C Street. Tacoma architect C.A. Darmer began designing the surviving complex around 1891.

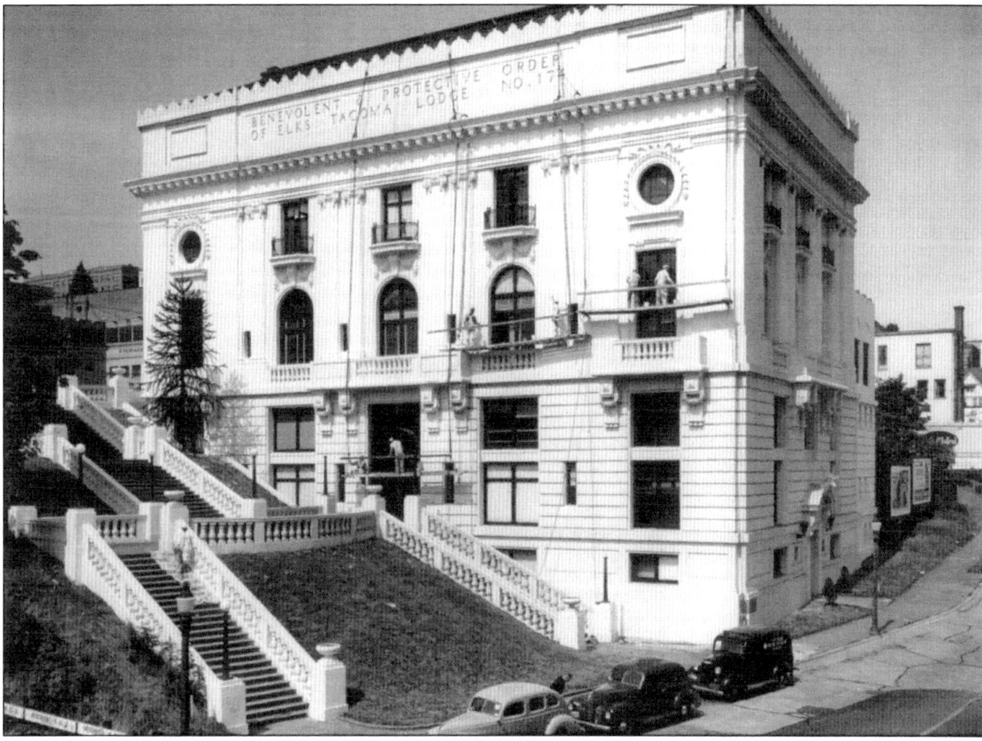

Tacoma's downtown Elks lodge, located at 565 Broadway, was designed by Edouard Frere Champney and was dedicated in 1916. The "Spanish Steps" on the south elevation of the building were designed as a required fire exit for the lodge. Regional developers and the City of Tacoma are currently (2013) working to preserve the building. (Richards Studio, Tacoma Public Library.)

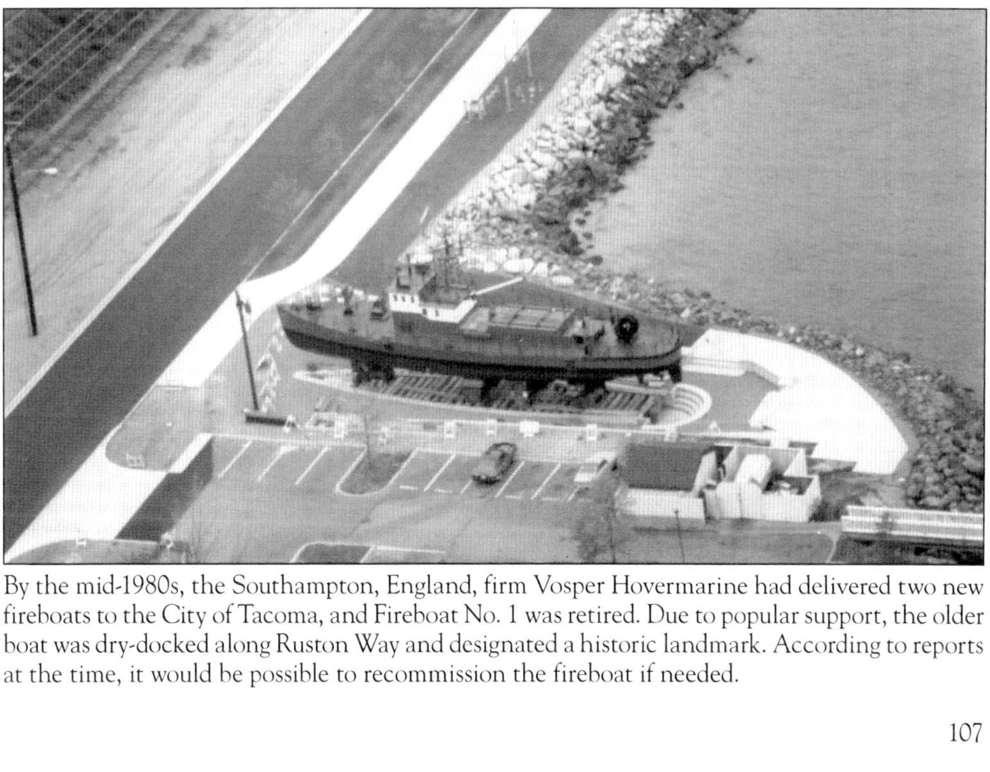

By the mid-1980s, the Southampton, England, firm Vosper Hovermarine had delivered two new fireboats to the City of Tacoma, and Fireboat No. 1 was retired. Due to popular support, the older boat was dry-docked along Ruston Way and designated a historic landmark. According to reports at the time, it would be possible to recommission the fireboat if needed.

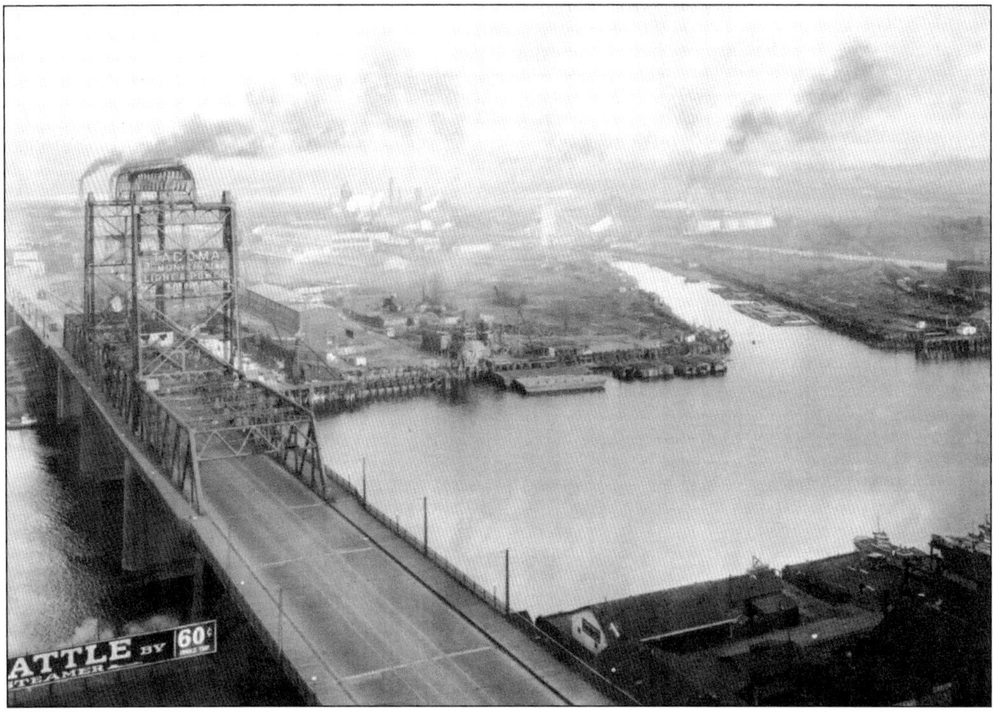

Saving the Murray Morgan Bridge was one of Tacoma's 21st-century success stories. Since its opening in 1913, it has served as a major link between the city's downtown and industries on the tidal flats. When the bridge was closed in 2007, it was already a designated landmark. With rumors of its possible demolition, Save Our Bridge was formed to spearhead its restoration. The bridge reopened to traffic in 2013.

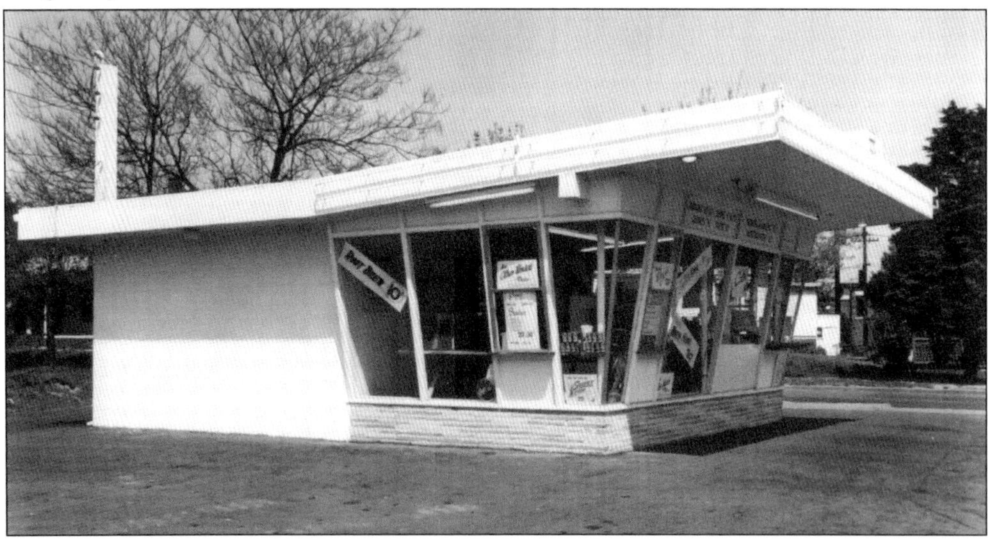

Perry W. Smith opened Frisco Freeze hamburger drive-in in 1950, one year before this photograph was taken. It was located at 1201 Division Avenue, and hamburgers were originally 30¢. Popular among students from nearby Stadium High School, it also had a regular adult clientele, including former governor Booth Gardner. Frisco Freeze became a historic landmark in 2008. (Richards Studio, Tacoma Public Library.)

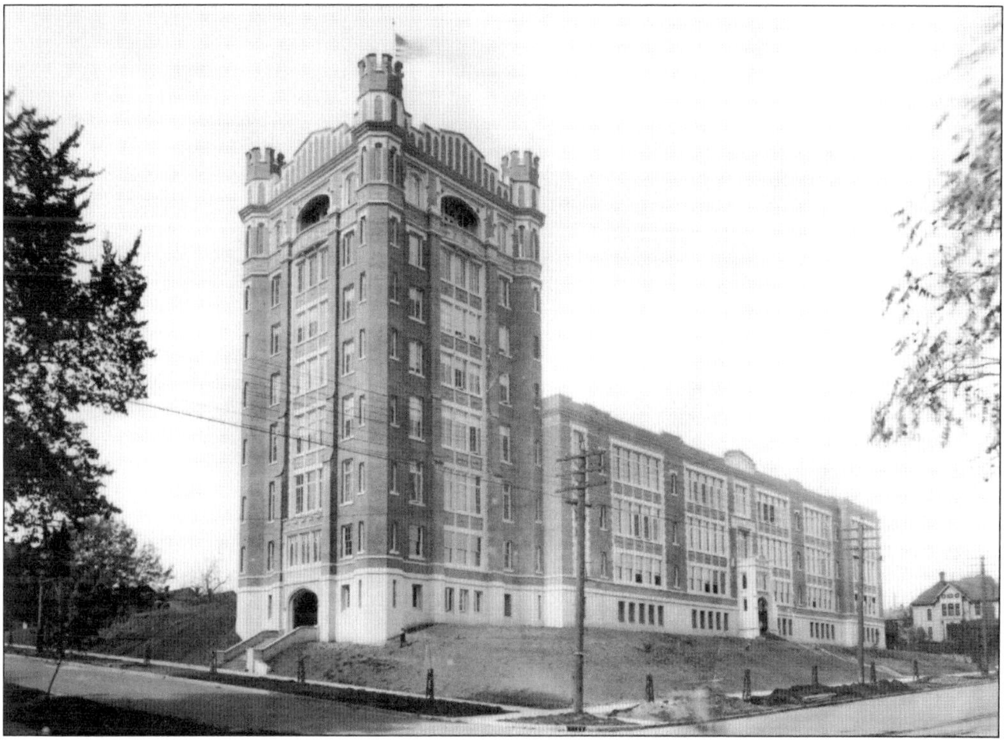

Central School was constructed in 1913, the year this photograph was taken. Elementary grades originally attended class in this building, designed by Heath and Gove and located at 601 South Eighth Street. Since 1968, the building has been the administrative headquarters for the Tacoma School District. It was designated as a landmark in 2010. (Tacoma Public Library.)

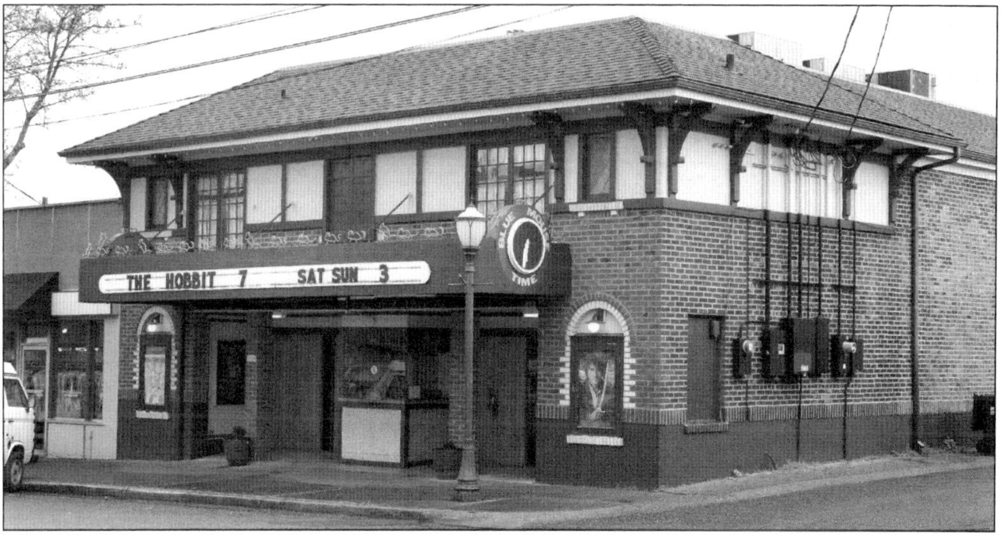

The Proctor Street Blue Mouse Theater, which opened in 1923, was one of several operated by John Hamrick in Tacoma. It has operated under various names since that time and is considered the oldest continuing neighborhood theater in Washington State. Noted glass artist Dale Chihuly designed the neon blue mice as a part of its restoration in 1994. The theater was designated as a landmark in 2008.

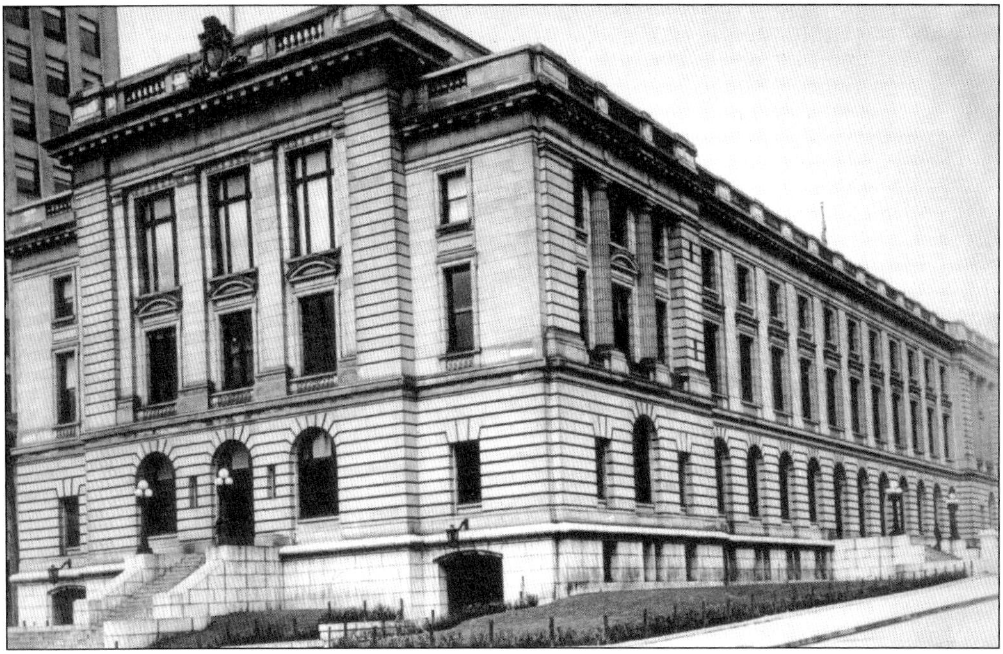

When the federal courthouse moved into Union Station after 1984, federal authorities declared this building, constructed in 1910 and located at 1102 South A Street, surplus and advertised it for sale. While there has been newspaper reporting on the future of the building, what will ultimately happen is unknown. The federal building became a historic property in 2010.

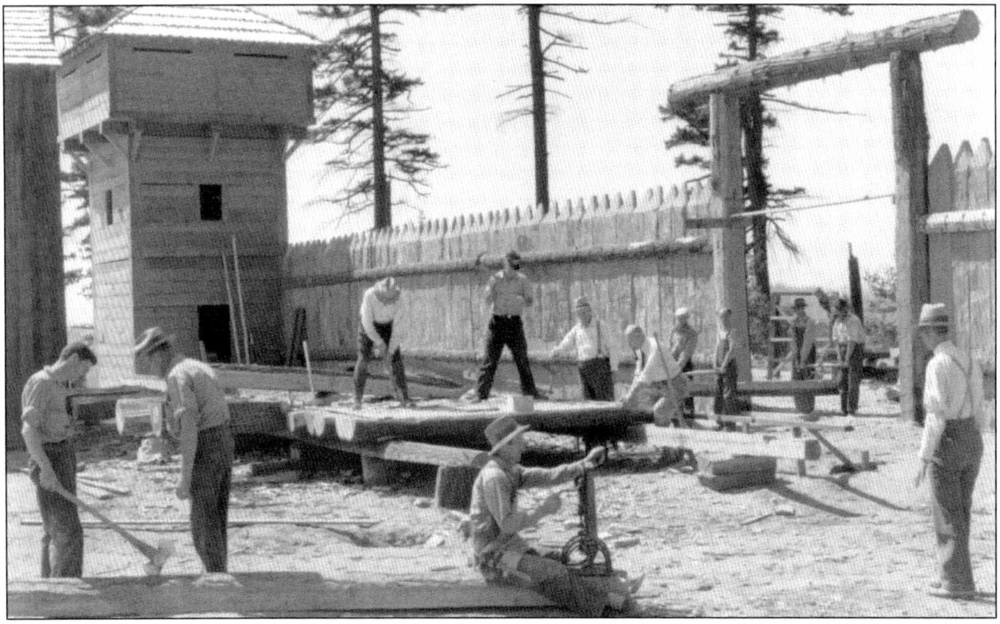

Many histories have been written about the significance of the original Fort Nisqually, located south of Tacoma. In 1934, the Tacoma Young Men's Business Club moved the deteriorated structure to available land in Point Defiance Park and began Fort Nisqually's restoration. This photograph shows them at work rebuilding a part of the palisades and bastion. The fort became a designated landmark in 1976. (Richards Studio, Tacoma Public Library.)

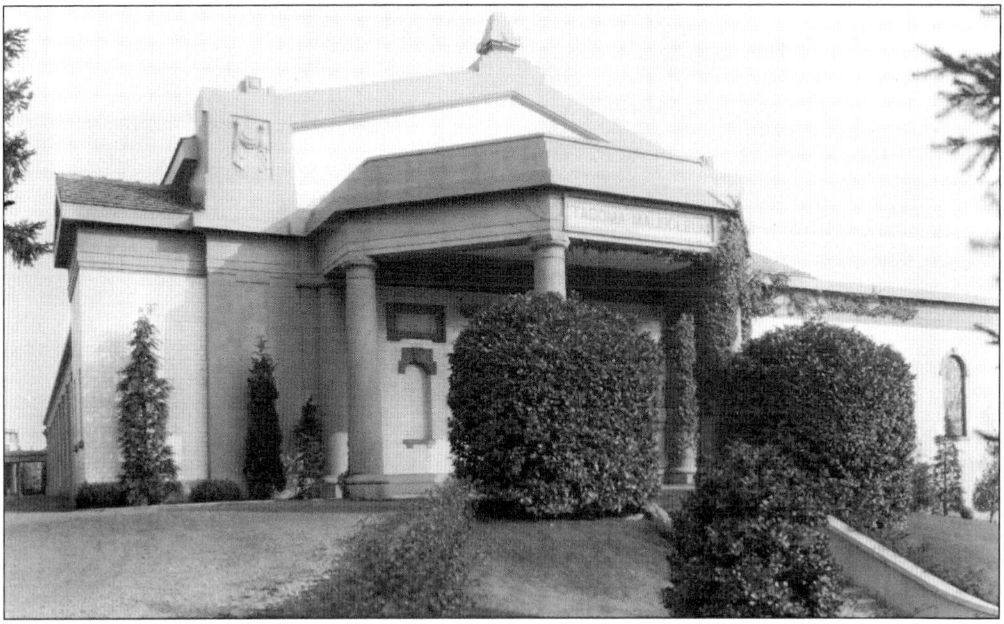

George Gove designed the Tacoma Mausoleum in 1909 near the entrance to Oakwood Cemetery at 5302 South Junett Street. Marvin Boland took this photograph in 1930, some 20 years after it opened its doors. While the National Register of Historic Places generally frowns upon designating properties related to cemeteries and burials, Tacoma created this landmark in 1998. (Marvin D. Boland Collection, Tacoma Public Library.)

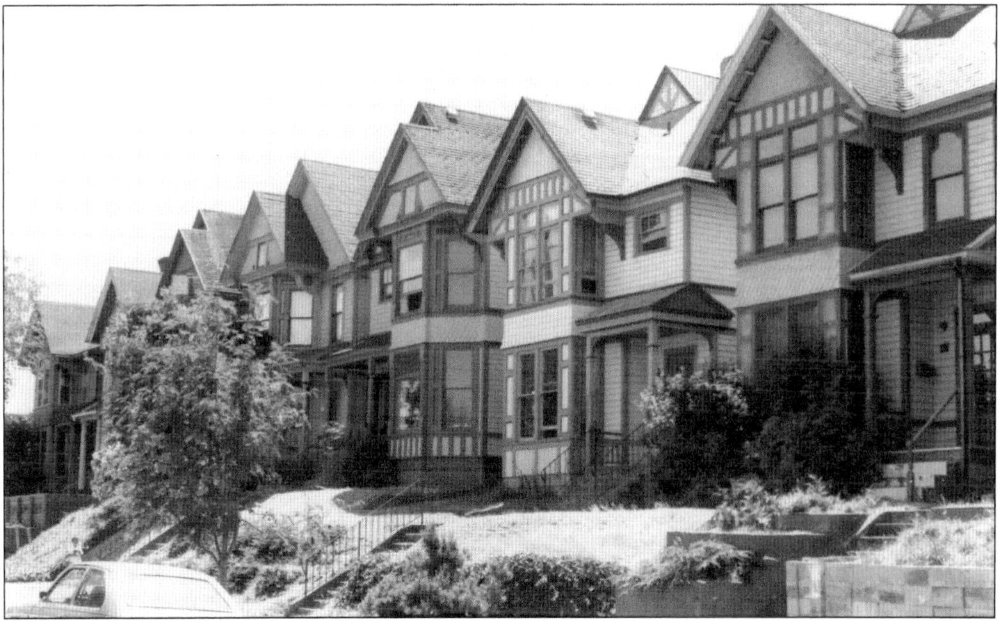

On the west side of the 700 block of South J Street, there is a group of houses called the South J Street Historic District that was placed in the Tacoma Register of Historic Places in 1992. Funded by the Washington Building Association, an early savings and loan institution, they present today a glimpse of a Tacoma streetscape in 1889, the year of construction. (Thomas R. Stenger collection.)

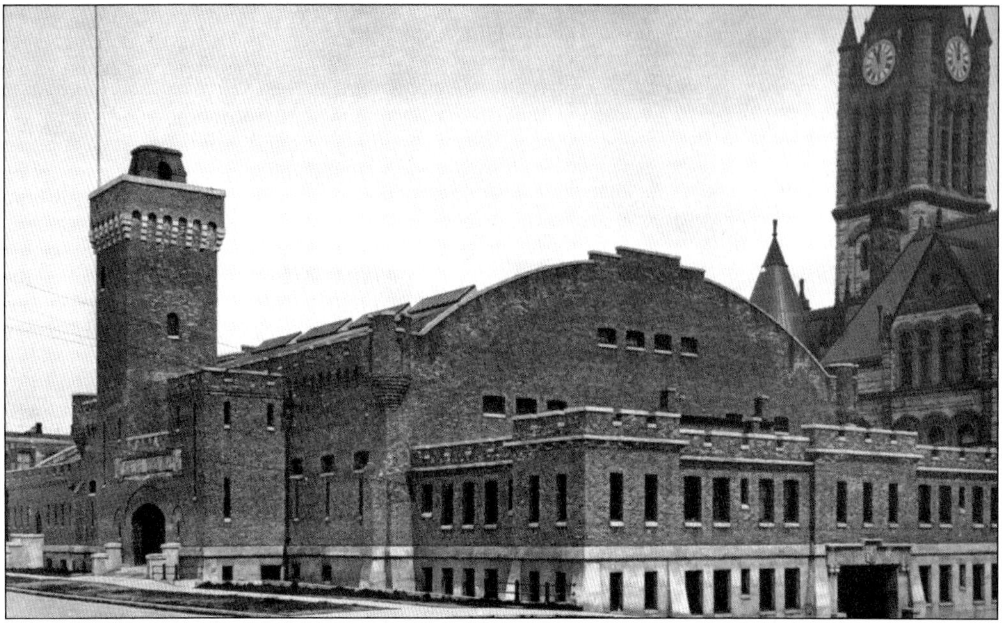

The Washington National Guard Armory, designed by architects Russell and Babcock in 1909 at 715 South Eleventh Street, is a designated local landmark. Known for its large mustering area used by both by men and their horses, the space was also a venue for everything from boxing matches to fancy dances. The National Guard left the building in 2011, and it now sits waiting for a new use.

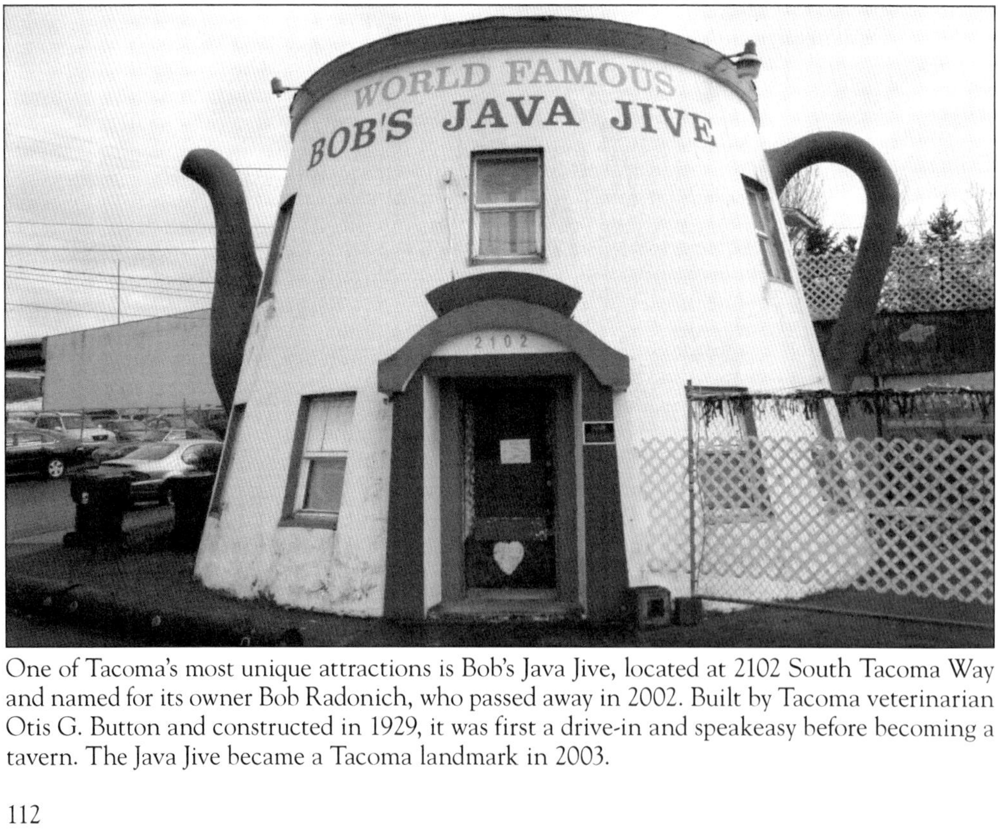

One of Tacoma's most unique attractions is Bob's Java Jive, located at 2102 South Tacoma Way and named for its owner Bob Radonich, who passed away in 2002. Built by Tacoma veterinarian Otis G. Button and constructed in 1929, it was first a drive-in and speakeasy before becoming a tavern. The Java Jive became a Tacoma landmark in 2003.

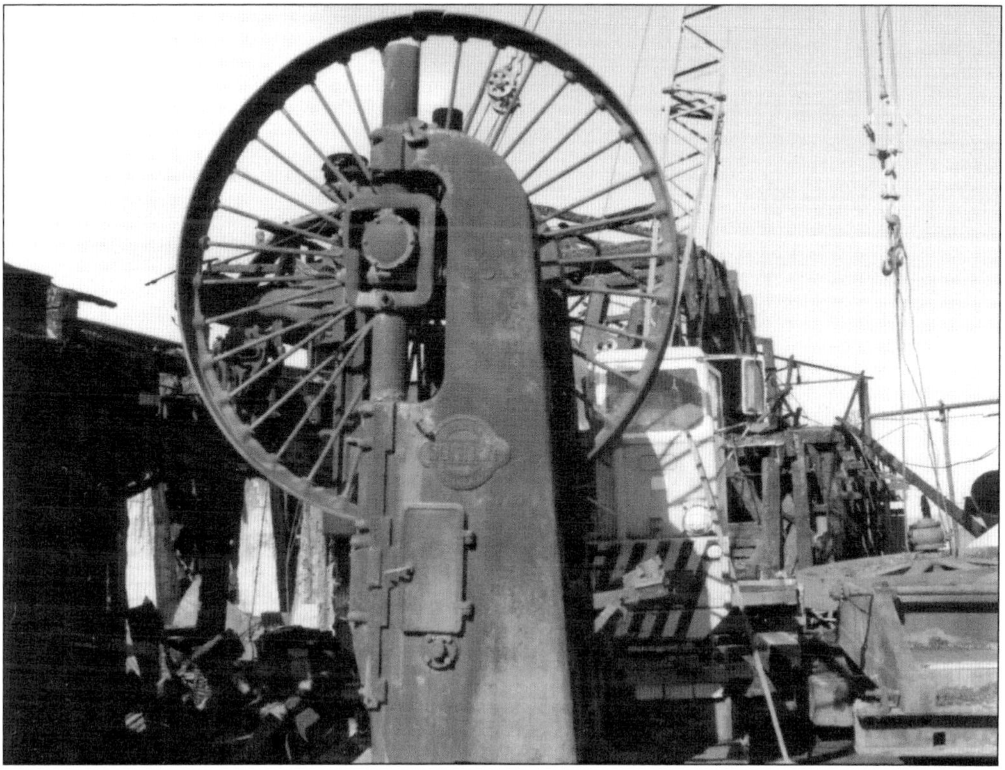

As noted in chapter two, the Dickman Lumber Company was destroyed by fire in 1979. The mill's headsaw, installed in 1923, survived among the debris. Through the efforts of the Old Town Improvement Club, the structure was placed in the Tacoma register in 1979 and ultimately became the property of the Metropolitan Park District. While exhibited for a while, it now sits rusting in a park storage yard.

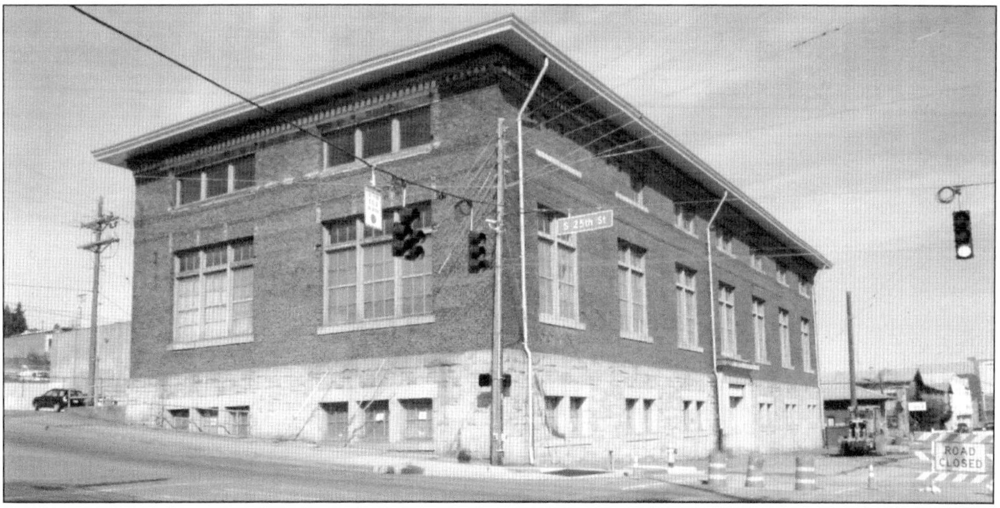

The 1911 Nisqually Power Substation, located at 2416 South C Street, historically represents the importance of public power in the development of the city. "Modern City Power Sub-Station Controls All of City's Current," headlined the *Tacoma Daily Ledger* in 1913. The building became a landmark in 2000.

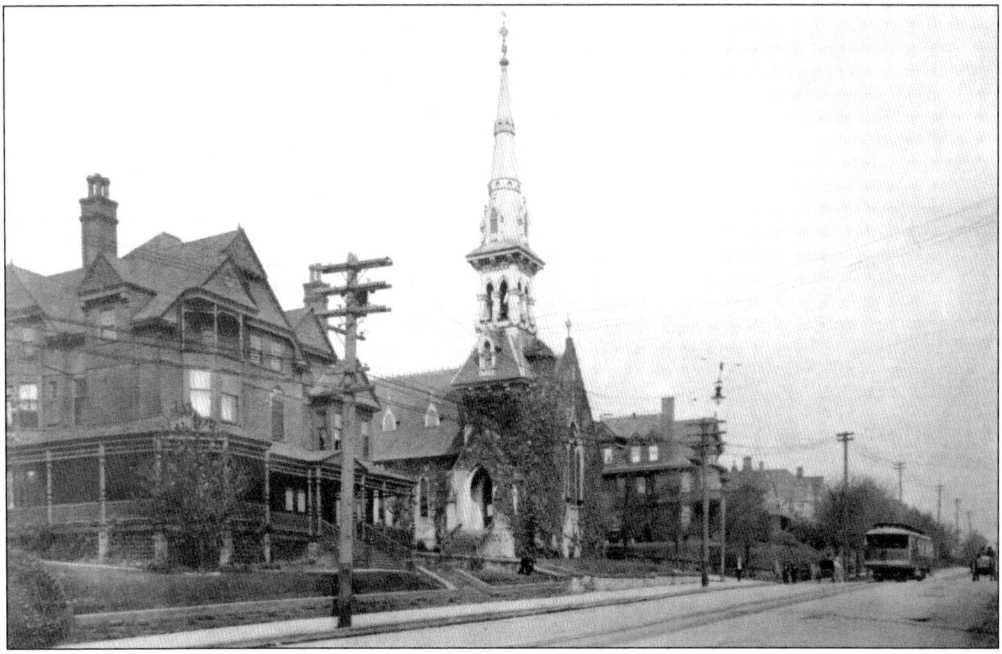

There is no greater success story in Tacoma than the salvation of St. Luke's Memorial Episcopal Church, built in 1883 and originally located at 602 Broadway Avenue. In 1934, the building was systematically dismantled and moved to a new site at 3601 North Gove Street, which was then the location of St. Mark's Episcopal Church. The brick-by-brick reconstruction was completed in 1947.

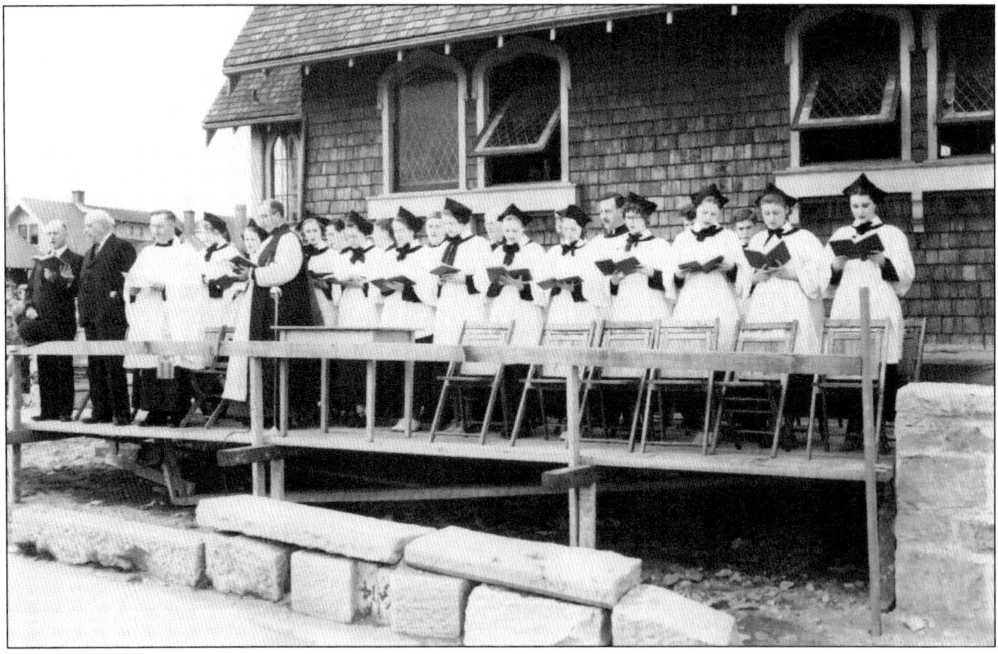

In 1935, St. Luke's congregation gathered at the new location to celebrate and dedicate the laying of the cornerstone. Dignitaries included various church leaders along with Tacoma mayor George Smitley. Rev. R.A. Walmsley brought a stone from Jerusalem to incorporate into the foundation. The St. Luke's Church became a landmark in 2008. (Richards Studio, Tacoma Public Library.)

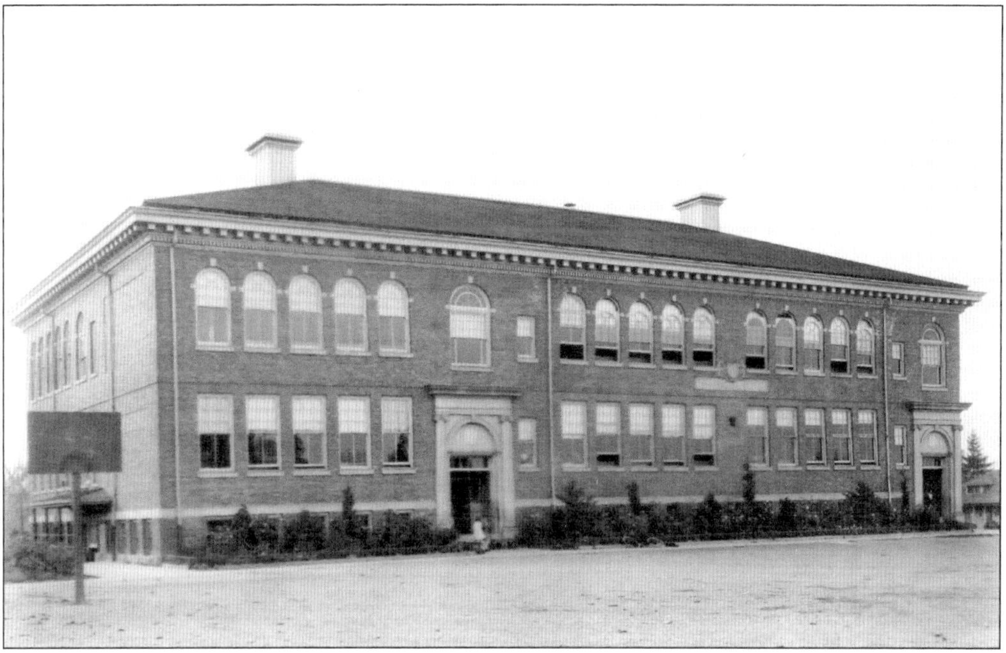

School architect Frederick Heath designed Washington School, located at 3701 North Twenty-sixth Street in the Proctor District, in 1906. The building replaced a 1901 two-room school that was originally on the site. Both it and Stadium School were opened on the same day in September 1906. Washington became a designated landmark in 2006 and is currently under restoration.

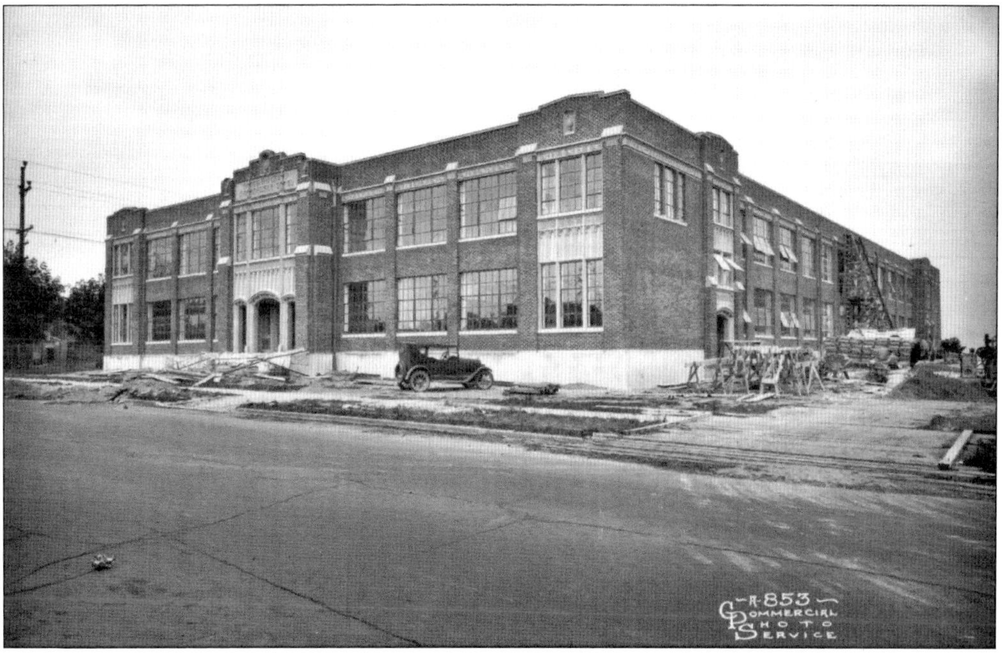

In this September 1925 photograph, the Morton M. McCarver Intermediate School is nearing completion scheduled for November of that year. The architectural firm of Hill and Mock designed the building at 2111 South J Street. It was designated a historic landmark in 2010, in part, because of its role in school desegregation in the 1960s. (Richards Studio, Tacoma Public Library.)

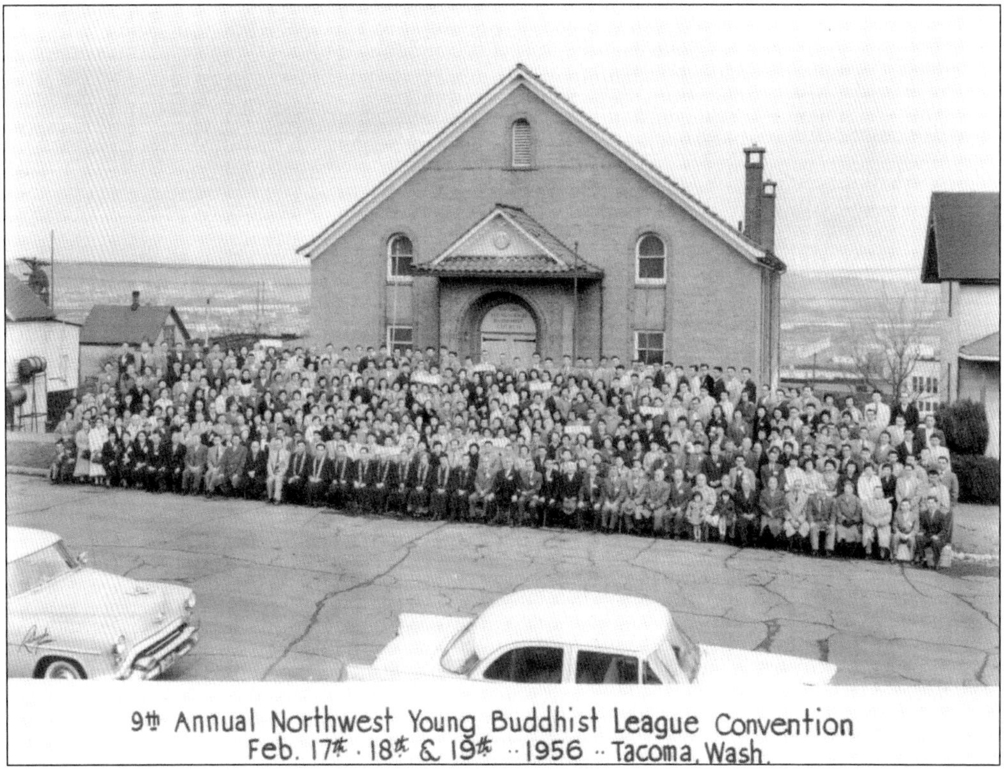

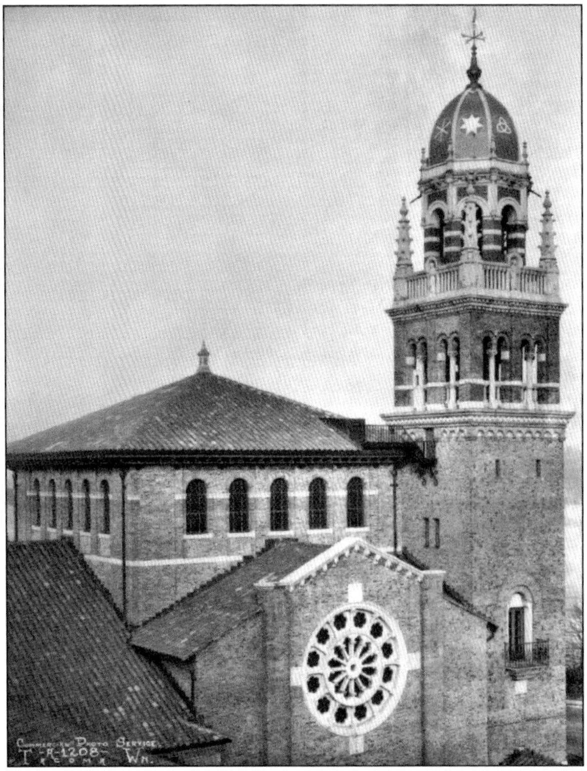

The Tacoma Buddhist Temple was constructed in 1930 and was designated as a landmark in 1995. Design by architect G.W. Bullard, it is located at 1717 Fawcett Avenue. In this 1956 photograph, members of the Northwest Young Buddhist League Convention pose in front of the church. (Richards Studio, Tacoma Public Library.)

Tacoma's First Presbyterian Church at 20 Tacoma Avenue South in the Stadium District was designed by the local architectural firm of Sutton, Whitney & Dugan based on original plans drawn by Ralph Adams Cram of Boston. It opened for services in 1924 and was designated as a landmark in 1975. In 1987, the congregation purchased the Buckley-King Mortuary next door, thus assuring its preservation. (Richards Studio, Tacoma Public Library.)

Eight

Memories

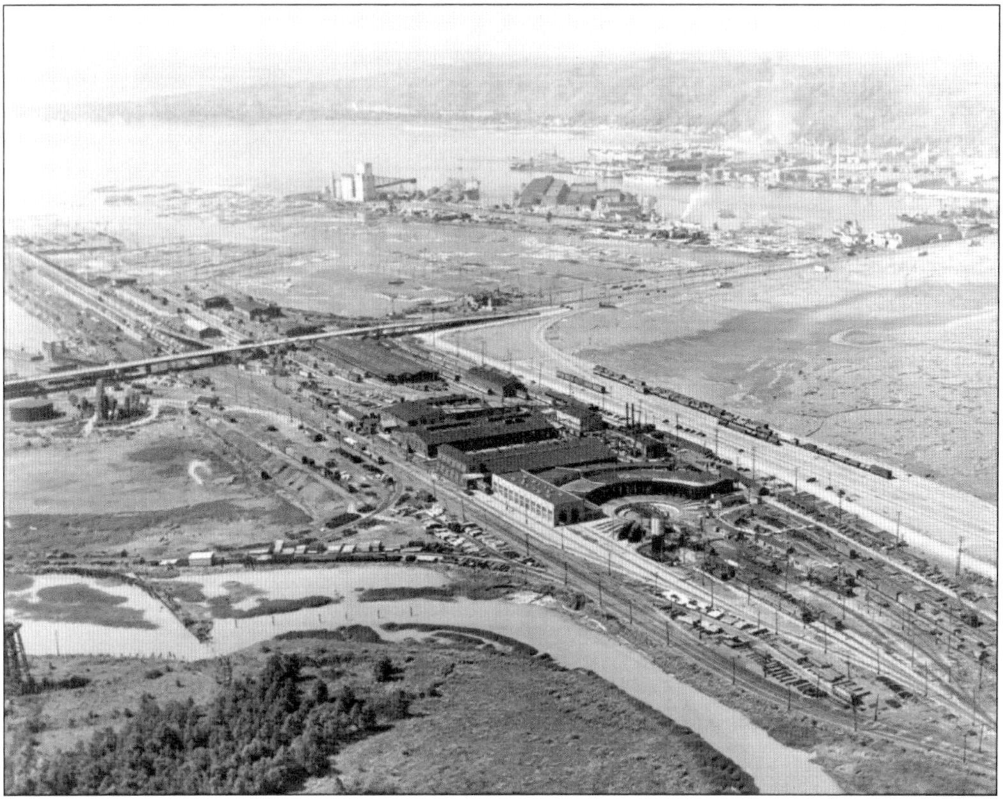

As noted in the introduction to this history, whether or not a building, or other aspect of the urban landscape, is there does not matter to some Tacomans. Memories and photographs are what matters. Some of these memories, such as mass transit, are transformed into today's urban amenities. Others remain as accepted memories that can never be replaced. In this chapter, there is an attempt to show images that illustrate some of the places and people that might spark memories in the reader. An image of the Chicago, Milwaukee, St. Paul and Pacific roundhouse taken by an unknown photographer around 1942 is seen here. Like the Northern Pacific before it, the Milwaukee Road chose Tacoma as its terminus, and while the roundhouse is no longer in Tacoma's port-industrial area, the terminus station survives as Freighthouse Square near the Tacoma Dome. While the railroad company is no longer in service, there are remnants throughout the West, showing the power stations used to run the trains. In some areas, portions of the abandoned rail line have been preserved as a trail.

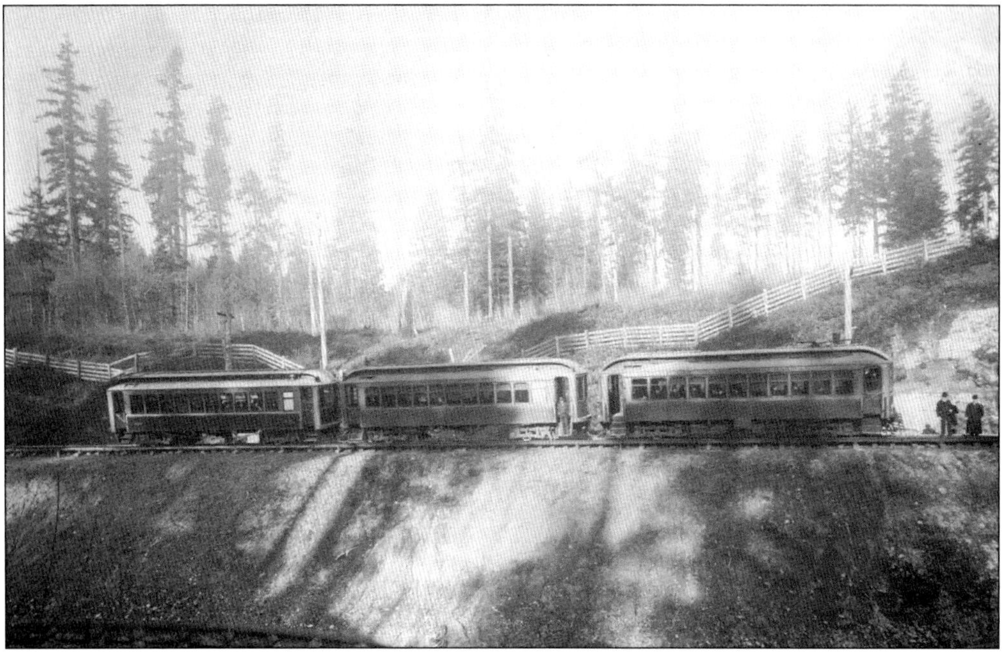

After World War II, the survival of the cable car in San Francisco caused urban dwellers in the West to wonder if the streetcar could be returned to their cities. Many in Tacoma could still remember the interurban rolling through undeveloped land to Seattle, as well as the streetcar lines where buses now follow the original routes. (Thomas R. Stenger collection.)

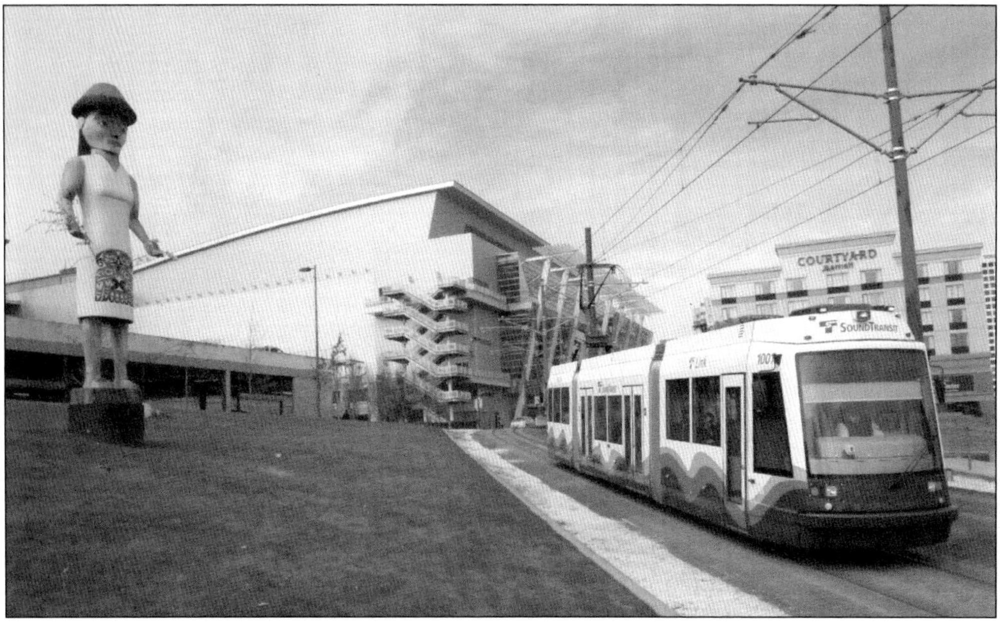

Light rail was the solution. Shown here is one moving through Tollefson Plaza toward the Convention Center prior to continuing on to the central business district. Tacoma's "welcome figure" is seen on the left. Carved by Puyallup Native American Shaun Peterson (Qwalsius) in Coast Salish style, the sculpture was placed as close as possible to one of the known Puyallup village sites.

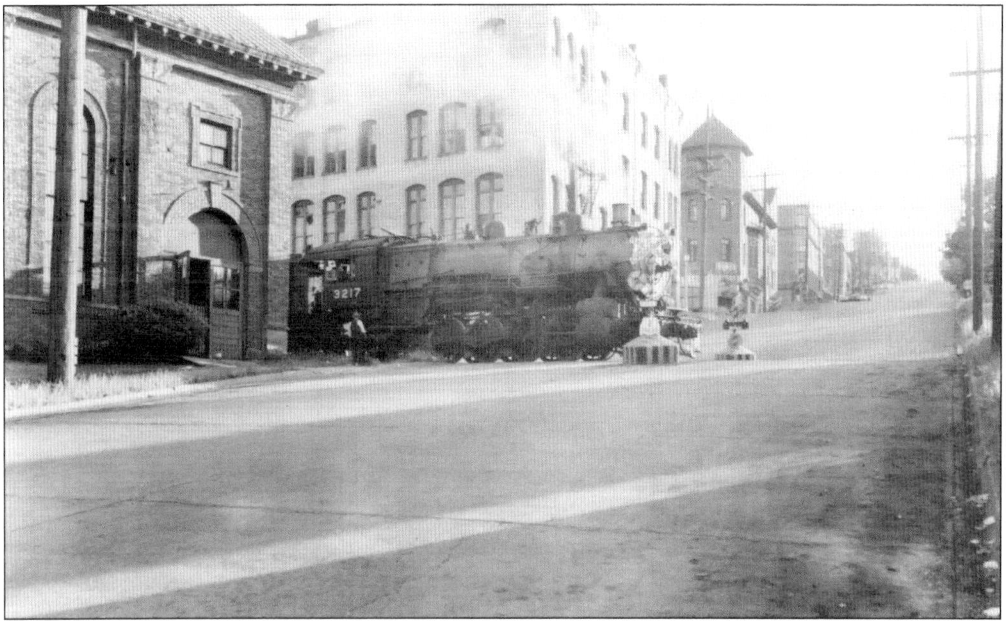

The first trains entering Tacoma during the later years of the 19th century followed the Prairie Line, and until the Northern Pacific changed its main route to front Commencement Bay, this was the only route in Tacoma. It passed through South Tacoma, crossed Pacific Avenue, and ended at the major shipping wharf close to where the present grain terminal is now located. Here, it is crossing South Nineteenth Street.

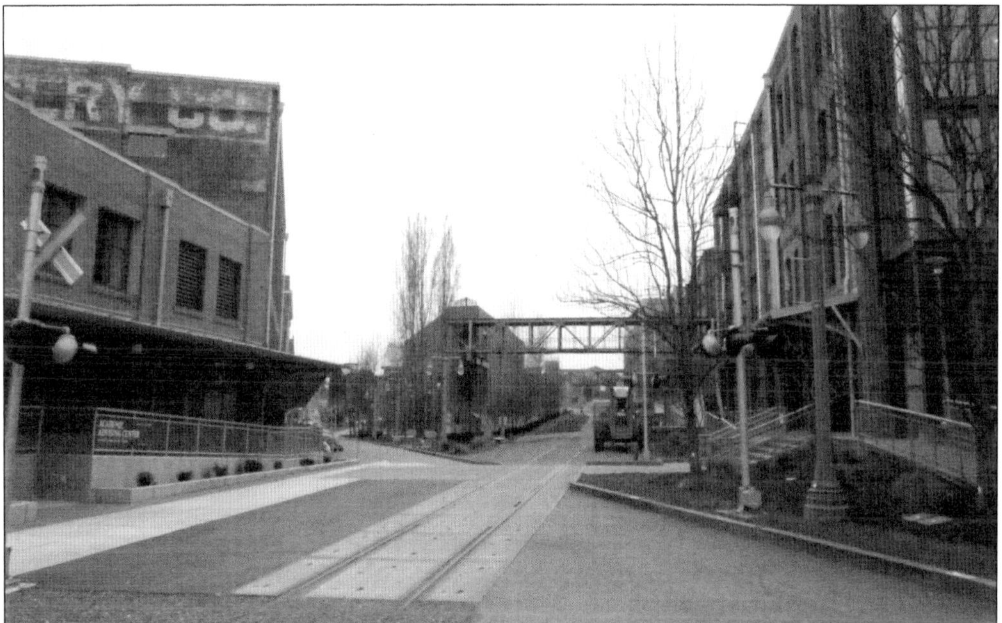

This view of the Prairie Line was taken in 2013 and shows that many buildings documented in the undated photograph at top still remain. This is the backside of the Union Station Warehouse Historic District (building fronts are to the left and face Pacific Avenue). The entire complex is now part of the University of Washington's Tacoma campus.

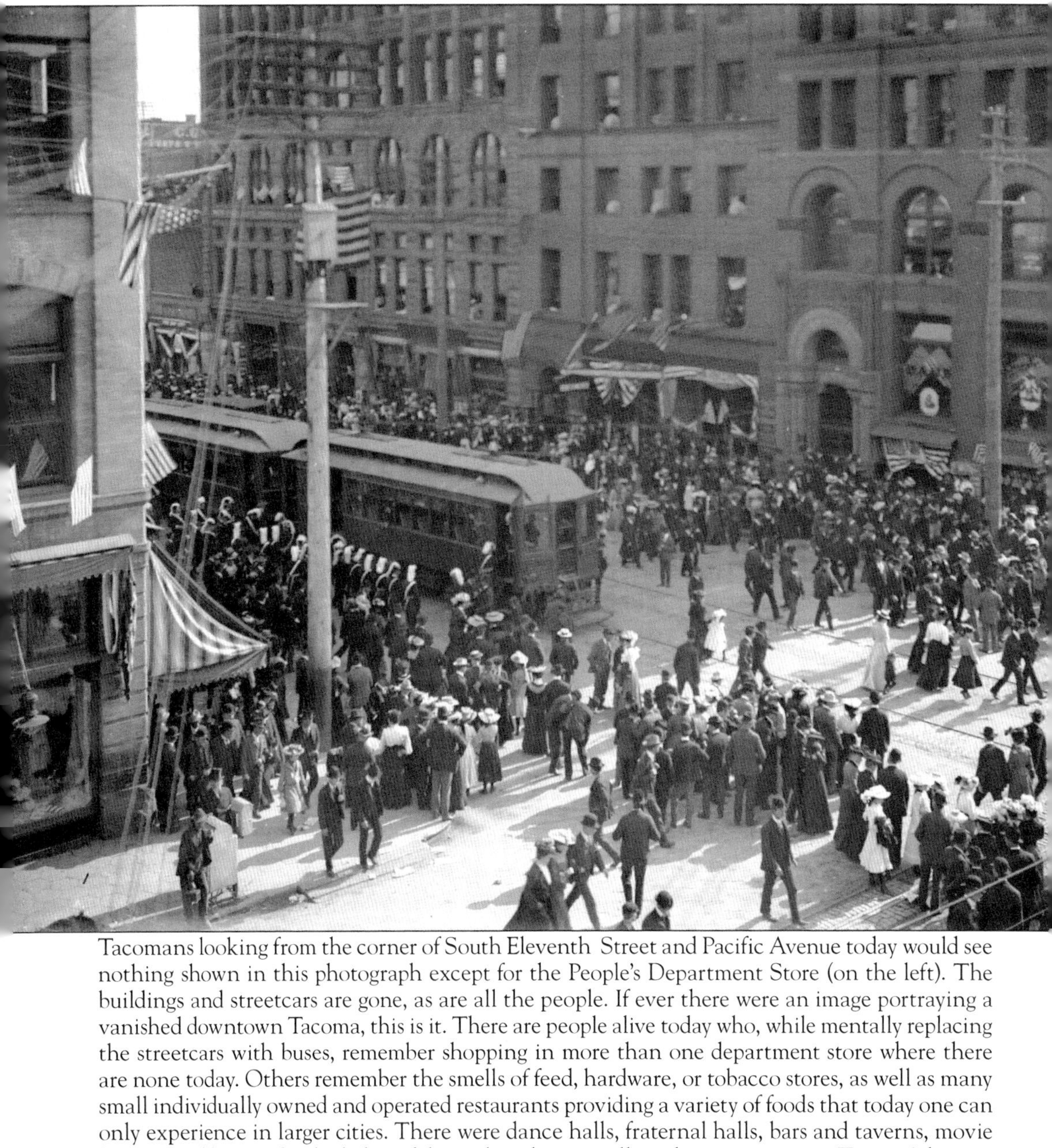

Tacomans looking from the corner of South Eleventh Street and Pacific Avenue today would see nothing shown in this photograph except for the People's Department Store (on the left). The buildings and streetcars are gone, as are all the people. If ever there were an image portraying a vanished downtown Tacoma, this is it. There are people alive today who, while mentally replacing the streetcars with buses, remember shopping in more than one department store where there are none today. Others remember the smells of feed, hardware, or tobacco stores, as well as many small individually owned and operated restaurants providing a variety of foods that today one can only experience in larger cities. There were dance halls, fraternal halls, bars and taverns, movie houses, and houses for the ladies of the night, who were allowed at some times in Tacoma's history to legally engage in their business. There was once something for everyone in downtown Tacoma, but now the area offers less variety. (Paul Richards Collection, Tacoma Historical Society.)

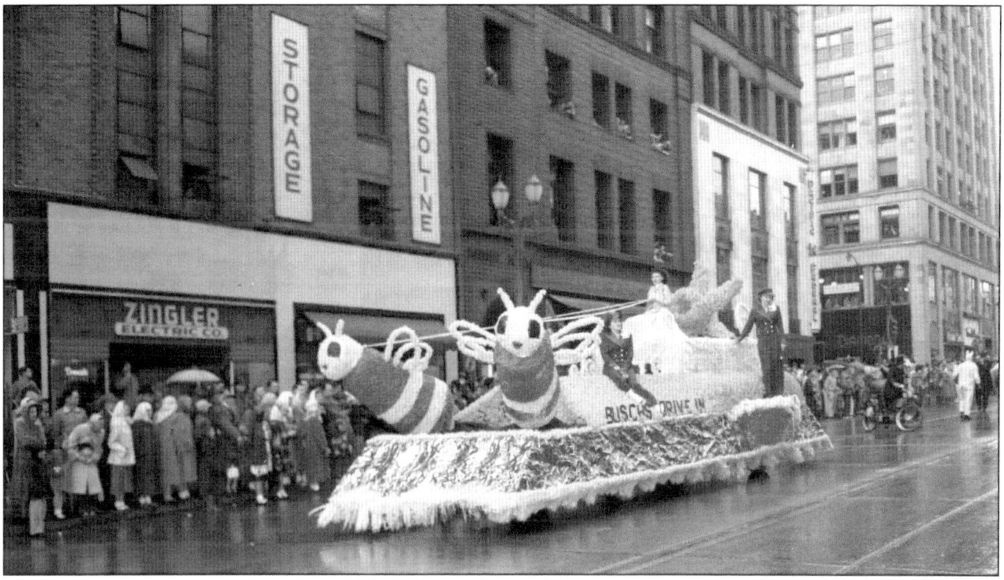

Small marching bands are no longer a part of the urban scene in Tacoma, but the Daffodil Festival and Parade is. Its foundation, with its first formal parade in 1934, evolved after the US Department of Agriculture introduced bulk horticulture to Puyallup Valley farmers. The date of this photograph of Busch's Drive-in float is unknown, but it is shown southward bound near Pacific Avenue and South Eleventh Street.

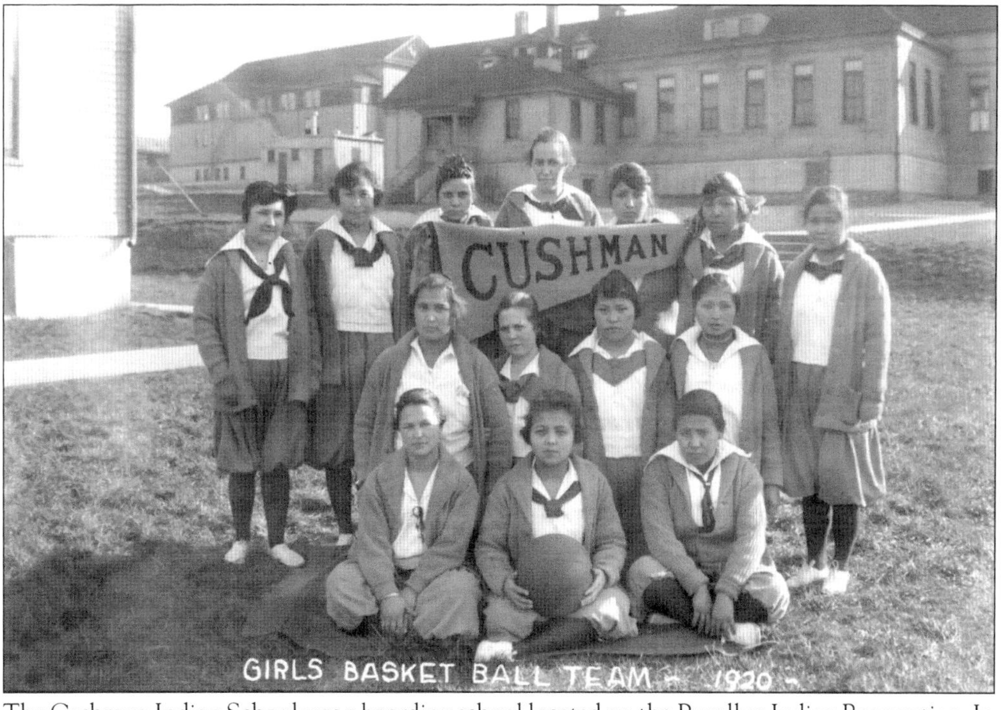

The Cushman Indian School was a boarding school located on the Puyallup Indian Reservation. In 1920, photographer Paul Richards took took this image of the girls' basketball team. Unlike today, girls' sports were rather limited and usually discouraged. Even so, this photograph does portray one instance where women could compete. (Paul Richards Collection, Tacoma Historical Society.)

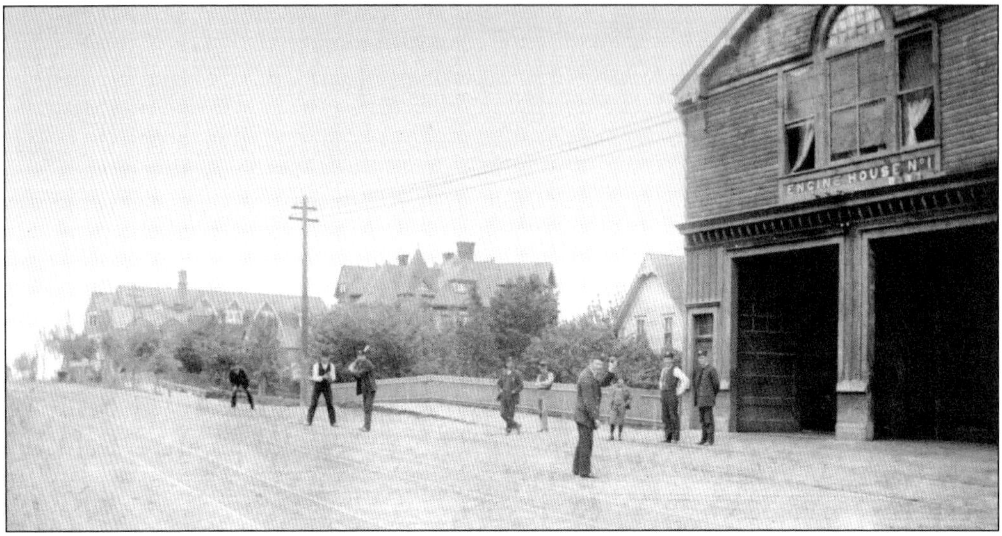

Semiprofessional baseball teams, like the marching bands, are a thing of the past. Many businesses and industries had their own teams that would compete for national championships. In this undated photograph, an unidentified photographer catches Engine House No. 1's firemen playing the game on St. Helens Avenue.

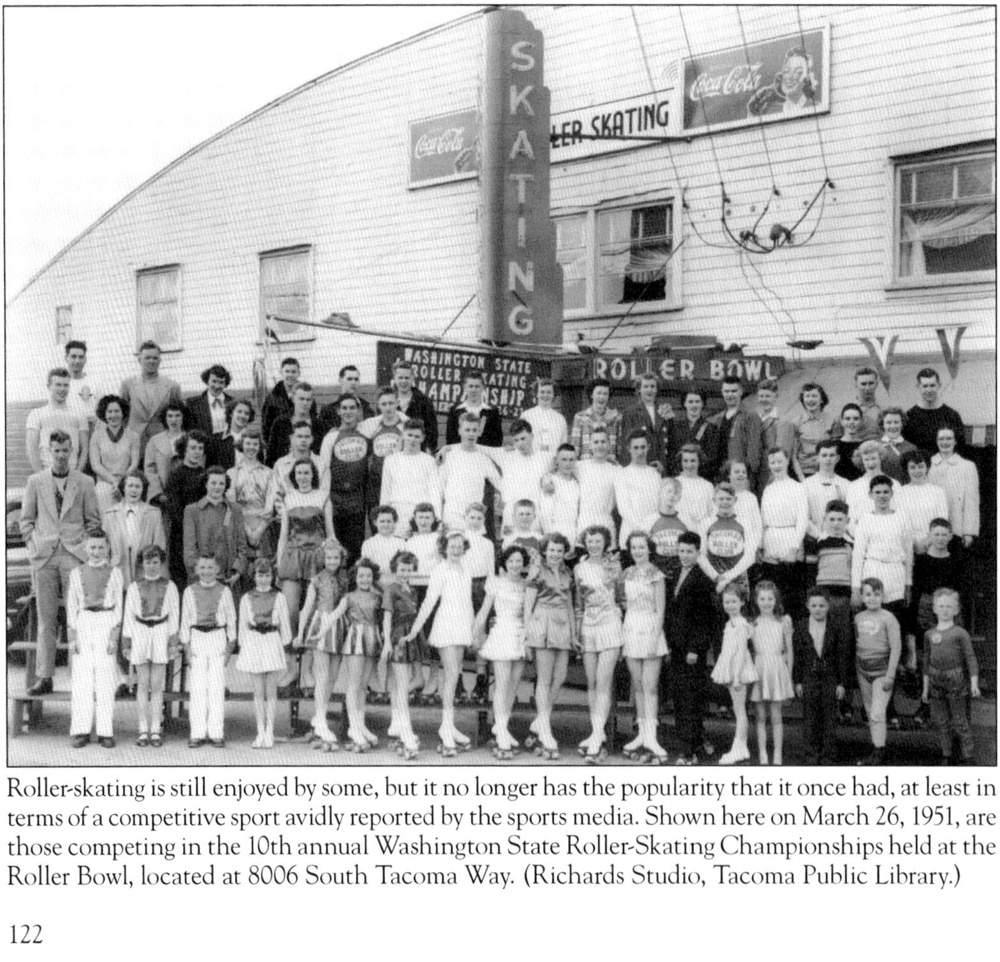

Roller-skating is still enjoyed by some, but it no longer has the popularity that it once had, at least in terms of a competitive sport avidly reported by the sports media. Shown here on March 26, 1951, are those competing in the 10th annual Washington State Roller-Skating Championships held at the Roller Bowl, located at 8006 South Tacoma Way. (Richards Studio, Tacoma Public Library.)

If a Tacoman is lucky, he or she can observe a game of lawn bowling played on the Sixth Avenue end of Wright Park. Unlike the noise and gaiety of regular bowling, this sport, whose roots traveled from ancient Rome and bocce, is a quiet affair, as these competitors from the Tacoma Bowling Association and officers from the British cruiser *Danae* document. (Richards Studio, Tacoma Public Library.)

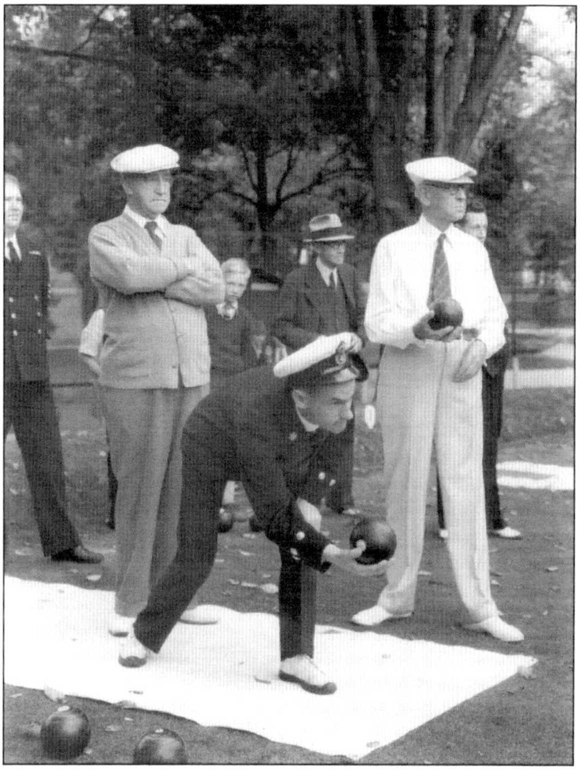

Little did local residents know that within a half century of the downtown Escalades opening in 1961, they would be gone as an outdated way to travel up the hills of downtown Tacoma. People, including that year's Daffodil Queen, pictured, gathered to take a ride on opening day. Today, those maneuvering the hills have developed an innovative route via building elevators and street overpasses. (Thomas R. Stenger collection.)

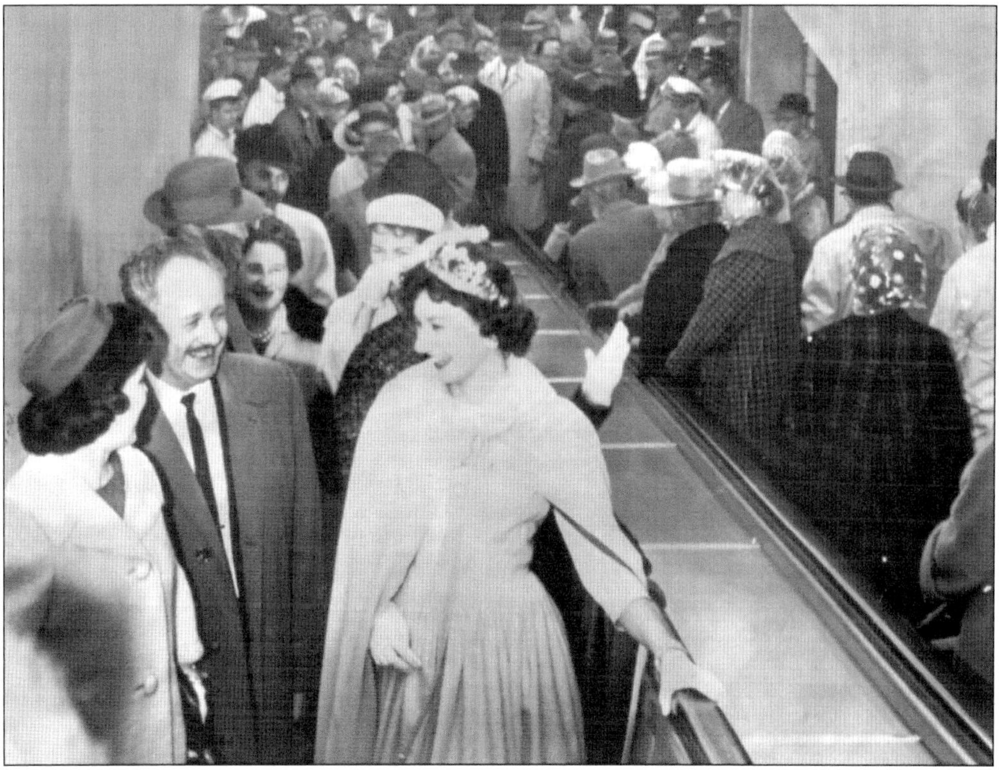

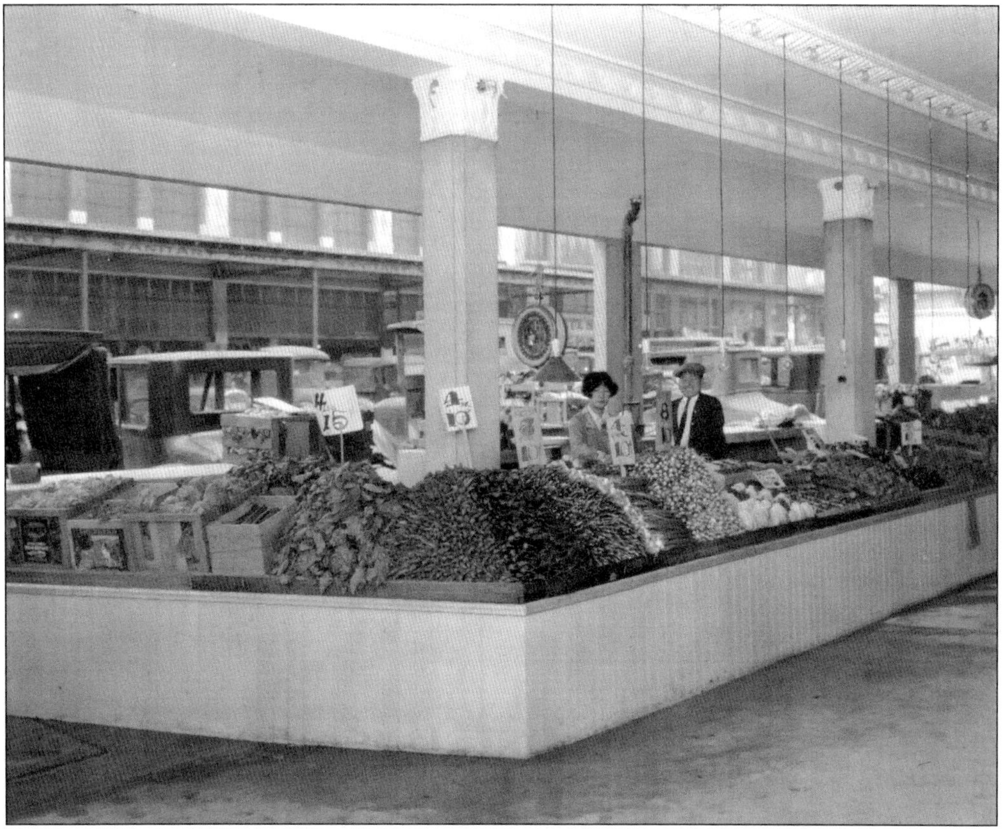

Like Seattle, Tacoma once had a complex of public markets. The Crystal Palace Public Market at 1101–1113 Market Street was the most well known. Shown here around 1927 is the interior. While the building was not demolished until 1973, it appears that the public markets, now replaced by neighborhood farmers' markets, did not survive World War II.

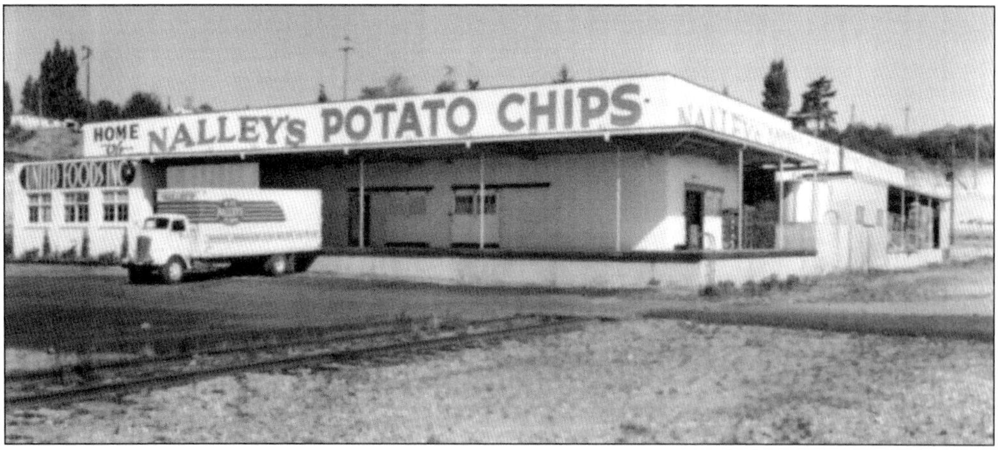

Croatian Marcus Nalley began making potato chips in the kitchen of his house in 1918 and was able to ultimately expand his South Tacoma location into a major plant for various products, including pickles. Over time, the business was sold to various business conglomerations, and the Tacoma plant was deemed unnecessary. Most of the buildings associated with Nalley's company have been demolished. (Richards Studio, Tacoma Public Library.)

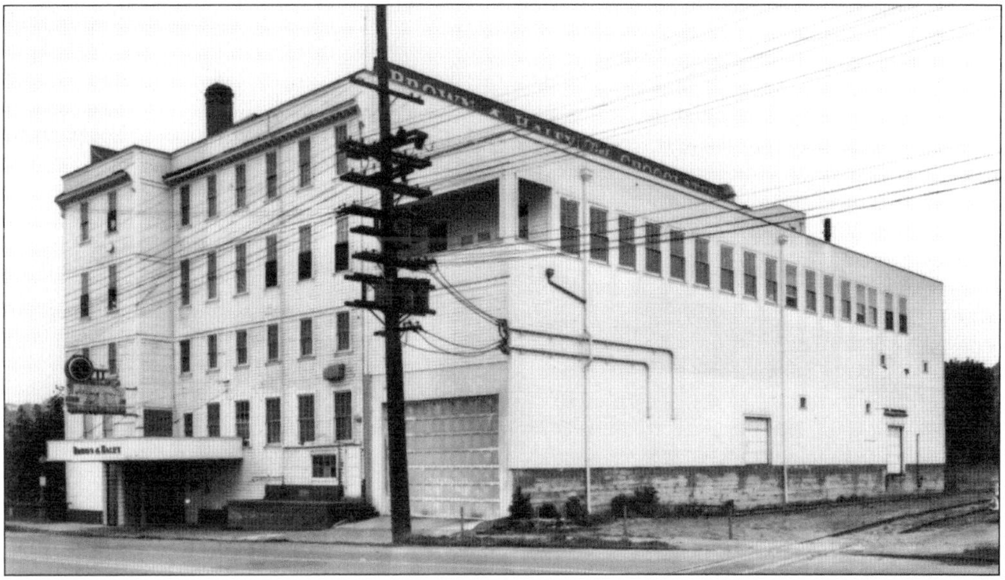

In June 1919, five years after the business organized, this building at 108 East Twenty-sixth Street became the manufacturing plant for the Brown and Haley Candy Company. For years, those enjoying the company's signature Almond Roca knew that their favorite candy originated in this building. It still exists, but its future is unknown. The candy is now manufactured in Fife. (Tacoma Public Library.)

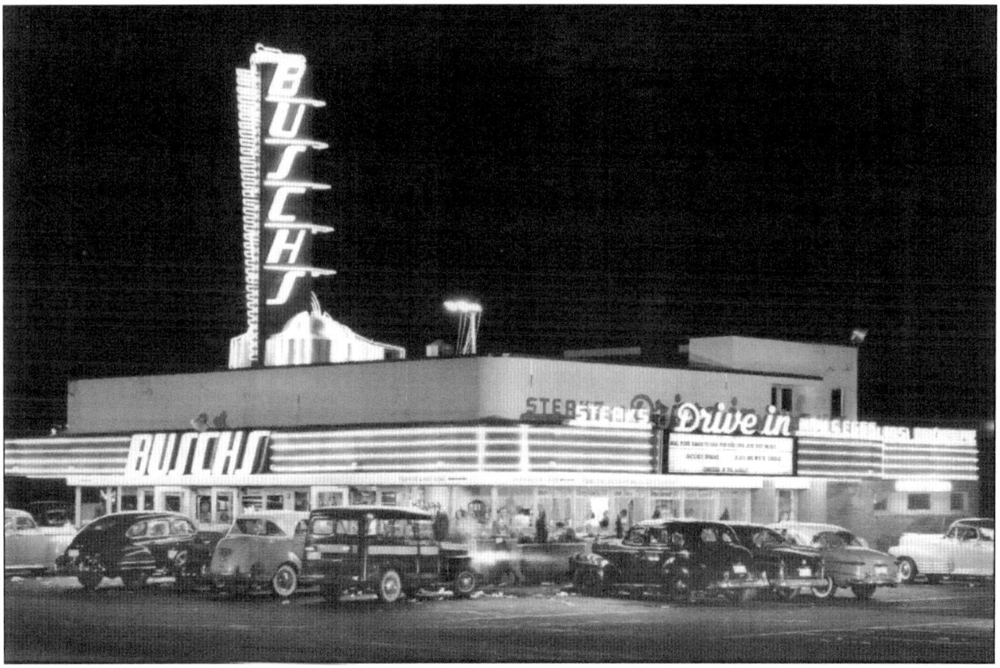

Busch's Drive-in was the place for a teenager to go in the 1950s. Located on South Tacoma Way, the hangout was originally Kruger's Triple XXX Root Beer Barrel drive-in, where carhops dressed in majorette costumes served customers. Bill and Thelma Busch purchased the building in 1943. The drive-in remained in business at this location until 1959. (Richards Studio, Tacoma Public Library.)

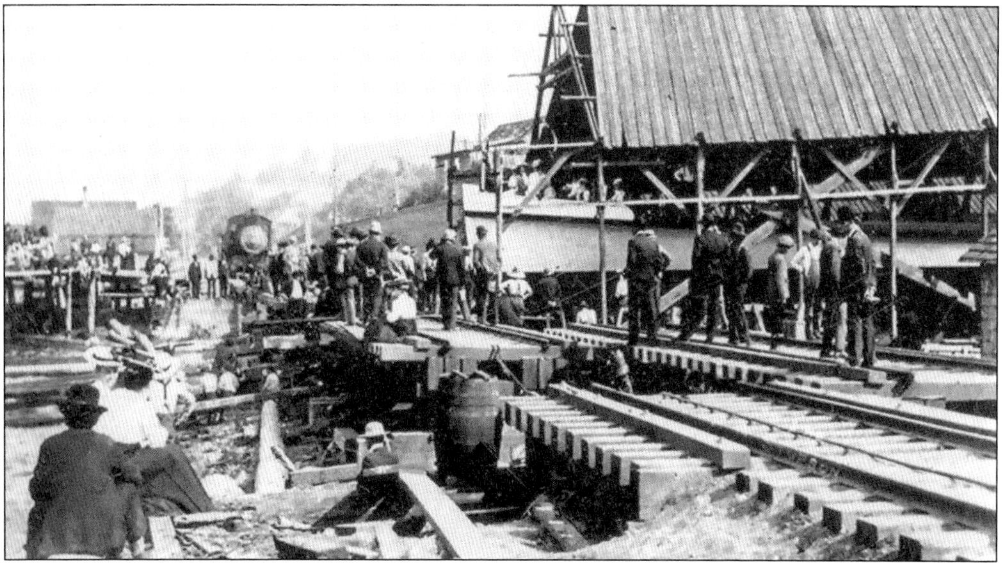

Those who have lived in Tacoma for a long time remember Old Town as a place of activity ranging from boat launchings (above) to events at the Top of the Ocean (below). The Crawford and Reid boatyard was located near the foot of North Carr Street. Note the train stopped in the distance. Every time there was a launching, the tracks were moved aside so that the boat could reach the water. Then they were rolled back into place, and the train proceeded. The event at the restaurant is unknown, but the photograph does document how popular the place was when it first opened. Also shown is the McCarver Street train station, a reminder that trains stopped in the neighborhood at one time. There have been three attempts to get the Old Tacoma neighborhood designated as a historic district. All have failed, leaving only memories of this once vibrant place. (Above, Robin Patterson collection; below, Richards Studio, Tacoma Public Library.)

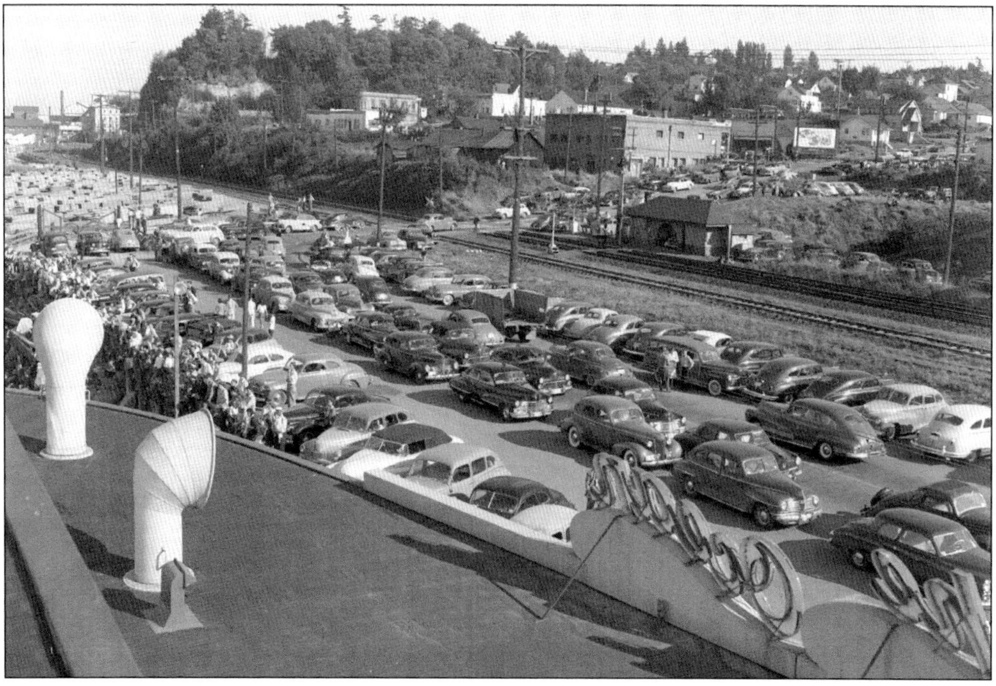

Steve Gay 90s, once located at 5238 South Tacoma Way, is gone as a business, but Tacoma-born Diana Schuur continues as one of the nation's foremost jazz singers. Pictured here as a teenager, Schuur performs at Steve Gay 90s. (Richards Studio, Tacoma Public Library.)

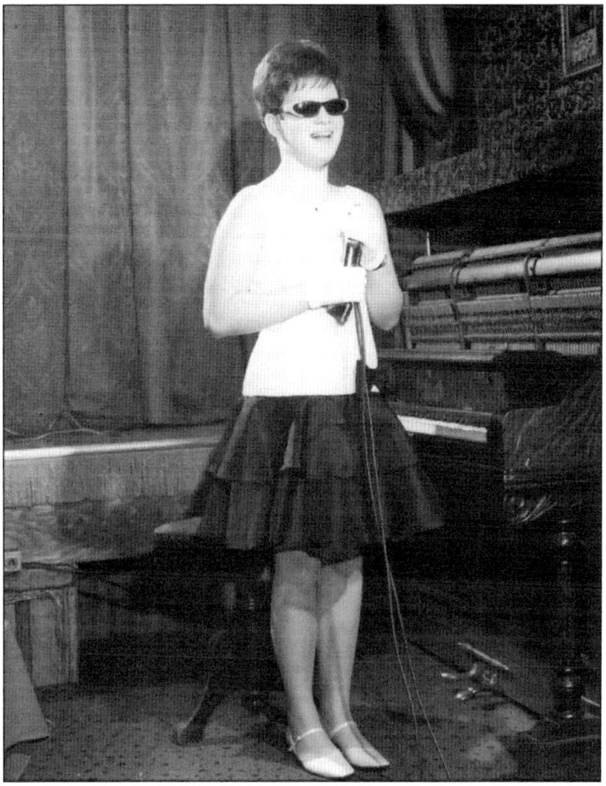

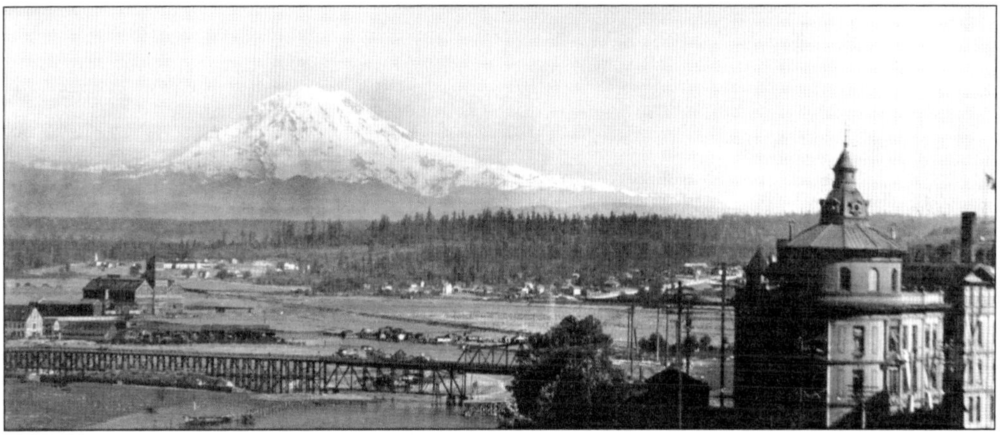

On May 18, 1980, Mount St. Helens, south of Mount Tahoma (aka Mount Rainier, pictured), erupted. At the time, those living in the Pacific Northwest had assumed that such an even could not happen. Historical accounts, however, record previous activity within the Cascade Range, especially around the time when settlers were first beginning to arrive in the region. If Mount Tahoma were to erupt again, disaster planners believe that is possible for the entire city of Tacoma to vanish in a massive mudflow. Such ponderings make much of what was written in this history minor by comparison. Even so, it is important to remember that environmental factors, be they earthquakes, storms, or floods do affect the urban landscape. So, too, do the decisions made by people over time. Some result in a loss to the landscape. But usually something arises in its place that newer generations cherish. The totality is a rich tapestry of old and new that is the essence of a city. (Thomas R. Stenger collection.)